My Memoirs

My Memoirs: 1878-1918

Ex-Kaiser William II

Impala

Published by
Impala
(International Media Publication and Literary Associates) Ltd
Registered Office:
c/o Davenport Lyons
30 Old Burlington Street
London W1S 3NL

First published in 1922 in Great Britain by Cassell & Company
Transferred to digital printing 2006

This edition © Impala Ltd 2006

COVER ILLUSTRATION, from a private collection, © Impala Ltd 2006

ISBN 1 905530 02 1

My Memoirs: 1878–1918

BISMARCK

§ 1

PRINCE BISMARCK'S greatness as a statesman and his imperishable services to Prussia and Germany are historical facts of such tremendous significance that there is doubtless no man in existence, whatever his party predilections, who would dare to question them. For this very reason alone it is stupid to accuse me of not having recognized the greatness of Prince Bismarck. The opposite is the truth. I revered and idolized him. Nor could it be otherwise. It should be borne in mind with what generation I grew up—the generation of the devotees of Bismarck. He was the creator of the German Empire, the paladin of my grandfather, and all of us considered him the greatest statesman of his day and were proud that he was a German. Bismarck was the idol in my temple, and I worshipped him.

But monarchs are also human beings of flesh and blood, hence they too are exposed to the influences emanating from the conduct of others. Therefore, looking at the matter from a human point of view, one will understand how, by fighting against me,

B

Bismarck himself destroyed, with heavy blows, the idol which I had set up; but my reverence for Bismarck, the great statesman, nevertheless remained unaltered.

While I was still Prince of Prussia, I often thought to myself: "I hope that the great chancellor will live for many years yet, for if I could govern with him I should be safe." My reverence for the great statesman, however, was not such as to make me, when I became Emperor, take upon my own shoulders political plans or actions of the prince which I considered to be mistaken. Even the Berlin Congress of 1878 was, to my way of thinking, a mistake, likewise the *Kulturkampf*. Moreover, the constitution of the empire was drawn up so as to fit in with Bismarck's extraordinary preponderance as a statesman; the big cuirassier boots did not fit every man.

Then came the labour protective legislation. I most deeply deplored the dispute which arose out of this, but, at that time, it was necessary for me *to take the road to compromise, a course I have generally followed both in domestic and foreign politics.* For this reason I could not wage the open warfare against the Social Democrats which the prince desired. Nevertheless, this quarrel concerning political measures cannot lessen my admiration for the greatness of Bismarck as a statesman. He remains the creator of the German Empire and, surely, no *one* man need have done more for his country than that.

Owing to the fact that the great matter of the unification of the empire was always before me, I did not allow myself to be influenced by the agitations which were the commonplaces of those days. In like manner, the fact that Bismarck was called " the majordomo of the Hohenzollerns " could not shake my trust in the prince, although he, perhaps, had visions of a political tradition for his family. As evidence of this, he was, for instance, unhappy that his son Bill showed no interest in politics and wished to pass on his chance of power to Herbert.

The tragic element for me in the matter of Bismarck lay in the fact that I became the successor of my grandfather—in other words that, to a certain extent, I skipped one generation. That is a serious thing. In such a case one is constantly forced to deal with deserving old men who live more in the past than in the present and cannot look into the future. When the grandson succeeds his grandfather and finds a revered but aged statesman of the calibre of Bismarck, it is not a matter of good luck for him, as one might suppose, and as I, in fact, did suppose. Bismarck himself points that out in the third volume of his memoirs (p. 40), when he refers, in the chapter on Bötticher, to the cautiousness of the old chancellor and of the young Emperor.

When Ballin directed the glance of the prince over the new harbour of Hamburg, Bismarck himself felt that a new era had begun, which he no longer thoroughly understood. On that occasion the prince remarked, in astonishment : " Another world, a new world ! "

This point of view also revealed itself on the

occasion of the visit of Admiral von Tirpitz to
Friedrichsruh, at the time when he wished to win the
old Imperial Chancellor over to favouring the first
Navy Bill.

As for me personally, I have the satisfaction of
recalling that Bismarck entrusted to me in 1886 the
very delicate Brest mission and said of me : " Some
day that man will be his own chancellor." This shows
that Bismarck must have had some belief in me.

I feel no grudge against him for the third volume
of his reminiscences. I released this volume after I
had sought and obtained my rights. To withhold
the volume any longer would have been pointless,
since the main contents had already become known
through indiscretions. Were this not true, there
might have been varying opinions as to the advisability in the choice of the time for publication. Bismarck would have turned in his grave if he could
have known at what time the third volume appeared
and what consequences followed. I should be
honestly grieved if the third volume should prove
to have damaged the memory of the great chancellor,
because Bismarck is one of the heroic figures needed
by Germany for its regeneration. My gratitude and
reverence for him cannot be extinguished or even
impaired by the third volume, or, indeed, by anything else whatever.

In the first half of the 'eighties I was sum-
moned to the Foreign Office at the behest of Prince
Bismarck. It was then presided over by Count
Herbert Bismarck. Upon reporting myself to the

prince he gave me a short sketch of the personages employed at the Foreign Office, and when he named Herr von Holstein, who was then one of the most prominent colleagues of the prince, it seemed to me that a slight warning against this man ran through the prince's words.

I had a room to myself, and all the documents concerning the preliminary history, origin and conclusion of the alliance with Austria (Andrassy) were laid before me in order that I might study them. I often went to the prince's home and to that of Count Herbert.

When I had thus become more intimate in the Bismarck circle I heard more open talk of Herr von Holstein. I heard that he was very clever, a good worker, inordinately proud, an odd sort of man who never showed himself anywhere and had no social relations, full of distrust, much influenced by whims, and, besides all this, a good hater and, therefore, dangerous. Prince Bismarck called him " The Man with Hyena's Eyes," and told me that it would be well for me to keep away from him. It was quite apparent that the bitter attitude which the prince adopted later towards Holstein, his former colleague, existed even then.

The Foreign Office was conducted with the strictest discipline by Count Herbert, whose rudeness to his subordinates particularly struck me. The members of the staff simply flew when they were summoned or dismissed by the count, so much so that a jocular saying arose at the time that " their coat-tails stood straight out behind them." The foreign policy was conducted and dictated by Prince Bismarck alone, after consultation with Count Herbert, who passed on the decisions of the chancellor and had them transformed into instructions. Hence, *the Foreign Office was nothing but an office of the great chancellor,* where work was carried out according to his directions. Able men, with independent ideas, were not schooled and trained there. This was in contrast to the General Staff under Moltke. There, new officers were carefully developed and trained to independent thinking and action, in accordance with approved principles, and by dint of preserving old traditions and taking into account all that modern events had taught. At the Foreign Office there were only executive instruments of a will, who were not informed as to the important inter-relationship of the questions turned over to them for treatment, and could not, therefore, act independently. The prince loomed up like a huge block of granite in a meadow ; were he to be dragged away, mostly worms and dead roots would be found beneath.

I won the confidence of the prince, who consulted me about many things. For instance, when the prince secured the first German colonial acquisitions (Great and Little Popo, Togo, etc.), I informed him, at his wish, concerning the state of mind created in the public and the navy by this move, and described to him the enthusiasm with which the German people had hailed the new departure. The prince remarked that the matter hardly merited this.

Later on I often spoke with the prince on the colonial question, and always found in him the intention to utilize the colonies for purposes of political barter, rather than to make them useful to the Fatherland or to utilize them as sources of raw materials.

As was my duty I called the prince's attention to the fact that merchants and capitalists were beginning energetically to develop the colonies and that, therefore—as I had learned from Hanseatic circles— they counted upon protection from a navy. For this reason, I pointed out that steps must be taken towards the construction of a fleet, in order that German foreign interests should not be without protection ; that, since the prince had unfurled the German flag in foreign parts, and the people stood behind it, there must also be a navy behind it. But the prince turned a deaf ear to my statements and merely used his pet phrase : " If the English should land on our soil, I should have them arrested." His idea was that the colonies would be defended by us at home. The prince attached no importance to the fact that the mere suggestion that the English could land without opposition in Germany—since Heligoland was English—was unbearable to Germany, and that we, in order to make a landing utterly impossible, needed a sufficiently strong navy and the possession of Heligoland.

The political interest of the prince was, in fact, concentrated essentially upon continental Europe ; England lay somewhat outside the daily cares that burdened him, all the more so since Salisbury stood well with him and had, in the name of England, hailed with satisfaction the Dual (i.e. Triple) Alliance, at the time of its formation. The prince worked primarily with Russia, Austria, Italy and Rumania, whose relations towards Germany and with each other he constantly watched. As to the prudence and skill with which he acted, Emperor William the Great once made a pointed remark to von Albedyll, his Chief of Cabinet. The general found His Majesty much excited after a talk with Bismarck, to such an extent, indeed, that he feared for the health of the old Emperor. He remarked, therefore, that His Majesty should avoid similar worry in future ; that, if Bismarck was unwilling to do as His Majesty wished, His Majesty should dismiss him. Whereupon the Emperor replied that, despite his admiration and gratitude towards the great chancellor, he had already thought of dismissing him, for the assertive attitude of the prince became at times too oppressive, but both he and the country needed Bismarck too badly ; he was the only man who could juggle with five balls of which at least two were always in the air. That trick, added the Emperor, was beyond his own powers.

Prince Bismarck did not realize that through Germany's acquisition of colonies, he would be obliged to look beyond Europe and automatically be forced to act politically on a large scale—with England especially. England, to be sure, was one of the five balls in his diplomatic game, but she was merely one of the five, and he did not grant her the special importance which was her due.

It was for this reason that the Foreign Office was entirely involved in the continental interplay of politics, and had not the requisite interest in colonies, a navy, or England, and possessed no experience in world-politics. English psychology and mentality, as shown in the pursuit—constant, though concealed by all kinds of little cloaks—of world hegemony, was to the German Foreign Office a book sealed with seven seals. Prince Bismarck once remarked to me that his main object was to prevent Russia and England arriving at an understanding. I took the liberty of observing that the opportunity to postpone such an understanding for a long time lay ready to hand in 1877–8, when the Russians might have been allowed to occupy Constantinople. Had this been done, the English fleet would have sailed in without further ado to defend Constantinople and the Russo-English conflict would have begun. Instead, I continued, the Treaty of San Stefano was forced upon the Russians, and they were compelled to turn about at the very gates of the city which they had reached after frightful battles and hardships. This, I went on, had created an inextinguishable hatred in the Russian army against us (as had been reported by Prussian officers, especially Count Pfeil), who had accompanied the Russian army on the Turkish campaign. Moreover, the San Stefano treaty had been cast aside and the Treaty of Berlin substituted for it, which had increased the hostility of the Russians

even more, who now looked upon us as the enemy of
their "just interests in the East." Thus the conflict between Russia and England, which the prince
desired, had been relegated far into the future.

Prince Bismarck did not agree with this judgment
of " his " congress, concerning the results of which
he, as the "honest broker," was so proud. He
earnestly remarked that he had desired to prevent a
general conflagration, and had been compelled to
offer his services as mediator. When, later on, I
told a member of the Foreign Office of this conversation, he replied that he had been present when the
prince, after the signing of the Berlin treaty, came
into the Foreign Office and received the congratulations of the assembled officials. After he had listened
to them the prince stood up and replied : " Now I
am driving Europe four-in-hand ! " In the opinion
of this gentleman, the prince was mistaken in this,
since, even at that time, there was the threat of a
Russo-French friendship in place of the Russo-Prussian—in other words, two horses were already to be
counted out of the four-in-hand. As Russia saw it,
Disraeli's statecraft had turned Bismarck's work as
" honest broker " into the negotiation of an Anglo-
Austrian victory over Russia.

Despite considerable divergencies in our opinions,
Prince Bismarck remained friendly and kindly dis-
posed to me, and, despite the great difference in our
ages, a pleasant relationship grew up between us.
In common with all those of my generation I was
an ardent admirer of the prince and won his trust

by my zeal and frankness. Nor have I ever betrayed that trust.

During the course of my association with the Foreign Office, Privy Councillor Raschdau, among others, discoursed with me on commercial policy, colonies, etc. In these matters, even at that early date, my attention was called to our dependence upon England, owing to the fact that we had no navy and that Heligoland was in English hands. To be sure, there was a project to extend our colonial possessions under the pressure of necessity, but all this could happen only with England's permission. This was a serious matter and certainly an unworthy position for Germany.

My work at the Foreign Office brought a very unpleasant happening in its wake. My parents were not very friendly towards Prince Bismarck and looked with disfavour upon the fact that their son had entered into the prince's circle. There was fear of my becoming influenced against my parents, of super-conservatism, of all sorts of perils, which talebearers from England and "Liberal circles," who gathered around my father, imputed against me. I never bothered my head with all this nonsense, but my position in my parents' house was rendered much more difficult for me and, at times, painful. Through my work under Prince Bismarck and the confidence reposed in me—often subjected to the severest tests—I have had to suffer much in silence for the sake of the chancellor. He, however, apparently accepted this quite as a matter of course.

I was on good terms with Count Herbert Bismarck.
He could be a very gay companion and knew how
to assemble interesting men around his table, partly
from the Foreign Office, partly from other circles.
True friendship, however, never ripened between us.
This was definitely proved when the count asked to
be relieved of office at the same time that his father
retired. My request that he should stay by me and
help me to maintain tradition in our political policy
elicited the sharp reply that he had become accustomed to report to his father and serve him, wherefore it was out of the question to demand that he
should come with his dispatch-case under his arm to
report to anybody other than his father.

§ 2

When Tsar Nicholas II—he who has been murdered—came of age, I was assigned at the instigation
of Prince Bismarck to confer upon the heir-apparent
at St. Petersburg the Order of the Black Eagle.
Both the Emperor and Prince Bismarck instructed me
concerning the relationship of the two countries and
the two reigning dynasties with each other, as well
as concerning customs, personages, etc. The Emperor
remarked in conclusion that he would give his grandson the same advice that was given to him by
Count Adlerberg, on the occasion of his first visit as a
young man to Russia, viz.: " In general, there, as
elsewhere, people prefer praise to criticism." Prince

Bismarck closed his remarks with these words : " In the East, all those who wear their shirts outside their trousers are decent people, but, as soon as they tuck their shirts inside their trousers, and hang a medal around their necks, they become pig-dogs."

From St. Petersburg I repeatedly reported to my grandfather and Prince Bismarck. Naturally I described, to the best of my ability, the impressions which I received there. I noticed especially that the old Russo-Prussian relations and sentiments had cooled to a marked extent and were no longer such as the Emperor and Prince Bismarck had assumed in their talks with me. After my return, both my grandfather and the prince praised me for my plain, clear report, which was all the pleasanter for me since I was oppressed by the feeling that I had been forced to disillusion these high personages of a number of matters.

In 1886—at the end of August and beginning of September—after the last meeting at Gastein of Emperor William the Great and Prince Bismarck with Emperor Franz Joseph, at which I also was present by command of my grandfather, I was commissioned to report personally to Tsar Alexander III concerning the decisions made at Gastein and to take up with him the questions relating to the Mediterranean and Turkey. Prince Bismarck gave me his instructions, sanctioned by Emperor William. These dealt more particularly with Russia's desire to reach Constantinople, to which the prince meant to raise no obstacles ; on the contrary, I received direct instructions to offer Constantinople and the Dardanelles to Russia. In other words, the San Stefano and Berlin treaties had been dropped. There was a plan to persuade Turkey in a friendly way that an understanding with Russia was very desirable for her.

The Tsar received me cordially at Brest-Litovsk, but I was present there at reviews of troops and fortress and defensive manœuvres which unquestionably suggested an anti-German policy.

In connexion with my conversations with the Tsar, the following remark by him is of importance : " If I wish to have Constantinople, I shall take it whenever I feel like it, without need of permission or approval from Prince Bismarck." After this rude refusal of Bismarck's offer of Constantinople, I looked upon my mission as a failure and made my report to the prince accordingly.

When the prince decided to make his offer to the Tsar, he must have altered his political conceptions which had led to San Stefano and the Berlin Congress, or else, on account of the development of the general political situation in Europe, he considered that the moment had come for shuffling the political cards in another way ; or, as my grandfather had put it, to " juggle " differently. Only a man of the world-importance and diplomatic ability of Prince Bismarck could embark on such a course. Whether the prince had planned his big political game with Russia in such a way that he might, first, by means of the Congress of Berlin, prevent a general war and cajole

England, and then, after having thus hindered Russia's Eastern aspirations by a stroke of genius, cater to these aspirations later in an even more striking manner, it is impossible for me to say. Prince Bismarck never told anyone about his great political projects. If the above theory is correct, Bismarck, trusting absolutely to his skill in statesmanship, must have reckoned upon bringing Germany still more into Russian favour, because Russian aspirations were brought to fulfilment by Germany alone—and that at a moment when the general European political situation was less strained than in 1877–8. In this case, nobody but Prince Bismarck could have played this tremendous game to a successful end ; and therein lies the weakness in the superiority of great men. Had he informed England of his offer to the Tsar, England, as in 1878, must have been opposed to it.

Be that as it may, the prince now adopted the policy which had occurred to me when I realized the disillusionment of the Russians when they stood before the gates of Constantinople and were not allowed to enter.

At Brest-Litovsk, in the course of the constant military preparations of all kinds, I could easily see that the conduct of the Russian officers towards me was essentially cooler and haughtier than on the occasion of my first visit to St. Petersburg. Only the small group of old generals, especially those at the Russian Court who were contemporary with Alexander II. and who knew and esteemed Emperor

William the Great, still showed their reverence for him and their friendly feeling towards Germany. In the course of a talk with one of them concerning the relations between the two courts, armies and countries, which I had found undergoing a change in comparison with former times, the old general said : " C'est ce vilain congrès de Berlin. Une grave faute du Chancelier. Il a détruit l'ancienne amitié entre nous, planté la méfiance dans les cœurs de la Cour et du Gouvernement, et fourni le sentiment d'un grave tort fait à l'armée russe après sa campagne sanglante de 1877, pour lequel elle veut sa revanche. Et nous voilà ensemble avec cette maudite République Française, plein de haine contre vous et rempli d'idées subversives, qui en cas de guerre avec vous, nous coûteront notre dynastie."* A prophetic foreshadowing of the downfall of the reigning Russian dynasty !

From Brest I went to Strassburg, where my grandfather was attending the Imperial manœuvres. In spite of the failure of my mission I found calm judgments of the political situation. My grandfather was pleased at the cordial greetings from the Tsar, which, in so far as the personal relationship of the two rulers was concerned, showed no change of heart. Also, to my surprise, I received a letter from

* " It is that confounded Congress of Berlin. A serious mistake on the part of the chancellor. He has destroyed the old friendship between us, sown distrust in the hearts of the Court and the Government, and engendered the idea of a great injustice to the Russian army after its bloody 1877 campaign, for which it desires revenge. And here we are by the side of that damned French Republic, full of hate for you and of subversive ideas, which, in case of a war with you, will cost us our dynasty."

Prince Bismarck wherein he expressed gratitude and appreciation to me for my actions and my report. This meant all the more to me since my statements could not have been agreeable to my grandfather and the chancellor. The Congress of Berlin had, especially in Russian military circles, destroyed the remnants of the brotherhood in arms still fostered among us and had engendered a hatred against everything Prussian and German, stirred up by association with French officers, and increased by the French until it had developed into the desire of vengeance by means of arms. That was the soil in which, later, the world-war ambitions of our foes found nourishment. " *Revanche pour Sedan* " combined with " *Revanche pour San Stefano.*" The words of the old general at Brest have remained unforgettably engraved upon my memory. They induced me to bring about my many meetings with Alexander III and Nicholas II, at which my grandfather's wish, impressed upon me on his death-bed, that I should watch over our relations with Russia, was always my guiding motive.

In 1890, at the Narva manœuvres, I was obliged to describe minutely to the Tsar the retirement of Prince Bismarck. The Tsar listened very attentively. When I had finished, the usually very cool and reserved sovereign, who seldom spoke about politics, spontaneously seized my hand, thanked me for this token of my confidence, regretted that I had been brought into such a situation and added, in exactly these words : " Je comprends parfaitement Ta ligne

c

d'action ; le prince avec toute sa grandeur n'était
après tout rien d'autre que Ton employé ou fonction-
naire.   Le moment ou il réfusait d'agir selon Tes
ordres, il fallait le renvoyer.   Moi pour me part je
me suis toujours méfié de lui, et je ne lui ai jamais
cru un mot de ce qu'il faisait savoir ou me disait
lui-même, car j'étais sur et savais qu'il me blaguait
tout les temps.   Pour les rapports entre nous deux,
mon cher Guillaume—[this was the first time that
the Tsar so addressed me]—la chute du prince aura
les meilleures conséquences, la méfiance disparaîtra.
J'ai confiance en Toi.   Tu peux te fier a Moi."*   I
recorded this important conversation immediately it
occurred.   I am sufficiently objective to ask myself
to what extent the courtesy of one ruler to another,
and possibly, in addition, the satisfaction at the
elimination of a statesman of Bismarck's importance,
can have influenced the Tsar, consciously or unconsciously, in making this statement.   Prince Bismarck's belief in the Tsar's trust in him was, sub-
jectively, undoubtedly genuine, and, moreover, there
can be no doubt as to the esteem in which Alexander III held Bismarck's ability as a statesman.

In any case, the Tsar remained true to his word
up to the day of his death.   This, to be sure, did

---

* " I understand perfectly Thy line of action ; the prince, with all his
greatness, was, after all, merely Thy employé or official.   As soon as he
refused to follow Thy orders, it was necessary to dismiss him.   As for me, I
always distrusted him, and I never believed a word of what he had told to me
or said to me himself, for I was sure and knew that he was hoaxing me all the
time.   As to the relations between us two, my dear William, the downfall of
the prince will have the best of results ; distrust will disappear.   I have confidence in Thee.   Thou canst trust Me."

little to change Russia's general policy, but Germany, at least, was safe from an attack from that quarter. The straightforward character of Alexander III guaranteed this—it became otherwise under his weak son.

Whatever one's attitude may be towards Bismark's Russian policy, one thing must be acknowledged : the prince, despite the Berlin Congress and the *rapprochement* of France to Russia, was able to avoid serious friction. That is equivalent to saying that, reckoning from the time of the Berlin Congress, he played a superior diplomatic and statesmanlike game for twelve years (1878–90). One must also lay stress upon the fact that it was a German statesman who, in 1878, prevented a general war, even at the cost of weakening the relations of Germany to Russia. As a statesman of genius, knowing exactly what he was aiming at, he held the justifiable belief that he would succeed in strengthening these relations once more, or, at least, in avoiding conflicts after he had overcome the crisis threatening all Europe. He succeeded in doing that for twelve years, and his successors at the helm of the ship of State succeeded in doing likewise for twenty-four years more.

When I was a prince I purposely held aloof from party politics, concentrating my entire attention upon my duties in the different branches of the army to which I was assigned. This afforded me satisfaction and filled my whole life. For this reason I avoided, while I was Prince of Prussia, all attempts

to drag me into party activities. Often enough
endeavours were made, under the cloak of harmless
functions, teas and the like, to ensnare me into
political circles or for electioneering purposes; but
I always held aloof.

The outcome of the treacherous malady which
killed Emperor Frederick III was frankly told me
in advance by the German physicians called into consultation as experts by the English physician, Sir
Morell Mackenzie. My deep grief and sorrow were
all the greater because it was almost impossible for
me to speak alone with my beloved father. He was
guarded like a prisoner by the English physicians
and, though reporters from all countries could look
upon the poor sick man from the physician's room,
every kind of obstacle was placed in my path to keep
me from my father's side and even to prevent my
keeping in constant touch with him by writing.
My letters were often intercepted and not delivered.
Moreover, from among the group of watchers, an
infamous, organized campaign of slander was conducted in the newspapers against me. Two journa-
lists were especially active in this; one Herr Schmid-
rowitz and Monsieur Jacques St. Cère, of the *Figaro*—
the latter a German Jew who slandered him who
was later Emperor, in the most poisonous way in
France, until the " Petit Sucrier " trial put an end
to his activities.

I gave the dying Emperor his last joy on earth
when I had the Second Infantry Brigade march past
him, led by me in person. These were the first and

last troops seen by Frederick III as Emperor. He
delighted his son on this occasion by writing on a
little card, that he was so grateful for having had the
pleasure of seeing these troops and was proud to call
them his own. This event was a ray of light during
those gloomy Ninety-Nine Days which brought upon
me, as Crown Prince, much grief, humiliation and
suspicion. In fulfilment of my duty during this
crisis, I kept a watchful eye upon all happenings in
military, official and social circles, and was inwardly
outraged at the signs of slackness which I noted
everywhere, and more especially at the hostility
against my mother, which was becoming more and
more noticeable. Moreover, I was naturally deeply
hurt at the constant campaign of slander directed
against myself, which depicted me as living in discord with my father.

§ 3.

After Emperor Frederick III had closed his
eyes for ever, the heavy burden of governing the
empire fell upon my youthful shoulders. First of
all I was confronted with the necessity of making
changes in the government personnel in various
quarters. The military entourage of the two emperors,
as well as the body of officialdom, had grown too old.
The so-called " *maison militaire* " (military household) of Emperor William the Great had been retained
in its entirety by Emperor Frederick III, without
being required to discharge military duties. In

addition, there was the entourage of Emperor Frederick III. I proceeded to dismiss, in the friendliest way, all those gentlemen who wished to go into retirement. Some of them received positions in the army, a few of the younger remained in my service for the transition period.

During the Ninety-Nine Days, while I was still Crown Prince, I had quietly considered a selection of those personages to whom I proposed later to give appointments, for the physicians had left me no doubt that my father had only a short time to live. I ignored Court or external considerations; nothing but previous achievements and character moved me in my choice. I did away with the term *maison militaire* and transformed it into " Main Headquarters of His Majesty." In choosing my entourage, I took the advice of only one man, in whom I reposed special confidence, my former chief and brigade commander, General—afterwards Adjutant-General—von Versen, a man of a straightforward, knightly, rather harsh character, an officer of the Old Prussian school, a typical chip of the old block. During his military service in line and Guard regiments he had noted with an observing eye the Court influences and tendencies which had often worked to the disadvantage of the officer corps in the old *maison militaire*. In this direction the circle of ladies of high position, jokingly known among the officers as " *trente et quarante* " on account of their age, also played a certain part. I wished to eliminate such influences.

I appointed General von Wittich my first adjutant-general and General von Hahnke, commander of the Second Infantry Guard Division, chief of my military cabinet. The latter was a friend of Emperor Frederick III and, while I was still serving with the First Infantry Guard Regiment, he was my brigade commander. These two were men of military experience and iron principles, who shared absolutely the sentiments of their master and remained bound to me to the end of their lives by the most exemplary fidelity.

At the head of my Court I appointed a man known to me from my youth, my father's former court-marshal, Count August Eulenberg, who remained at the head of the Ministry of the Royal House until his death in June, 1921, at the age of 82 years. He was a man of fine tact, uncommon ability, clear insight in Court as well as political matters, sincere character, and golden fidelity to his King and his King's family. His manifold abilities would have enabled him, to the same degree that they had made him known as court-marshal throughout Europe, to act with equal success as ambassador or as Imperial Chancellor. Working with unswerving zeal, endowed with winning politeness, he stood by me with helpful counsel in many matters—dynastic, family, Court, public life. He had to do with many men in all social strata and all walks of life, by all of whom he was revered and esteemed, and he was treated by me likewise with friendship and gratitude.

After consultation with Prince Bismarck, Herr

von Lucanus, from the Ministry of Public Worship and Instruction, was appointed Chief of the Civil Cabinet. Prince Bismarck observed jokingly that he was pleased with this choice, since Herr von Lucanus was known to him as an able and enthusiastic huntsman, which was always a good recommendation for a civilian official. He added that a good huntsman was a regular good fellow. Herr von Lucanus took over his post from His Excellency von Wilmowski. He discharged his duties admirably, and, being well endowed in everything pertaining to art, technical matters, science and politics, he was to me a counsellor, untiring collaborator, and friend. He combined with a healthy knowledge of men a strong dash of refined humour, which is so often lacking in men of the Germanic race.

With Prince Bismarck I had stood on very good and trustful terms ever since my association with the Foreign Office. Then, as previously, I revered the powerful chancellor with all the ardour of my youth, was proud to have served under him and to have the opportunity now to work with him as my chancellor.

The prince was present during the last hours of the old Emperor and had listened with me to the latter's political testament to his grandson—i.e. his desire regarding the special care to be lavished upon our relations with Russia. In accordance with the last wish of my dying grandfather, and in order to emphasize our relations with Russia, the prince brought about my summer trip to St. Petersburg as my first political act in the eyes of the world. He also drew up the programme for my journey.

An obstacle was placed in the way of carrying out this plan by a letter from Queen Victoria of England, who, upon hearing of the projected visit to St. Petersburg, expressed to her eldest grandson in a good-humoured but authoritative tone, her disapproval of the contemplated journey. She said that a year of mourning must first elapse, after which my first visit was due to her as my grandmother, and to England as my mother's native country, before other lands should be considered. When I placed this letter before the prince, he gave way to a violent fit of anger. He spoke about "family dictation in England," of interference from that quarter, which must cease. The tone of the letter showed, he said, how the Crown Prince and Emperor Frederick had been ordered about and influenced by his mother-in-law, wife, etc. Thereupon the prince wished to draw up the text of a reply to the Queen. I remarked that I would prepare the appropriate answer, steering the proper middle course between the grandson and the Emperor, and that I would show it to the prince before dispatching it.

The answer paid heed, in its outward form, to the close relationship between a grandson and his grandmother—who had carried him in her arms when he was a baby and, in view of her age alone, commanded great respect—but, in its essentials, it laid stress upon the position and duty of the German Emperor, compelled to carry out unconditionally a command of his dying grandfather affecting Germany's most vital interests. It stated that the grandson was obliged to respect this command of his grandfather in the interests of the country, that the representation of those interests had now devolved upon him by the will of God, and that his royal grandmother must leave to him the question of deciding in what manner this was to be done. I added that, otherwise, I was her loving grandson, who would always be grateful for any advice from his grandmother, who had derived so much experience from her long reign; but that I was, nevertheless, in matters affecting Germany, compelled to retain my freedom of action. The visit to St. Petersburg, I said, was politically necessary, and the command of my Imperial grandfather was consonant with the close family relations between me and the Russian Imperial house; therefore it would be carried out.

The prince approved of the letter. The answer, which arrived after a while, was surprising. The Queen agreed that her grandson was in the right; he must act in accordance with the interests of his country; she would be glad to see him, even if it were later on, at her own home. From that day onward my relations with the Queen, who was feared even by her own children, were of the best imaginable; from that day onward she never treated her grandson except as a sovereign of equal rank with herself!

On my first journeys I was accompanied by

Count Herbert, as the representative of the Foreign Office. He drew up the speeches and conducted the political conferences, in so far as they were of an official nature, in accordance with his father's instructions.

Upon my return from Constantinople in 1889 I described to the prince, at his request, my impressions of Greece, where my sister Sophie was married to the heir-apparent, the Crown Prince Constantine, and also my impressions of Constantinople. In doing this, it struck me that Prince Bismarck spoke quite disdainfully of Turkey, of the men in high positions there and the conditions of the country. I thought I might inspire him in part with essentially more favourable opinions, but my efforts were of little avail. Upon asking the prince the reason why he held such an unfavourable opinion, he answered that Count Herbert had reported very disapprovingly on Turkey. Prince Bismarck and Count Herbert were never favourably inclined towards Turkey and they never agreed with me in my Turkish policy—the old policy of Frederick the Great.

During the last period of his tenure of office as chancellor, Bismarck declared that the maintenance of friendly relations with Russia, whose Tsar reposed special trust in him, was the most important reason for his remaining at his post. It was in this connexion that he gave me the first hints concerning the secret reinsurance treaty with Russia. Until then I had heard nothing about it, either from the prince or the Foreign Office, although I had associated myself particularly actively with Russian matters.

When I assumed the reins of government after the early death of my father, the generation of the grandson, as I have already remarked, followed upon the generation of the grandfather, which meant that the entire generation of Emperor Frederick was passed over. This generation, through its dealings with the Crown Prince Frederick William, was imbued with many Liberal ideas and projects of reform which were to be carried out under the direction of the Emperor Frederick. Upon his death, this entire generation, especially the politicians, found itself deceived in its hopes of exerting influence, and felt itself, to a certain extent, in the position of an orphan. Those belonging to it, despite the fact that they did not know my inner thoughts and aims, adopted a distrustful and reserved attitude towards me, instead of transferring their interest from the father to the son, for the purpose of furthering the welfare of the Fatherland.

There was one exception to this, a representative of the National Liberals—Herr von Benda, a man still in the full bloom of youth. While I was yet a prince I had made his acquaintance at the great hare-hunts promoted by Councillor Dietze at Barby. There Herr von Benda had won my affection and confidence when I, surrounded by older men, had listened to discussions on political, agricultural and national economic questions. In the course of these discussions, Herr von Benda held my attention by reason of his independent, interesting judgment. I accepted with pleasure an invitation to Benda's country seat, Rudow, near Berlin, and from this arose the custom of a regular yearly visit. The hours spent in the family circle at Rudow stand out pleasantly in my memory. Benda's talented daughters used to regale us industriously with music. The political conversations there proved Herr von Benda to be a man of great foresight, with a freedom from partisan considerations that gave him an open mind as to the general needs of the State, to an extent seldom found among members of political parties. He gave me many a helpful piece of advice for the future, drawn from the depths of his faithful, genuinely Prussian heart. Herr von Benda was firmly attached to the family of his sovereign; yet he was able to feel broad tolerance for men of other parties.

The later periods of my reign proved that I was not hostile to any party, with the exception of the Ultra-Socialists; also, that I was not anti-Liberal. My most important Finance Minister was the Liberal, Miquel; my Minister of Commerce was the Liberal, Moeller; the leader of the Liberals, Herr von Bennigsen, was Chief President of Hanover. I stood very close, especially in the second half of my reign, to an elderly Liberal deputy, whose acquaintance I made through Herr von Miquel. This was Herr Seydel (Celchen), owner of an estate in eastern Germany—a man with two clever eyes, which gazed forth from a clean-shaven face. He worked with Miquel in railway and canal matters, and was a

thoroughly able, simple, practical man—a Liberal
with a streak of Conservatism.

Naturally, I had numerous dealings and points of
contact with the Conservative Party, for the members of the country nobility often met me at Court
and other hunts, or else came to Court and served in
Court positions. Through them I could become
thoroughly informed on all agrarian questions and
learn where the farmer's shoe pinched him.

The Free-thinkers, under their " unswerving "
leader, entered into no relations with me ; they
limited themselves to opposition.

In my conversations with Benda and Bennigsen,
we often spoke of the future of Liberalism, and, on
one occasion, Benda made this interesting observation : " It is not necessary and also not advisable to
have the Prussian heir-apparent dabble in Liberalism
—we have no use for that sort of thing. He must be
essentially conservative, though he must, at the same
time, combine this with breadth of mind, and avoid
narrowness and prejudice against other parties."

Bennigsen agreed with me when I spoke to him
of the necessity for the National Liberals to revise
their programme—the original motto on which :
" Maintenance of the German Empire and Freedom
of the Press," had long served to rally the members
around the Liberal banner ; by such revision the
proselytizing power of the old brand of Prussian
Liberalism would not be lost among the people.
Both the Prussian Liberals and the Conservatives,
I continued, made the mistake of remembering too

well the old period of conflict of 1861–6 ; and, at elections and other political fights, they were prone to fall back into the habits of those days. That period, I said, so far as our generation was concerned, had already passed into history and come to an end ; the present had begun for us with the year 1870 and the new empire ; our generation had drawn a line under the year 1866 ; we must build anew upon the foundations of the empire ; political parties must shape their course also in this direction and not take over from the past stuff that was outworn and, moreover, calculated to create discord. Unfortunately all this has not come to pass. Bennigsen made a very telling point when he said : " Woe to the North German Liberals if they come under the leadership of the South German Democrats, for that will mean the end of real, genuine Liberalism ! Then we shall get the masked democracy arising from below, for which we have no use hereabouts."

The Conservative Party, honourable and faithful to its King, unfortunately has not always produced leaders of superior endowments who were, at the same time, skilful, tactically-trained politicians. The agrarian wing was at times too strongly assertive and was a burden to the party. Moreover, memories of the period of conflict were still too lively. I counselled union with the Liberals, but found little support. I often pointed out that the National Liberals in the empire were true to the empire and to the Emperor, for which reason they should be

thoroughly welcome to the Conservatives as allies ;
that I could not and did not wish to govern without
them in the empire, and was absolutely unwilling to
govern against them ; that North German Conservatism was misunderstood in some parts of the empire,
because of differences in historical development ; and
that, therefore, the National Liberals were its natural
allies. It was owing to these views of mine, for
instance, that I removed Court Preacher Stocker—a
man of brilliant achievement as a social missionary—
from his post, because he made a demagogical provocative speech in South Germany, aimed against
the Liberals there.

The Centre Party was welded together by the
Kulturkampf and was strongly anti-Protestant and
hostile to the empire. Notwithstanding this, I had
dealings with many important men of the party and
managed to interest them in practical collaboration
for the good of all. In this, Schorlemer (the father)
was especially helpful to me. He never made a
secret of his Prussian loyalty to his King. His son,
the well-known Minister of Agriculture, even joined
the Conservative Party. In many matters, the
Centre co-operated ; at one period it possessed, in
its old leader, Windthorst, the keenest politician in
the legislature. Nevertheless, in spite of all this,
one could not help being aware of the underlying
Centreist conviction that the interests of the Roman
Church must always be maintained and never be
relegated to a secondary place.

§ 4

When I was Prince William, I was placed for a long time under the Chief President of the province of Brandenburg, von Achenbach, in order that I might study questions of home administration, and gain experience in economic questions while taking an active part in the work. Spurred on by the captivating discourses of Achenbach, I derived from this period of my life a special interest in the economic side of the inner development of the country, whereas the purely juridical side of the administration interested me to a lesser degree. Canal construction, highway building, forestry, improvement in all kinds of transportation facilities, betterment of dwellings, introduction of machines into agriculture and their co-operative development—all these were matters with which I busied myself later on ; this was especially true in regard to hydraulic work and the development of the network of railways, particularly in the badly neglected territory of eastern Germany.

I discussed all these matters with the ministers of State, after I had ascended the throne. In order to urge them on, I allowed them free rein in their various domains. This turned out to be hardly possible so long as Prince Bismarck remained in office, for he reserved to himself the main decision in everything, and thereby impaired the independence of those working with him. I soon saw that the ministers, being entirely under Bismarck's thumb, could not declare themselves in favour of

D

" innovations " or ideas of the " young master " of which Bismarck disapproved. The ministry, in short, was nothing but a tool in the hand of Bismarck, and acted completely in accordance with his wishes. In itself, it was natural enough that a Premier of such overwhelming importance, who had won for Prussia and Germany such great political victories, should dominate his ministers completely and lead them despotically. Nevertheless, I found myself in a difficult position. The typical answer with which my suggestions were met was : " Prince Bismarck does not want that done ; we cannot get him to consent to that ; Emperor William I would not have asked such a thing ; that is not in accordance with tradition, etc." I realized more and more that, as a matter of fact, I had no Ministry of State at my disposal ; that the gentlemen composing it, from long force of habit, considered themselves officials of Prince Bismarck.

Here is an example to show the attitude of the cabinet towards me in those Bismarckian days. The question arose of the renewal of the Socialist Law, a political measure devised by Prince Bismarck for fighting Socialism. A certain paragraph therein was to be toned down, in order to save the law. Bismarck opposed the change. There were sharp differences of opinion. I summoned a Crown Council. Bismarck spoke in the antechamber with my adjutant ; he declared that His Majesty completely forgot that he was an officer and wore a sword-belt ; that he must fall back upon the army and lead it against the

Socialists in the event of the Socialists resorting to revolutionary measures ; that the Emperor should leave him a free hand, and he would restore quiet once for all. At the Council meeting Bismarck stuck to his opinion. The individual ministers, when asked to express their views, were lukewarm. A vote was taken—the entire ministry voted against me.

This vote showed me once again the absolute domination exerted by the chancellor over his ministers. Deeply dissatisfied, I talked over the matter with His Excellency Lucanus, who was as much struck as I was by the situation. Lucanus called upon some of the ministers and took them to task for their attitude, whereupon they made it clear that they were " not in a position " to oppose the prince, and declared that it was quite impossible that they should be expected to vote against his wishes.

The great strike of Westphalian coal workers in the spring of 1889 took the civil administration by surprise, and caused great confusion and bewilderment, especially among members of the Westphalian provincial administration. From all sides came calls for troops ; every mine-owner wanted, if possible, to have sentries posted outside his room. The commanders of the troops which were summoned immediately made reports on the situation as they found it. Among them was one of my former barrack comrades, belonging to the Hussar Guard Regiment, von Michaelis by name, who was famous as a wit. He rode alone and unarmed among the crowds of strikers,

who—the early spring being remarkably warm—
were camped upon the hillsides, and soon managed,
by his confidence-inspiring, jovial ways, to set up a
harmless intercourse with the workmen. By ques-
tioning them he obtained much valuable information
about the grievances—real and imaginary—of the
workers, as well as about their plans, hopes and
desires for the future. He soon won for himself
general appreciation and affection among the workers
and handled them so well that complete quiet reigned
in his territory. When, on account of nervous and
worried telegrams from the big industrial leaders and
officials, received at the office of the Imperial Chancellor, I inquired of Michaelis how the situation stood,
the following telegraphic answer came from him:
" Everything quiet, excepting the Government
officials."

During the spring and summer a mass of material
was collected from the announcements and reports
received, which showed clearly that all was not well
in industrial circles; that many a demand of the
workers was justified and, to say the least, entitled to sympathetic investigation both on the part
of the employers and the officials. The realization
of this, which was confirmed when I questioned
my former tutor, Privy Councillor Dr. Hintzpeter—
a man particularly well informed on social phenomena,
especially those in his own province—caused the
resolve to ripen in me to summon the State Council,
include employers and employees in its deliberations,
and to bring about, under my personal direction, a

thorough investigation of the labour question. I
decided that by this method there would be acquired
guiding principles and material which would serve the
chancellor and the Prussian Government as a basis
for working out appropriate projects for new laws.

Inspired by such thoughts I went to His Excellency von Bötticher, who at once prophesied opposition on the part of the chancellor to such action,
and advised strongly against it. I stuck to my ideas,
adducing, in support of them, the maxim of Frederick
the Great: " Je veux être un Roi des gueux." [" I
wish to be a King of the rabble."] I said that it was
my duty to take care of those Germans who were
exhausted by industry, to protect their strength and
better their chances of existence.

The predicted opposition from Prince Bismarck
was soon forthcoming. There was much trouble
and fighting before I put through what I wanted,
owing to the fact that some of the big industrial
interests ranged themselves on the side of the chancellor. The State Council met, presided over by me.
At the opening session the chancellor unexpectedly
appeared. He made a speech in which he ironically
criticized and disapproved of the whole undertaking
set in motion by me, and refused his co-operation.
Thereupon he walked out of the room.

After his departure, the strange scene had its
effect on the assembly. The fury and ruthlessness
which the great chancellor brought to the support of
his own policy and against mine, based upon his
absolute belief in the correctness of his own judgment,

made a tremendous impression upon me and all those
present. Nevertheless, it stood to reason that I was
deeply hurt by what had occurred. The assembly
proceeded to take up its work again and turned out a
wealth of material for the extension of that social
legislation called into being by Emperor William the
Great, which is the pride of Germany, in that it
evinces a protective attitude towards the labouring
classes such as is not to be found in any other country
on earth.

Thereupon I decided to summon an International
Social Congress. Prince Bismarck opposed this also.
Switzerland was contemplating something similar
and had thought of convening a congress at Berne.
Roth, the Swiss Ambassador, hearing of my scheme,
advised the cancellation of the invitations to Berne
and acceptance of an invitation to Berlin. What he
wished occurred. Thanks to the generosity of Herr
Roth it was possible to convene the congress at
Berlin. The material collected as a result of it was
worked out and applied in the form of laws—only
in Germany, however.

Later on I talked with Bismarck concerning his
project of fighting the Socialists with cannon and
bayonets in the event of their resort to revolutionary acts. I sought to convince him that it was
out of the question for me, almost immediately
after William the Great had closed his eyes after a
blessed reign, to stain the first years of my government with the blood of my own people. Bismarck
was unmoved ; he declared that he would assume

responsibility for his actions; that all I need do was to leave the matter to him. I answered that I could not square such a course with my conscience and my responsibility before God, particularly as I knew perfectly well that conditions among the labouring classes were bad and must be bettered at all costs.

The conflict between the views of the Emperor and the chancellor relative to the social question— i.e. the furtherance of the welfare of the labouring classes of the population with participation therein by the State—was the real cause of the break between us, and caused a hostility towards me lasting for years on the part of Bismarck and a large part of the German nation—especially of the official class—that was devoted to him.

This conflict between the chancellor and myself arose because of his belief that the social problem could be solved by severe measures and, if the worst came to the worst, by means of soldiers; not by following principles of general love for mankind or " humanitarian nonsense " which, he believed, he would have to adopt in conforming to my views.

Bismarck was not a foe to the labouring classes— on that I wish to lay stress, in view of what I have previously said. On the contrary! He was far too great a statesman to underrate the importance of the labour question to the State; but he considered the whole matter from the standpoint of pure expediency for the State. The State, he believed, should care for the labourer, as much and in whatever manner

it deemed proper ; he would not admit of any co-
operation of the workers in this. Agitation and
rebellion, he believed, should be severely suppressed ;
by force of arms, if necessary. Government protection on the one hand, the mailed fist on the other—
that was Bismarck's social policy.

I, however, wished to win over the soul of the
German working man, and I fought zealously to
attain this goal. I was filled with the consciousness
of a plain duty and responsibility towards my entire
people—also, therefore, towards the labouring classes.
What was theirs by right and justice should become
theirs, I thought ; moreover, I believed that this
should be brought about, wherever the will or power
of the employers ceased, by the lord of the land and
his government, in so far as justice or necessity
demanded. As soon as I had recognized the necessity
for reforms, to some of which the industrial elements
would not consent, impelled by a sense of justice I
took up the cudgels for the labouring classes.

I had studied history sufficiently to guard myself
against the delusion of believing in the possibility of
making an entire people happy. I realized clearly
that it was impossible for *one* human being to make
a nation happy. The truth is that the only nation
that is happy is the one that is contented or, at
least, is willing to be contented ; a willingness which
implies a certain degree of realization of what is possible—a sense of the practical, in short. Unfortunately, this is often lacking.

I was well aware that, in the unbounded demands

of the Socialist leaders, unjustified greed would be increasingly developed; but for the very reason that I wished to be able to combat unjustifiable aspirations with a clear conscience and in a convincing way, it behoved me not to deny recognition and aid to justifiable aspirations.

The policy that kept in view the welfare of the workers unquestionably imposed a heavy burden upon all the industrial elements of Germany in the matter of competition in the world-market, through the well-known laws for the protection of working men. This was especially true in relation to an industrial system such as the Belgian, which could, without hindrance, squeeze the last drop out of the human reserves of Belgium and pay low wages, without feeling any pangs of conscience or compassion for the sinking *moral* of the exhausted, unprotected people. By means of my social legislation I made such conditions impossible in Germany, and I caused it to be introduced by General von Bissing in Belgium also, during the War, in order to promote the welfare of the Belgian workers. First of all, however, this legislation is—to use a sporting term—a handicap upon German industry in the battle of world competition; it alienated many big leaders of industry, an attitude which, from their point of view, was quite natural. But the lord of the land must always bear in mind the welfare of the whole nation; therefore, I went my way unswervingly.

On the other hand, those workers who blindly followed the Socialist leaders gave me no word of thanks for the protection created for them nor for the work I had done. Between them and myself lies the motto of the Hohenzollerns : *Suum cuique.* That means " To each his own "—not, as the Social Democrats would have it, " To everyone the same ! "

I also harboured the idea of preventing to some extent competitive warfare, at least in the industrial world of the European continent, by bringing about a sort of quota-fixing arrangement in foreign countries, thereby facilitating production and making possible a healthier mode of life among the working classes.

There is great significance in the impression which foreign workers got in studying Germany's social legislation. A few years before the War people in England, under the pressure of labour troubles, woke up to the conviction that better care must be taken of the workers. As a result of this, commissions visited Germany, some of them composed of working-men. Guided by representative Germans, Socialists among them, they visited the industrial districts, factories, benevolent institutions, sanatoria of insurance companies, etc., and were astonished at all the things they saw. At the farewell dinner given them the English leader of the working-men's deputations turned to Bebel, and made this concluding remark : " After all we have seen of what is done in Germany for the workers, I ask you : are you people still Socialists ? " And the Englishmen remarked to a German that they would be quite satisfied if they could succeed, after long fights in Parliament, in putting through one-tenth of what had already been accomplished years before in Germany towards bettering the condition of the labouring classes.

I had observed with interest these visits of the English deputations and marvelled at their ignorance of German conditions. But I marvelled even more at a question on the same subject asked by the English Government, through the channel of the English Embassy, which betrayed an absolutely amazing lack of knowledge of the progress made in Germany in the province of social reform. I questioned the English Ambassador, remarking that as England was represented in 1890 at the Berlin Social Congress the Government must certainly have been informed, at least through the embassy, of the Reichstag debates, which had dealt in a detailed manner with the various social measures. The ambassador replied that the same thing had also occurred to him and caused him to have the earlier records of the embassy investigated, whereupon it had transpired that the embassy had sent the fullest reports on the subject to London and that exhaustive reports had been forwarded home concerning every important stage in the progress of social reform; but, " because they came from Germany, nobody ever read them ; they were simply pigeon-holed and had remained there ever since; it is a downright shame ; Germany does not interest people at home." Thus the Briton, with a shrug of his shoulders. Neither the British King nor Parliament had enough conscience or time or desire to work for the betterment of the working class. The " policy of encirclement " for the annihilation of Germany, especially of its industry and, thereby, of its working population, was, in their eyes, far more important and rewarding. On November 9, 1918, the German Radical Socialist leaders, with their like-minded followers, joined forces with this British policy of annihilation.

In a small way, in places where I had influence, as, for instance, in the administration of my Court, and in the Imperial Automobile Club, I laid stress upon the social point of view of the question. For instance, out of the tips given by visitors to palaces, I caused a fund to be established which was destined solely for the benefit of the domestic staff, and which, in the course of time, reached a magnificent total. From this fund, the servants and their families received money for trips to bathing resorts, costs of taking cures, burial expenses, dowries for their children, confirmation expenses, and similar payments.

When, at the request of the newly-founded Imperial Automobile Club, I took it under my protection, I accepted an invitation to a luncheon in the beautiful rooms of the club-house, built by Ihne. In addition to magnates such as the Duke of Ratibor, the Duke of Ujest, etc., I found there a number of gentlemen from Berlin's high financial circles. Some of them behaved rather wildly. When the conversation turned to the subject of drivers, I suggested establishing a fund which, in case of accident, illness

or death befalling these men, should provide means
of livelihood for those whom they left behind. The
suggestion met with unanimous approval and the fund
has had most excellent results. Later on I brought
about the establishment of a somewhat similar fund
for the skippers and pilots attached to the Imperial
Yacht Club at Kiel.

Special pleasure was afforded me by the Kaiser
Wilhelm Children's Home, founded by me at
Ahlbeck, at which, in peace times, between May and
the end of September in each year, a large number of
children from the most poverty-stricken working-
class districts in Berlin were accommodated, in suc-
cessive detachments, each party staying four weeks.
This home is still under the experienced direction
of the admirable superintendent, Miss Kirschner,
daughter of the former Chief Burgomaster of Berlin,
and it has achieved most brilliant results, both
physically and psychically. Weakened, pale, needy
children were there transformed into fresh, bloom-
ing, happy little beings, of whose welfare I often
joyfully convinced myself by personal visits.

For the very reason that I have spoken of my
quarrel with Bismarck as an outcome of labour
questions, I wish to add to what I have already said
about his basic position in the matter, one instance
showing how brilliantly the prince behaved in something that concerned the workers. In this, certainly, he was impelled by nationalistic motives,
but he also realized at once that it was necessary
to protect a large section against unemployment,

which caused him to intervene with the full weight of his authority.

Some time around 1886, while I was still Prince William, I had learned that the great Vulcan shipping firm at Stettin, owing to lack of orders, was confronted with bankruptcy, and its entire staff of workmen, numbering many thousands, with starvation, which would mean a catastrophe for the city of Stettin. Only by an order for the building of a big ship could the Vulcan yard be saved. Spurred on some time before by Admiral von Stosch, who wished to free us once and for all from the English shipbuilders, the Vulcan people had set to work courageously to build the first German armoured ship, christened by my mother in 1874 on her birthday, on which occasion I was present. Ever since that time the warships built at the Vulcan yards had always satisfied naval experts. The firm, however, seldom built warships.

The German mercantile marine, on the other hand, had not dared to follow the path courageously blazed by Admiral von Stosch. And now the brave German shipyard company was faced with ruin, since the North German Lloyd had refused its offer to build a passenger steamer, alleging that the English, because of their years of shipbuilding traditions, could build it better.

It was a serious emergency. I hastened to Prince Bismarck and laid the matter before him.

The chancellor was furious; his eyes flashed, his fist came crashing down on the table.

" What ! Do you mean to say that these shop-keepers would rather have their boats built in England than in Germany ? Why, that is un-heard of ! And is a good German shipyard to fail for such a reason ? The devil take this gang of traders ! "

He rang the bell and a servant entered.

" Have Privy Councillor X. come here immediately from the Foreign Office ! "

In a few minutes—during which the prince stamped up and down the room—the man summoned appeared.

" Telegraph to Hamburg, to our envoy—the Lloyd in Bremen is to have its new ship built by the Vulcan Company in Stettin ! "

The privy councillor vanished in hot haste, with " his coat-tails sticking straight out " behind him. The prince turned to me, and said : " I am greatly obliged to you. You have done the Fatherland, and also myself, an important service. Henceforth ships will be built in *our* yards—I'll take care to make this clear to the Hanseatic crowd. You may telegraph to the Vulcan people that the chancellor will guarantee that the ship will be built in the Vulcan yards. May this be the first of a whole lot of such ships ! As for the workers whom you have thus saved from unemployment, I hope that they will express their thanks to you ! "

I passed on the news to Privy Councillor Schlutow at Stettin and great was the joy caused thereby. This was the first step upon the road destined to lead to the construction of the magnificent German express steamers.

When, after I had ascended the throne in 1888, I went to Stettin, in order to place honorary insignia on the flags of my Pomeranian Grenadiers, I also visited the Vulcan shipyard, at the invitation of the directors. After my reception by the directors outside the yards, the great doors were flung open, and I walked inside; but, instead of work and pounding hammers, I found deep silence. The entire body of workmen was standing in a half-circle, with bared heads; in the middle stood the oldest workman of all, a man with a snow-white beard, bearing a laurel wreath in his hand.

I was deeply moved. Schlutow whispered to me: " A little pleasure for you, which the workmen themselves have thought of." The old workman stepped forward and, in pithy, plain words, expressed to me the gratitude of the workmen to me for having saved them, and, above all, their wives and children, from hardship and hunger, by my appeal to Bismarck about the building of the ship. As a token of their gratitude he asked my permission to hand over the laurel wreath. Most deeply moved, I took the wreath and expressed my pleasure at receiving my first laurels, without the shedding of a drop of blood, from the hands of honest German workmen.

That was in the year 1888! In those days the German working-classes knew how to appreciate the blessing of labour.

II

CAPRIVI

WHEN I began my reign, General von Caprivi was Chief of the Admiralty. He was the last general to hold this post. I at once energetically took in hand the development and reform—in fact, one may say the foundation anew—of the Imperial German Navy, based on my preliminary studies in England and at home. That action was not to the liking of the general, who was able but rather self-willed and not entirely devoid of pride.

Unquestionably he had rendered valuable services in mobilization, improvement of the officer corps and the development of the torpedo-boat organization. On the other hand, the building of ships and the replacement of outworn material were in a deplorable state, to the detriment of the fleet and to the dissatisfaction of the shipbuilding industry, which was growing and looking about for employment. As an Old Prussian general, Caprivi's way of thinking was that of his day—that of his comrades of 1864–5 and 1870–1. In his eyes, the army had always done everything and would continue to do so in future; ·therefore, no great demands for money to be devoted to the navy should be imposed upon the country, since should this be done, there was danger that the

sums destined for the army might be decreased and
its development thereby hampered. This idea, from
which he was not to be dissuaded, was altogether
wrong. The amounts granted did not flow into a
reservoir from which they might be directed, by
the mere opening of a valve, now into army, now into
navy channels. Whenever Caprivi was unwilling to
demand anything for naval construction, in order, by
so doing, to divert more money towards the army,
events did not happen as he foresaw. By his action
the army received not one penny more, but merely
whatever the Minister of War asked for and received
in accordance with his budget.

There was need of a Secretaryship of State for the
Navy which should be entirely independent of the
Ministry of War, part of whose duty it would be to
demand and obtain for the navy as much as was
required for the protection of our commerce and
colonies. That is what came to pass later on.

Caprivi soon came to me with the request that I
should relieve him of his post. He stated that he
was not satisfied with it in itself; that, moreover,
I had all kinds of plans for the future affecting the
navy which he considered impossible of realization;
in the first place, because there existed no means of
replacement for the officer corps—at that time the
yearly influx of cadets was between 60 and 80—and
a large navy without a large officer corps was un-
thinkable. In addition to this, he informed me, he
had soon realized in the course of His Majesty's tours
of inspection that the Emperor knew more about

naval matters than he did, a fact which placed him in an impossible situation in relation to his subordinates.

In view of these circumstances, I parted with him, placing him in command of an army corps. Following the motto "The navy for the seamen!" I chose, for the first time, an admiral as its chief, a step which was received in maritime circles with great joy. The man chosen was Admiral Count Monts.

When, soon afterwards, I was confronted with the rather unexpected retirement of Prince Bismarck, I found the choice of his successor a difficult one. Whoever he might be, he was sure to have a difficult task without any prospect of appreciation for what he might achieve—he would be looked upon as the usurper of a post to which he was not entitled and which he was not qualified to fill. Criticism, criticism, nothing but criticism—that was sure to be the daily bread upon which the new chancellor must reckon ; and he was also certain of becoming the target for the hostility of all those who favoured Prince Bismarck as well as of the many who, previously, could not do enough in opposition to him. There was bound to be a strong current of enmity towards the new chancellor, in which the old prince himself would not be the least serious factor.

After taking all this into consideration, it was decided to choose a man belonging to Prince Bismarck's generation, who had held a leading position in the wars and had already filled a government position

under him. Hence Caprivi was chosen. His age
was a guarantee that he would be a careful and calm
adviser for the "orphaned" young Emperor.

Very soon the question arose of the extension of
the reinsurance treaty with Russia. Caprivi declared
that, out of consideration for Austria, he was unable
to renew it, since the threat against Austria contained
therein, when it became known in Vienna—as it
almost unavoidably would—was such as to lead to
very unpleasant consequences. For this reason the
treaty lapsed. In my opinion it had already lost its
main value from the fact that the Russians no longer
stood whole-heartedly behind it. I was confirmed
in this view by a memorandum written by Count
Berchem, Under-Secretary of State, who had worked
with Prince Bismarck.

The agrarian Conservatives opposed Caprivi as a
man without landed property, and a violent fight
raged around the commercial treaties. These difficulties were greatly enhanced because Prince Bismarck,
ignoring his former maxims, took part in the fight
against his successor with all his characteristic energy.
Thus arose the opposition of the Conservatives against
the Government and the Crown, and the prince in
person sowed the seed from which later grew the
" misunderstood Bismarck " and that *Reichsverdros-
senheit* [unfriendliness to the empire] so often ex-
hibited in the Press. The " misunderstood Bismarck "
created permanent opposition throughout my reign
to my suggestions and aims by means of quotations,
speeches and writings, as well as by passive resistance

and thoughtless criticism. Everything that was done was painted in dark colours, made ridiculous and criticized from top to bottom, by a Press that placed itself quite willingly at the disposal of the prince and often out-Bismarcked Bismarck in its behaviour.

This phenomenon became most apparent at the time of the acquisition of Heligoland. This island, lying close in front of the great waterways leading to the principal Hanseatic commercial ports, was, in the hands of the British, a constant menace to Hamburg and Bremen and rendered futile any project for building a navy. Owing to this, I had firmly resolved to win back this aforetime German island to its Fatherland.

The means of securing the surrender from England of the red rock of Heligoland was found in the colonial domain. Lord Salisbury proved inclined to exchange the " barren rock " for Zanzibar and Witu in East Africa. From commercial sources and the reports of the commanders of German cruisers and gunboats which were stationed there and cruised along the coast of the recently acquired German East African colonies, I knew that, as soon as Tanga, Dar-es-Salaam, etc., rose to prosperity, the importance of Zanzibar as the principal port of transshipment would be a thing of the past. It was evident that as soon as these other harbours were made deep enough and provided with sufficient cargo-loading equipment for trading steamers, there would no longer be any need to ferry goods from the interior in dhows to Zanzibar, in order to have them

reloaded on vessels there, since they could be loaded
direct at the new harbours along the coast.

I was convinced, therefore, that we had, first, an
acceptable asset for purposes of exchange, and,
secondly, a good opportunity to avoid colonial friction with England and come to a friendly understanding with her. Caprivi agreed ; the negotiations were
concluded, and one evening, shortly before dinner, I
was able to tell the Empress and a few intimates the
exceedingly joyful tidings that Heligoland had become
German. A preliminary, and very important, extension of the empire had been achieved without bloodshed ; the first condition for the extension of the fleet was fulfilled, something which the
natives of the Hanseatic towns and the rest of the
North Germans had desired for centuries had
come to pass. In silence, an important event had
occurred.

Had Heligoland been acquired in the chancellorship of Prince Bismarck, it would probably have been
valued very highly. Having happened under Caprivi
it loosed a flood of criticism. It was merely Caprivi,
the usurper, who had had the audacity to sit in the
prince's chair, and the " irresponsible," " ungrateful,"
" impulsive " young master who had done such a
thing ! Had Bismarck only wished he could have
had the old rock any day, but he never would have
been so unskilful as to give up to the English for it
the very promising African possessions, and he never
would have allowed himself to be thus worsted.
That was the sort of thing heard almost everywhere.

The newspapers of the prince joined loudly in this note of criticism, to the great grief of the people of the Hanseatic cities.

Curious, indeed, were the criticisms of this exchange of Zanzibar and Witu, indulged in by the Bismarckian Press, which previously, when I worked under him, had always explained that the prince had not much belief in the value of colonies in themselves and looked upon them merely as objects of barter, possibly in deals with the British. His successor acted according to these ideas in the matter of Heligoland ; and was therefore most violently criticized and attacked. Not until the world war was on did I see articles in the German Press which unreservedly admitted the acquisition of Heligoland to be an act of far-sighted statesmanship and added reflections as to what would doubtless have happened if Heligoland had not become German.

The German nation has every reason to be thankful to Count Caprivi for this achievement, since thereby the building of its navy and its victory at the Skager Rak were made possible. As for the German navy it long ago acknowledged this.

The school law of Count Zedlitz aroused violent new conflicts. When they led to Zedlitz's retirement the cry arose among his adherents : " If the count goes, so must the chancellor."

Caprivi left his post, in a calm, dignified manner. He tried honestly, within the measure of his powers and abilities, to continue the traditions of Prince

Bismarck. In this he found little support among political parties, and, for this reason, had to endure the criticism and hostility of the public and of those who, had they acted for the right and the interests of the State, should have stood by him. Without one word of resentment, Caprivi, in noble silence, lived the remainder of his life in almost solitary retirement.

III

HOHENLOHE

§ 1

AGAIN I was confronted with the difficult task of choosing a chancellor. His position and activities were to be under somewhat the same auspices, and subject to the same conditions, as those of his predecessor. But now there was a definite desire that he should be a statesman, an elderly man of course, qualified to inspire Prince Bismarck with greater confidence than a mere general could do. It was assumed that a statesman would know better how to walk in the footsteps of the prince, politically speaking, and afford Bismarck fewer opportunities for criticism and attacks. These latter had tended to create gradually among all Government officials— who dated mostly from the period of Bismarck—an unmistakable nervousness and dissatisfaction, by which the work of the entire governmental system was impaired to an appreciable extent. Moreover, they lent to the Opposition in the Reichstag a constantly renewed strength drawn from elements previously faithful to the Government, and effected a generally detrimental influence. Especially was this the case in the Foreign Office; the spirit of Holstein, the supposed representative of the " old, tried

Bismarckian traditions," began to assert itself, so that there the unwillingness to collaborate with the Emperor became particularly strong, and the belief grew up that it was necessary to carry on, independently, the policy of Bismarck.

After mature deliberation, I decided to entrust the post of chancellor to Prince Hohenlohe, who was then governor of Alsace-Lorraine. At the outbreak of the war of 1870 he had succeeded, as Bavarian Minister, in prevailing upon Bavaria to enter the war on the side of Prussia. Ever since he had been highly esteemed by Prince Bismarck on account of his fidelity to the empire. It was natural to expect that Bismarck's opposition would cool off when confronted with such a successor. Thus, the choice of Hohenlohe as chancellor was strongly influenced by consideration for Prince Bismarck and for the public opinion inspired by him.

Prince Hohenlohe was the typical old-style *grand seigneur*. He was thoroughly urbane by nature and in his dealings with others ; a man of refined mind, with a slight touch of playful irony sometimes glinting through, keen on account of his years, a level-headed observer and judge of men. Despite the great difference in age between us he got along very well with me ; a circumstance made apparent by the fact that he was treated both by the Empress and myself as our uncle, and addressed as such, which brought about a certain atmosphere of intimate confidence in our intercourse. In his talks with me, especially when voicing his opinion as to appointments of officials, he gave very characteristic descriptions of the gentlemen under discussion, often combined with philosophical observations which proved that he had reflected deeply on life and humanity and were evidence of a mature wisdom grounded on experience.

Something happened during the first period of Hohenlohe's regime as chancellor which throws an interesting light upon the relations between France and Russia. At the time of the fraternization between Russia and France, I received reliable information from the General Staff, as well as from our embassy at Paris, to the effect that France contemplated the withdrawal of a number of her troops from Algeria, in order to shift them to southern France, for possible use either against Italy or against Alsace. I accordingly apprised Tsar Nicholas II of this news, adding the remark that I should be compelled to adopt counter-measures unless the Tsar could dissuade his ally from so provocative a step. At that time the Russian Minister for Foreign Affairs was Prince Lobanoff, formerly ambassador at Vienna, and well known for his pro-French proclivities. During the summer of 1895 he had visited France and had been cordially entertained. In the autumn, just as I was starting for the hunting at Hubertusstock on the Schorfheide near Eberswalde, Prince Lobanoff, on his return journey from Paris, requested to be received in audience by me, at the behest of the Tsar. Upon being received by me, he described the calm

and sensible frame of mind which he had found in
Paris, and sought to reassure me with regard to the
reported movement of troops, which, according to
him, was mere empty rumour and chatter without
any real foundation. He added that he was bringing
to me the most quietening assurances, that there
was no reason for me to feel the slightest alarm.
I thanked him heartily for his report, remarking
that the word " alarm " did not occur in the dic-
tionary of a German officer, and added that, if
France and Russia wished to make war, I could
not prevent it. Whereupon the prince, piously
casting up his eyes towards heaven, made the sign
of the Cross and said : " Oh, la guerre ! quelle idée
qui y pense, cela ne doit pas être." [" Oh, war,
what an idea, who thinks of such a thing ? It must
not be."] To that I replied that *I*, in any event,
was not thinking of it, but that an observer—and
he need not be very keen-eyed—must assuredly consider the constant celebrations and speeches, as well
as the official and unofficial visits exchanged between
Paris and St. Petersburg, as significant symptoms
which could not be ignored, and which were calculated to arouse great dissatisfaction in Germany ;
that, should it come to war, against my own will and
that of my people, I felt that, trusting in God and
in my army and people, it would be possible for
Germany to get the better of both opponents.

To this I added still another statement, reported
to me from Paris, which had been made by a Russian
officer who was in France as a member of a deputa-

tion of officers. Having been asked by a French comrade whether the Russians believed that they could beat the Germans, the gallant Slav replied: " Non, mon ami, nous serons battus à plate couture, mais qu'est-ce que ça fait ? Nous aurons la république." ["No, my friend, we shall be thoroughly beaten, but what does that matter ? We shall get a republic."] At first the prince eyed me, speechless, then, shrugging his shoulders, he remarked : " Oh, la guerre, il ne faut pas même y penser." ["Oh, war, one must not even think about it."] The officer had merely expressed the general opinion of the Russian intelligentzia and social circles. As far back as my first visit to St. Petersburg, in the early 'eighties, a grand duchess said to me at dinner, quite calmly : " Here we sit all the time on a volcano, we expect the revolution any day ! The Slavs are not faithful, they are not at all monarchical, all of them are republicans at heart ; they disguise their sentiments, and they lie, every one of them, all the time."

Three important events, related to foreign politics, came within the period of Prince Hohenlohe's chancellorship : the opening, in 1895, of the Kaiser Wilhelm Canal (North Sea–Baltic Canal), begun under Emperor William the Great, to which squadrons or individual ships representing countries all over the world were invited ; the annexation, in 1897, of Tsing-tao ; and the much-discussed Kruger dispatch.

Prince Hohenlohe played an especially important role in the annexation of Tsing-tao. He, too, was of the opinion that Germany needed some coaling stations for her ships, and that the demands of commercial bodies that the opportunity for opening up China to international trade be not allowed to pass, were justified. It was resolved that, under unimpaired Chinese sovereignty and after payment of the *Likin* (internal revenue tax), a trading port, with a naval coaling-station as protection, was to be founded, wherein it was contemplated that China be allowed to co-operate to the utmost possible extent. The station was to serve the ends of commerce, before all else, the military measures being limited solely to the protection of the trading centre as it developed; they did not constitute an end in themselves or a base for further military enterprises.

Already several places had been considered, but these, upon more careful investigation, had proved to be unsuitable, because they either had bad connexions or none at all with the interior regions, or were not promising from a commercial-political standpoint, or were encumbered by privileges already granted to other countries. Finally, it was agreed—because of the reports of Admiral Tirpitz, who was, at that time, in command of the East Asiatic Cruiser Squadron, and because of the opinion of the geographical expert, Freiherr von Richthofen, who, having been questioned on the subject, had drawn a most promising picture of the possibilities of development in Shantung—to found a settlement on the Bay of Kiao-chou.

The chancellor proceeded to collect data on the

political questions which arose as a result of this and consequently had to be taken into consideration. It was particularly necessary not to disturb Russia or interfere with her designs. Further information was obtained, some of it from our East Asiatic Division; from this source favourable reports came in as to anchorages and the ice-free nature of the Bay of Kiao-chou, and as to the prospects, if a port were to be founded there. From conversations among the officers of the Russian-China Division which had come to our ears during intercourse with them, we learned that the Russian admiral, in accordance with orders from his Government, had anchored one winter in the bay, but had found it so desolate and so atrociously lonesome—there were no tea-houses with Japanese geisha girls, which the Russians deemed absolutely indispensable to winter quarters—that the Russian squadron would never go back there again. It was also reported that the Russian admiral had advised his Government most earnestly against further prosecuting its intention of founding a settlement on this bay, because there was absolutely no advantage to be derived from it. Hence, the Russians had no intention of establishing a foothold there.

This last piece of information arrived at about the same time as the answer from the Russian Foreign Minister, Count Muravieff, sent through the German Ambassador, relative to the sounding of Russian opinion which had been made pursuant to instructions from the chancellor. Muravieff set forth that

Russia certainly had no direct claims, based on treaty with China, to the bay, but that she, nevertheless, laid claim to it on the basis of the *droit du premier mouillage* [right of first anchorage], seeing that the Russian ships had anchored there before those of any other fleet. This answer, it will be seen, ran counter to the report of our East Asiatic Division relative to the statements made by the Russian admiral.

When I, together with Hollmann, met the chancellor, in order to discuss the above answer, the prince listened to the reading of it with his little ironical smile and remarked that he had been unable to find any jurist at the Foreign Office who could tell him anything about this wonderful claim; was the navy in a position to do so ? Admiral Hollmann declared that he, in all his experience of foreign service, had never heard of it; that it was nonsense and an invention of Muravieff, whose only motive was unwillingness to have some other nation settle on the shores of the bay. I advised that Privy Councillor of the Admiralty, Perels, one of the most famous living experts, and an acknowledged authority on international maritime law, in this domain, be asked to deliver an opinion in order to clarify the question. This was done. The opinion tore Muravieff's contention to pieces, corroborated that of Hollmann, and completely did away with the legend of the " right of first anchorage."

Months elapsed; my visit to Peterhof of August, 1897, was imminent. In agreement with the prince, my uncle, I decided to discuss frankly the entire matter in person with the Tsar, and, if possible, put an end to Muravieff's notes and evasions. The conversation took place at Peterhof. The Tsar stated that he had no interest in the territory south of the Tientsin—Peking line, which meant that there was no reason why he should place obstacles in our path in Shantung; that his interest was concentrated upon the territory on the Yalu, around Port Arthur, etc., now that the English had made difficulties for him at Mokpo; that he would, in fact, be pleased if Germany should locate herself in future on the other side of the Gulf of Chih-li as Russia's welcome neighbour.

Afterwards, I had a talk with Muravieff. He employed all his arts, wriggled backwards and forwards in his statements, and finally brought up his famous " right of first anchorage." That was all I wanted. I now passed to the offensive myself, striking out at him squarely with the opinion delivered by Perels. When I told him, finally, as the Tsar desired, the result of the conversations between us two sovereigns, the diplomat was even more embarrassed, lost his assumed calm, and capitulated.

Thus was the soil prepared, politically speaking. In the autumn came the news from Bishop Anzer of the murder of the two German Catholic missionaries in Shantung. The entire German Catholic world, particularly the " colonials " in the Centre Party, demanded energetic measures. The chancellor proposed to me immediate intervention. While

F

I was engaged in the winter hunting at Lotalingen, I consulted with him, in one of the little towers of the castle there, as to what steps were to be taken. The prince proposed to entrust Prince Henry of Prussia, who was present, with the command of the squadron that was to be sent out to reinforce the East Asiatic Division. I informed my brother of this in the presence of the chancellor, whereat the prince and the others present were highly pleased. The chancellor sent the news to the Foreign Office and the new Secretary of State for Foreign Affairs, Herr von Bülow, who was away on a journey.

Kiao-chou was occupied in November, 1897. In December of that year Prince Henry, on board the *Deutschland,* sailed with his squadron to eastern Asia, where he later took over the command of the entire East Asiatic Division. On March 6, 1898, the agreement with China concerning Kiao-chou was signed. At the same time, Mr. Chamberlain in London brought up before the Japanese Ambassador, Baron Kato, the idea of the conclusion of an Anglo-Japanese alliance, in order to bar Russia's advance in the East.

One will naturally inquire why, in the discussion of our audacious move, there is no mention of England, since she was certainly deeply interested therein. Preliminaries, however, had already been gone into with England. In order to meet the necessity for German coaling stations, I had intended to found, lease, or buy some in agreement with England, so far as might be possible. In view of the fact that my uncle, the chancellor, was, as a member of the Hohenlohe family, related to Queen Victoria, known to her personally for years and highly esteemed by her, I hoped that this might tend to facilitate the negotiations which were entered into with the English Government for the above-noted purpose. My hope was disappointed. The negotiations dragged along without any prospect of a successful termination.

I took occasion, therefore, at the behest of the chancellor, to discuss the matter with the English Ambassador at Berlin. I complained of the treatment received from the English Government, which everywhere opposed German aspirations, even such as were justified. The ambassador agreed frankly with this, and expressed his astonishment at England's failure to meet Germany half way, and at English short-sightedness, since Germany, a young, rising nation, whose development, after all, was not to be prevented, turned directly to England in order to acquire territory with her consent, instead of going straight ahead or allying itself with other nations; it was certainly more than England could reasonably ask. Moreover, he added that, since England already owned almost all the world, she could certainly find a place where she might permit Germany to establish a station; that he was unable to understand the gentlemen in Downing Street; that in case Germany should not succeed in obtaining England's approval, she would probably occupy, on her own account, such places as were suited to her ends, because, after all, there was no law against it.

I laid stress upon the fact that this agreed entirely with my own view and, in conclusion, once more I summed up my standpoint for the ambassador. I told him that Germany was the only country in the world which, despite its colonial possessions and its rapidly growing commerce, possessed no coaling stations ; that we were quite willing to acquire these with England's consent ; that, should she refuse to show a realization of our situation and fail to meet us half way, we should be compelled to turn to some other great Power, in order, with its help, to found settlements.

This talk, likewise, was fruitless. Finally, the negotiations with England were broken off, without result, in a rather impolite manner. Thereupon the chancellor and I decided to appeal to Russia.

The occupation of Kiao-chou aroused surprise and anger in the English Government. Having refused us her support, England had definitely reckoned on the belief that nobody would help Germany in attaining her goal. Now that events had turned out differently, there was no lack of recriminations from London. When the English Ambassador assumed this tone he was referred to the conversations with me, and it was made clear to him that it was solely the fault of his Government that it had come to no understanding with Germany.

England's attitude of aloofness surprised us at that time. An occurrence which was unknown to me then may serve to throw light on the matter. In a book entitled " The Problem of

Japan," which appeared anonymously at The Hague in 1918 and was said to have been written by an " Ex-Diplomat from the Far East," an excerpt was published from a work of the American Professor Usher, of Washington University, St. Louis. Usher, like his former colleague, Professor John Bassett Moore of Columbia University, New York, has often been called into consultation as an adviser on foreign relations by the State Department at Washington, because he has a knowledge possessed by few other Americans on international questions affecting the United States. Professor Usher, in his book published in 1913, made known for the first time the existence and contents of an " agreement " or " secret treaty " between *England, America* and *France*, dating from the spring of 1897. In this it was agreed that, in case Germany or Austria, or both of them, should begin a war for the sake of " Pan-Germanism " the United States should at once declare in favour of England and France and go to the support of these Powers with all its resources. Professor Usher cites at length all the reasons, including those of a colonial character, which inevitably imposed upon the United States the necessity of taking part, on the side of England and France, in a war against Germany, which Professor Usher, in 1913, prophesied as imminent!

The unknown author of " The Problem of Japan " went to the trouble of publishing, in tabulated form, the agreements between England, France and America in 1897, in order thereby to show, in a way

easily understood, the extent of the reciprocal obligations.   This chapter is extraordinarily well worth
reading ; it gives a good glimpse into the preliminary
history and *preparation of the world war on the part
of the Entente,* which even at that time was uniting
against Germany, although not yet appearing under
the name of " Entente Cordiale." The " Ex-Diplomat "
remarks in this connexion :—

Here is a treaty that Prof. Usher alleges to have been
entered into as long ago as 1897, in which every phase of
activity and participation in future events by England,
France and the United States is provided for, including the
conquest of the Spanish dependencies, control over Mexico and
Central America, the opening up of China and the annexation of coaling stations.   And all these measures Prof.
Usher wishes us to believe were taken to defend the world
against Pan-Germanism.

It is unnecessary to remind Prof. Usher or anybody
else for that matter, that Pan-Germanism, if we go so far as
to assume that such a thing actually exists, had certainly
never been heard of in 1897, at which time Germany had not
yet adopted her programme for naval construction on a
large scale, the same having been bruited for the first time in
1898.   If, therefore, it is true that England, France and the
United States harboured the mutual designs imputed to
them by Prof. Usher, and entered into an alliance to accomplish them, it will scarcely do to attribute the conception of
the idea and the stimulus to its consummation to so feeble
a pretext as the rise of a Pan-Germanism.

Thus the "Ex-Diplomat"!
This is truly amazing.   A definite treaty of parti-
tion directed against Spain, Germany, etc., arranged
even to minute details, was planned between Gauls

and Anglo-Saxons, in a time of the profoundest peace, and concluded without the slightest twinge of conscience, in order to annihilate Germany and Austria and eliminate their competition from the world-market! *Seventeen years* before the beginning of the world-war *this* treaty was made by the united Anglo-Saxons and its goal was systematically envisaged throughout this entire period! Now one can understand the ease with which King Edward VII could pursue his policy of encirclement; for years the principal actors had been united and in readiness. When he christened the compact " Entente Cordiale," its appearance was for the world, especially for Germany, an unpleasant novelty [*novum*], but, in the countries on the other side, it was merely the official acknowledgment of facts long known there.

In view of this agreement, one can understand the opposition of England in 1897 to an agreement with Germany regarding coaling stations, and the anger aroused because Germany managed, in agreement with Russia, to gain a firm foothold in China, concerning the exploitation of which country *without* German participation a tripartite treaty had already been concluded.

Usher talked out of school and conclusively proved *at whose door lies the guilt for the world war.* The treaty directed against Germany—sometimes called the " Gentlemen's Agreement "—of the spring of 1897, is the basis, the point of departure, for this war, which was systematically developed by the Entente countries for seventeen years. When they had succeeded in winning over Russia and Japan likewise for their purposes, they struck the blow, after Serbia had staged the Serajevo murder and had thus touched the match to the carefully filled powder-barrel.

Professor Usher's statements are likewise a complete refutation of all those who were impelled, during the war, to find the reason for the entry of the United States in certain military acts on the part of Germany, as, for instance, the *Lusitania* case, the expansion of U-boat warfare, etc. None of that is right. The recently published, excellent book of John Kenneth Turner, " Shall It Be Again ? " points out, on the basis of convincing proofs, that Wilson's alleged reasons for going to war and his war aims were not the real ones. America—or rather President Wilson—was resolved probably from the start, certainly from 1915, to range herself against Germany and to fight. She did the latter, alleging the U-boat warfare as a pretext—in reality under the influence of powerful financial groups—and yielding to the pressure and prayers of her partner, France, whose resources in man-power were becoming more and more exhausted. America did not wish to leave a weakened France alone with England, whose annexation designs on Calais, Dunkirk, etc., were well known to her.

It was a fateful thing for Germany—let this be stated here, in a general way—that our Foreign Office was unable to meet the broad policy of encirclement of England and the cunning of Russia and France with an equal degree of diplomatic skill.

This was partially because it had not really been trained under Prince Bismarck ; and, therefore, when, after the retirement of the prince and Count Herbert, the all-dominating will and spirit were lacking, it was not capable of the task of conducting foreign affairs on its own independent initiative. Moreover, it is difficult to train good diplomats in Germany for our people lack the taste and endowment for diplomacy, which have shone forth brilliantly but from few German minds, such as Frederick the Great and Bismarck. Unfavourable, also, to the Foreign Office were the very frequent changes of secretaries of State. Imperial Chancellors, following the example of Bismarck, maintained their influence upon the Foreign Office and suggested the secretaries of State who should direct its affairs. I acquiesced in the proposals of the Imperial Chancellors as to these posts, for I admitted their right to choose for themselves their leading collaborators in the domain of foreign affairs. That these frequent changes were not calculated to work towards the continuity of political policy was a disadvantage that had to be taken into account.

The Foreign Office was largely influenced by the axiom : " No disagreeable quarrels with other Powers ! "—" Surtout pas d'histoires " ["Above all, no yarns ! "], as the French general said to a company of soldiers which, he had heard, designed to mutiny. One of the secretaries of State told me once when, in placing some matter before me, I had called his attention to the apparently serious situation in connexion with some foreign question, that this simply *must* be righted, that the Foreign Office based its acts primarily upon the axiom : " Let us have quiet ! " Given this attitude, one can also understand the answer which the German representative gave to a German merchant in a South American Republic who had asked him for help and intercession with the authorities after his shop had been plundered and his property stolen : " Oh, don't bother me with these things ! We have established such pleasant relations with this Republic that any action undertaken in your behalf would only serve to upset them ! " I need scarcely add that whenever such a conception of duty came to my notice, I removed the official concerned from his post.

The Foreign Office enjoyed general unpopularity both with the people and the army. I worked repeatedly, during the tenure of office of various chancellors, for thorough reform, but in vain. Every new chancellor, especially if he himself did not come from the ranks of the foreign service, needed the Foreign Office in order to inform himself of foreign affairs, and this took time. But, once he had worked himself in, he was under obligations to the officials, and was reluctant to make extensive changes, burdened as he was by other matters and lacking detailed knowledge regarding the Foreign Office personnel, particularly as he still believed that he needed the advice of those who were " orientated."

But let us return to Tsing-tao. Here everything was done to promote commerce and industry, and done jointly with the Chinese; moreover, the flag of the Chinese Empire was hoisted over the custom-house at Tsing-tao. The development there was such that the port, during the years immediately preceding the war, ranked sixth among all Chinese trading centres in the commercial register of the great Chinese merchants and of the merchants' guild, coming just after Tientsin. Tsing-tao was a pros-pering German commercial colony, where many Chinamen worked side by side with Germans; it was, so to speak, a great sample warehouse of Ger-man ability and German achievement, to which the Chinese, who formerly had not known Germany, her capabilities of achievement and her products, could repair for selection and emulation; it was a contrast to the naval stations of Russia and England, which were purely military posts directed solely towards domination and conquest.

The rapid rise of Tsing-tao as a trading centre aroused the envy of the Japanese and English, but this did not prevent swarms of the latter from journey-ing with their families to the splendid beach, enjoy-ing its cool air and the beautiful Strand Hotel and devoting themselves to playing polo and lawn tennis, after they had escaped from the heat of Hong-kong, Canton and Shanghai. Envy prompted England in 1914 to demand that Japan should take Tsing-tao, although it was *de facto* Chinese. Japan did this joy-fully, promising to return it to China, but it was not returned until the beginning of 1922, after much pressure, although Japan had agreed with America that she was not to be allowed to make any territorial acquisitions in China without previous consultation with Washington.

Thus a great German cultural work in a foreign land, which stood as a model of the method and manner that a cultured nation should employ in extending the advantages of its culture to another nation, was annihilated by English commercial envy. Some day, when Hong-kong has gone the same way, England will repent of her act, and bitterly reproach herself for having abandoned her old maxim, in accordance with which she has acted for so many years : " White men together against coloured men ! " When once Japan has made a reality of her watchword, " Asia for the Asiatics," and brought China and India under her sway, England will cast her eyes about in search of Germany and the German fleet.

As to the " *Yellow Peril*," I had the following interview with the Tsar after the Russo-Japanese War.

The Tsar, at that time, was visibly impressed by the growing power of Japan and its increasing menace to Russia and Europe, and requested my opinion concerning the matter. I answered that, if the Russians counted themselves among the cultured nations of Europe, they must be ready to rally to the defence of these nations against the " Yellow Peril " and to fight for, and by the side of, Europe for their own and Europe's existence and culture ; but that, if the Russians, on the other hand, considered themselves Asiatics, they would unite with the " Yellow Peril," and, joining forces with it, would assail Europe. The Tsar, said I, must bear this in mind in providing for the defence of his land and in organizing his army.

When the Tsar asked me what course I thought the Russians would take, I replied : " The second."

The Tsar was outraged and at once wished to know on what I based this opinion. I answered that my opinion was based on Russia's construction of railways and on the arraying of the Russian army along the Prussian—Austrian frontier. Thereupon the Tsar protested that he and his house were Europeans, that his country and his Russians would certainly cleave to Europe, that he would look upon it as a matter of honour to protect Europe from the " yellow men." To this I replied that, if this was the Tsar's attitude, he must make his military preparations conform to it without delay. The Tsar said nothing.

At all events, I sought to utilize Tsar Nicholas II's anxiety at the growing power of Japan to the advantage of Germany and general European culture. Russia, despite the fact of her taking sides with Japan, was the first nation to collapse among all those participating in the war.

The able statesmen of Japan, of whom there are quite a number, must be in some doubt as to whether they ranged their country on the right side in the war. Yes, they will perhaps ask themselves whether it would not have been more advantageous for Japan to have prevented the world war. This would have been within her power, had she ranged herself firmly and unequivocally on the side of the Central Powers, from which, in former times, she learned so willingly and so much. Had Japan adopted soon enough such an orientation in her foreign policy and, like Germany, fought by peaceful means for her share in world trade and activity, I should have put the " Yellow Peril " away in a corner and joyfully welcomed into the circle of peacefully inclined nations the progressive Japanese nation, the " Prussians of the East." Nobody regrets more than I that the " Yellow Peril " had not already lost its meaning when the crisis of 1914 arose. The experience derived from the world war may yet bring this about.

Germany's joint action with France and Russia at Shimonoseki was based upon Germany's position in Europe. Wedged in between on-marching Russia, threatening Prussia's frontier, and France, fortifying her borders anew with forts and groups of fortresses, confronted with a friendship between these two nations resembling an alliance, Berlin looked with anxiety into the future. The war-like preparations of the two Powers were far ahead of ours, their navies far more modern and powerful than that of Germany, which consisted of a few old ships, almost without fighting value. Therefore it seemed to us wise to acquiesce in the suggestion of this strong group, in order that it might not—should we decline—turn immediately to England and cause the entry of the latter into the combination. This would

have meant the formation, at that time, of the combination of 1914, which would have been a serious
matter for Germany. Japan, on the other hand,
was about to go over to England, at least in her
sympathies. Moreover, Germany's making common
cause with the Franco-Russian group offered the
possibility of achieving gradually a more trusting
and less strained relationship in Europe and of living
side by side with our two neighbours there in greater
friendliness, as a result of the common policy adopted
in the Far East. The policy adopted by us at this
juncture was also consistently based on the maintenance of world peace.

In the entire Kiao-chou question, Prince
Hohenlohe, despite his age, evinced a capacity for
sticking steadily to his purpose and a degree of
resolution which must be reckoned as greatly to his
credit.

§ 2

Unfortunately, in the matter of the Kruger dispatch, his prudence and his vision, so clear on other
occasions, abandoned him ; on such an assumption
only is his obstinate insistence on the sending of
this dispatch to be understood. The influence of
such an energetic and eloquent personage as Herr
von Marschall, former State Attorney, may have
been so powerful, the siren song of Herr von Holstein
so convincing, that the prince yielded to them. In
any event, he did his country an ill turn in this

matter and damaged me seriously both in England and at home.

Since the so-called Kruger dispatch made a big stir and had serious political consequences, I shall tell the story of it in detail.

The Jameson Raid caused great and increasing excitement in Germany. The German nation was outraged at this attempt to overpower a little nation, which was Dutch—and, hence, Lower Saxon-German in origin—and to which we were sympathetic because of racial relationship. I was much worried at this violent excitement, which also seized upon the higher classes of society, foreseeing possible complications with England. I believed that there was no way to prevent England from conquering the Boer countries, should she so desire, although I also was convinced that such a conquest would be unjust. I was unable, however, to overcome the prevailing excitement, and on account of the attitude I adopted, was even harshly judged by my intimates.

One day, when I had gone to my uncle, the Imperial Chancellor, for a conference, at which the Secretary of State for the Navy, Admiral Hollmann, was present, Freiherr Marschall, one of the secretaries of State, suddenly appeared in high excitement, with a sheet of paper in his hand. He declared that the excitement among the people—in the Reichstag, even—had grown to such proportions that it was absolutely necessary to give it outward expression, and that this could best be done by a telegram to Kruger, a rough draft of which he had in his hand.

I objected to this and was supported by Admiral Hollmann. At first the Imperial Chancellor remained passive in the debate. In view of the fact that I knew how ignorant Freiherr Marschall and the Foreign Office were of English national psychology, I sought to make clear to Freiherr Marschall the consequences which such a step would have among the English; in this, likewise, Admiral Hollmann seconded me. But Marschall was not to be dissuaded.

Then, finally, the Imperial Chancellor took a hand. He remarked that I, as a constitutional ruler, must not stand out against the national consciousness and against my constitutional advisers; otherwise, there was danger that the excited attitude of the German people, deeply outraged in its sense of justice and also in its sympathy for the Dutch, might cause it to break down the barriers and turn against me personally. Already, he said, statements were flying about among the people; it was being said that the Emperor was, after all, half an Englishman, with secret English sympathies; that he was entirely under the influence of his grandmother, Queen Victoria, that the dictation emanating from England must cease once for all, that the Emperor must be freed from English tutelage, etc. In view of all this, he continued, it was his duty as Imperial Chancellor, notwithstanding the fact that he admitted the justification of my objections, to insist that I should sign the telegram, in the general political interest, and, above all else, in the interest of my relationship to my people. He and also Herr von

G

Marschall, he went on, in their capacity of my constitutional advisers would assume full responsibility for the telegram and its consequences.

Sir Valentine Chirol, at that time correspondent
of the *Times,* wrote in the *Times* of Sept. 11 that
Herr von Marschall, directly after the sending of the
dispatch, had stated to him that the dispatch did
not give the personal opinion of the Emperor but
was a governmental act for which the chancellor and
himself assumed full responsibility.

Admiral Hollmann, appealed to by the Imperial
Chancellor for corroboration of this point of view,
and asked by him to uphold it to me, declined to do
so with the remark that the Anglo-Saxon world
would unquestionably attribute the telegram to the
Kaiser, since nobody would believe that such a provocative act could come from His Majesty's elderly
advisers and that all would consider it an " impulsive
act of the youthful Emperor."

Then I tried again to dissuade the ministers from
their project ; but the Imperial Chancellor and
Marschall insisted that I should sign, reiterating
that they would be responsible for the consequences.
It seemed to me that I ought not to refuse after
their presentation of the case. I signed.

Not long before his death Admiral Hollmann
recalled the occurrence to me in full detail, as it is
described here.

After the Kruger dispatch was made public the
storm broke in England, as I had prophesied. I
received from all circles of English society, especially

from aristocratic ladies unknown to me, a veritable flood of letters containing every possible kind of reproach ; some of the writers did not hesitate even at slandering me personally and insulting me. Attacks and calumnies began to appear in the Press, so that soon the legend of the origin of the dispatch was as firmly established as the " Amen " at church. If Marschall had but announced in the Reichstag what he stated to Chirol, I personally would not have been drawn into the matter to such an extent.

In February, 1900, while the Boer War was in progress, and while I was with the fleet at Heligoland attending the manœuvres of ships of the line, after having been present at the swearing-in of recruits at Wilhelmshaven, I received news by telegraph from the Wilhelmstrasse, via Heligoland, that Russia and France had proposed to Germany to make a joint attack on England, now that she was involved elsewhere, and to cripple her sea traffic. I objected and ordered that the proposal should be declined.

Since I assumed that Paris and St. Petersburg would present the matter at London in such a way as to make it appear that Berlin had made this proposal to both of them, I immediately telegraphed from Heligoland to Queen Victoria and to the Prince of Wales (Edward) the facts of the Russo-French proposal, and its refusal by me. The Queen answered expressing her hearty thanks, the Prince of Wales with an expression of astonishment. Later, Her

Majesty let me know secretly that, shortly before the receipt of my telegram from Heligoland concerning the proposal from Paris and St. Petersburg, the false version of the matter foreseen by me had indeed been told, and that she was glad to have been able—thanks to my dispatch—to expose the intrigue to her Government and quieten it as to the loyal attitude of Germany; she added that she would not forget the service I had done England in troublous times !

When Cecil Rhodes came to me, in order to bring about the construction of the Cape-to-Cairo Railway and the telegraph line through the interior of German East Africa, his proposals were approved by me, in agreement with the Foreign Office and the Imperial Chancellor, with the proviso that a branch railway should be built via Tabora, and that German material should be used in the construction work on German territory. Both conditions were most willingly accepted by Rhodes. He was grateful at the fulfilment of his pet ambition by Germany, only a short time after King Leopold of Belgium had refused his request.

Rhodes was full of admiration for Berlin and the tremendous German industrial plants, which he visited daily. He said that he regretted not having been in Berlin before, in order to have learned about the power and efficiency of Germany and to have got into touch with the German Government and prominent Germans in commercial circles; that he had desired, even before the Jameson Raid, to visit Berlin, but had been prevented in London at that time from so doing; that, had he been able to inform us before of his plan to get permission to build the Cape-to-Cairo line through the Boer countries, as well as through our colonies, the German Government would probably have been able to help him by bringing persuasion to bear upon Kruger, who was unwilling to grant this permission; that "the stupid Jameson Raid" would never have been made, in that case, and the Kruger dispatch never written, and, as to that dispatch, he had never borne me a grudge on account of it. He added that as we, in Germany, could not be correctly informed as to his aim and actual purposes, the said raid must have looked to us like "an act of piracy," which naturally and quite rightly had excited the Germans; that all he had wanted was to have such stretches of land as were needed for his railway—such, in fact, as Germany had just granted to him in the interior of her colonies—a demand which was not unjust and would certainly have met with German support. I was not to worry, he added, about the dispatch and not bother myself any more about the uproar in the English Press. Rhodes did not know about the origin of the Kruger dispatch and wanted to console me, imagining that I was its originator.

Rhodes went on to advise me to build the Bagdad Railway and open up Mesopotamia, after having simultaneously introduced irrigation there. He said that this was Germany's task, just as his was the

Cape-to-Cairo line. In view of the fact that the
building of this line through our territory was also
made dependent upon the cession to us of the Samoan
Islands, Rhodes worked actively in London towards
having them turned over to us.

§ 3

In home politics, Prince Hohenlohe, as chancellor,
showed a mildness which was not generally favourable. Owing to his long acquaintanceship with Herr
von Hertling, he was able to establish friendly relations with the Vatican. His mildness and indul-
gence were also exercised towards Alsace-Lorraine,
in which, as an expert of long standing, he showed
particular interest. But he received little thanks
for this, since the French element, indirectly benefited thereby, behaved with ever-increasing arrogance.
Prince Hohenlohe loved to employ mediation, compromise and conciliation—towards the Socialists likewise—and he employed these methods on some
occasions when energetic measures would have been
more fitting.

He hailed with much joy my Far East trip to
Constantinople and Jerusalem. He was pleased at
the strengthening of our relations with Turkey and
considered the plan for the Bagdad Railway arising
from them as a great cultural work worthy of
Germany.

He also gave his most enthusiastic approval to my

visit to England in 1899, made by me with my wife
and two sons at the desire of my royal grandmother,
who, growing steadily weaker on account of her
years, wished to see her eldest grandson once more.
He hoped that this journey might serve to efface
somewhat the consequences of the Kruger dispatch,
and also to clear up some important questions by
means of conferences between him and English
statesmen. In order to avoid any unpleasantness
from the English Press, which, angered by the Boer
War and the partially unjustified attacks of certain
German newspapers, had been answering in like
tone, the Queen had commissioned the author of
" The Life of the Prince Consort," Sir Theodore
Martin, to inform the English Press of Her Majesty's
desire that a friendly reception be accorded to her
Imperial grandson ; and that is what indeed came
to pass. The visit ran its course harmoniously and
caused satisfaction on all sides. I held important
conferences with various leading men.

Not once in the entire visit was the Kruger dispatch mentioned. On the other hand, my royal
grandmother did not conceal from her grandson how
unwelcome the whole Boer War was to her ; she made
no secret of her disapproval of, and aversion for, Mr.
Chamberlain and all that he represented, and thanked
me again for my prompt and sharp refusal of the
Russo-French proposal to interfere and for my
immediate announcement of this proposal. One
could easily see how much the Queen loved her
splendid army and how deeply she had been grieved

by the heavy reverses suffered by it at the outset of
the war, which had caused by no means negligible
losses.   Referring to these, the aged field marshal,
the Duke of Cambridge, coined the fine phrase :
" The British nobleman and officer have shown that
they can die bravely as gentlemen."

On my departure, the Queen bade me farewell with
cordial and grateful greetings to her " much cherished
cousin," the Imperial Chancellor, whose ability and
experience, she hoped, would continue to maintain
good relations between our two countries.

My report entirely satisfied Prince Hohenlohe as
to the success of my journey ; at the same time, however, I was the object of the most violent attacks
from a certain section of the Press and from many
excited " friends of the Boers."   The German lacks
the very quality with which the English people has
been inoculated, and to which it has been trained
by long political self-discipline : when a fight is on,
even though it be merely upon the field of diplomacy,
the Englishman unquestioningly follows the flag, in
accordance with the proverb : " You can't change
the jockey while the horse is running."

§ 4

In the autumn of 1900, Prince Hohenlohe retired
from the chancellorship, for the work had become
too arduous for a man of his advanced age.   Moreover, the constant quarrels and disputes of the

Hohenlohe

political parties with each other were disagreeable
to him and it went against the grain with him to
make speeches before them in the Reichstag. Equally
disagreeable to him was the Press, part of which
had taken the bit between its teeth, and imagined
that it could conserve the Bismarckian tradition by
quoting sayings of Bismarck, and had greatly jeopar-
dized relations with England, especially during the
Boer War.

The hope, aroused by the choice of Prince Hohenlohe as chancellor and his assumption of the office,
that Prince Bismarck would place fewer obstacles in
his path, had been only partially fulfilled. The
atmosphere had been much relieved and Prince
Bismarck brought to a much milder frame of mind
by my reconciliation with him, which had received
outward expression in his solemn entry into Berlin
and his stay at the old Hohenzollern palace, but
his adherents and those rallying around him for the
sake of opposition were not to be dissuaded from
their activities. Moreover, the political representatives of the people succeeded, while I was on my
way to Friedrichsruh to celebrate Bismarck's
eightieth birthday, in refusing to pay homage to the
old Imperial Chancellor, a matter which naturally
deeply hurt the sensitive Prince Hohenlohe and
filled him with indignation. He, like myself, was
deeply moved by the death of his great predecessor,
and we, together with the German people, sincerely
mourned Prince Bismarck as one of the greatest of
the sons of Prussia and Germany, in spite of the

fact that he had not always made our task easy.
I insisted upon hurrying back from my trip to
Norway in order to pay honour to him who, as a
faithful servant of his old master, had helped the
German nation to unity, and under whom I, when
I was prince, had had the proud privilege of
working.

It is said that one of the reasons for Prince
Hohenlohe's retirement from his post was the advice
of his son Alexander, who was much at his father's
house ; he was known in society as " the Crown
Prince," and was essentially different from his
lovable father.

Prince Hohenlohe could look back upon a series
of successes during his term as chancellor : the settlement of the disputes concerning the " Citizens'
Book of Laws," the reform of military punishment procedure, the Naval Law, the appointment of
Waldersee to the command in China at the time
of the Boxer War, Tsing-tao, and the Yangtse
treaty.

He bade me farewell on the 15th of October, 1900.
Both of us were greatly moved, for not only was the
chancellor and faithful co-worker parting from his
Emperor, but also the uncle from his nephew, who
looked up with grateful esteem to the old man, who,
at the age of 75 years—an age when others have long
since retired to rest and contemplation—had not
hesitated to obey the summons of the Emperor to
subject himself to even more exacting labours and to
devote his time and strength to the German Father-

land. When about to leave my room, he grasped
my hand once again with the request that I might
grant him, during the years of life still remaining to
him which he meant to spend in Berlin, the same
plain, faithful friendship which he had so long
noted and admired between me and Admiral von
Hollmann. I shall always preserve him faithfully
in my memory.

IV

BÜLOW

§ 1

ON the day after Prince Hohenlohe's farewell, the man summoned by me as his successor—Count Bülow, Secretary of State for Foreign Affairs—arrived. His choice for the post was imminent, because he was thoroughly cognizant of our foreign policy, and especially of our relations with England—which policy was becoming constantly livelier and more complicated—and because he had already proved himself a skilful orator and ready debater in the Reichstag. The fact that the second of these qualities was lacking in his predecessor had often been painfully noticeable. When Prince Hohenlohe's intention to retire became known in the Imperial Council, the Bavarian Ambassador at Berlin, Count Lerchenfeld, very pointedly remarked to me, " Do not for Heaven's sake choose another South German," for South Germans were not fitted for the leading post at Berlin ; North Germans were naturally better able to fill it and, therefore, it would be better for the empire to select a North German.

I had been personally acquainted with Bülow for a long time, ever since, indeed, the period of his ambassadorship at Rome, and I had followed closely his work as secretary of State. I had often visited him at his home and held many a conference with him in his garden. He came into close relationship with me when he accompanied me on my journey to the Far East, where, in co-operation with our ambassador, Freiherr Marschall, he assisted me in getting into personal touch with the leading men of the Turkish Government. Hence, the relations of the new chancellor with me were already begun and, to a certain extent, established, since we had for years discussed all political problems and spheres. Moreover, he stood much nearer to me in age than his predecessors, most of whom were old enough to have been my grandfather. He was the first " young chancellor " of Germany, and this made our common task easier for both of us.

When I was in Berlin, scarcely a day went by without my taking a long morning walk with the chancellor in the garden of the Imperial Chancellor's palace, during which outstanding business was cleared up and problems of the day discussed. I often had a meal with him and always found at his table, where I was most hospitably received by the count and his amiable wife, a group of the most interesting men, in choosing whom the count was a master. He was likewise unsurpassed in his skilful control of conversation and in his witty handling of the various topics that arose. To me it was always a pleasure to be in the company of the chancellor. I enjoyed his bubbling wit, his exchange of views with many professors, savants and artists, as well as government officials of all kinds, in informal, unofficial intercourse, and stimulating interchange of ideas.

The count was an excellent narrator of anecdotes, drawn both from books and his own personal experience, which he told in several languages. He liked to tell stories of the days when he was a diplomat, especially of those spent at St. Petersburg.

The count's father was an intimate friend of Prince Bismarck, and had been one of his closest co-workers. Young Bülow also had begun his career under the great chancellor; he had been brought up on Bismarckian ideas and traditions and strongly influenced by them, but, nevertheless, had not adhered to them to such an extent as to lose his independence.

In the course of one of the first talks I had with Bülow as Imperial Chancellor he informed himself concerning my views of how best to handle the English in our dealings with them. I told him that I considered absolute frankness to be the most important thing in all matters relative to England and Englishmen; that the Englishman, in presenting his point of view and working for his interests, was inconsiderate to the point of brutality, for which reason he thoroughly appreciated anybody who acted similarly towards him; that there must be no playing the diplomatic game, or "finesseing," with an Englishman, because it made him distrust those with whom he was dealing and suspect that they were not honest, and were secretly designing to cheat him; that such devious methods could be successful only with Latin and Slavic nations; that, once the Englishman had become suspicious, there was nothing more to be done with him, despite the most honeyed words and most obliging concessions ; that the only advice, therefore, which I could give the chancellor was that he should confine himself entirely to straight-forwardness in his English policy. I said this with particular emphasis, for " finesseing " was especi-ally dear to the diplomatic character of Count Bülow and had become second nature to him.

I also took occasion, during this talk, to warn the chancellor against Holstein. In spite of my warn-ing—which was merely a repetition of that previously given to me by Bismarck—Bülow worked a great deal, or was obliged to work, with Holstein. This remark-able man had been able gradually—especially from the time that the Foreign Office had been, so to speak, orphaned by Bismarck's retirement—to create for himself a position that became steadily more influential, and to maintain it under three chancellors with such skill that he was considered indispensable. Holstein was unquestionably possessed of great shrewdness, seconded by a phenomenal memory and a certain talent for political combinations, which, without doubt, often became a hobby with him. His position was also based largely on the fact that he was looked upon in many quarters, especially among the older officials, as the " upholder of the Bismarckian traditions," the man who maintained these in the teeth of " the young master." Above all, his importance rested on his wide personal know-ledge in the entire domain of the foreign service.

Since he wielded, on account of this, an authoritative influence on all proposals relative to the appointment of officials and, hence, also on the careers of the younger officials, it may be easily understood why he, little by little, had obtained for himself a dominating position at the Foreign Office. But, at the same time, he sought more and more to obtain a decisive influence upon the conduct of foreign policy; he had, in fact, become the guiding spirit both of the Foreign Office and of German foreign policy.

The serious point of this was that he exerted his far-reaching influence entirely from under cover and avoided all official responsibility as an adviser. He preferred to remain in the dark and exert his influence from there. He refused every responsible post—many stood open to him—every titular honour, every promotion. He lived in complete seclusion. For a long time I tried in vain to become personally acquainted with him, for which purpose I used to invite him to meals, but Holstein steadily declined. On one occasion only, in the course of many years, did he consent to dine with me at the Foreign Office, and it was characteristic of him that, whereas on this occasion all the other gentlemen present wore full evening dress, he appeared in a frock coat and excused himself on the plea that he had no dress suit. The secrecy with which he surrounded himself in his work, so as not to be held responsible for it, became also apparent at times in the character of the memorials drawn up by him; they were unquestionably ingenious and attractive, but often as involved and ambiguous as the oracle of Delphi; there were occasions when, after a decision based on the contents of one of these documents had been made, Herr von Holstein would prove to a nicety that he meant exactly the opposite of what had been thought.

I considered it a serious matter that an irresponsible counsellor should exercise such powerful influence, especially as he did so from under cover and, in so doing, eluded the officials who were nominally responsible. It often happened, particularly in the von Richthofen era, that I would advise a foreign ambassador to discuss with the Secretary of State some political question which he had taken up with me, and he would reply : " J'en parlerai avec mon ami Holstein." ["I shall speak about it with my friend Holstein."] The very fact that an official of the Foreign Office dealt with foreign ambassadors over the head of his superior did not seem right to me ; but that he should be dubbed " friend " by these foreigners seemed to me to go beyond what I deemed advisable.

Matters had, in fact, gradually developed to such a stage that Holstein conducted a good part of our foreign affairs. True, he still listened to the chancellor in connexion with them, but what the Emperor thought or said about foreign affairs seemed altogether unimportant. If matters turned out successfully, the Foreign Office reaped the reward ; if they went wrong, then it was the fault of the " impulsive young master."

H

In spite of all this, Bülow, too, apparently thought Herr von Holstein indispensable at first ; he worked with him for a long time, until, at length, he realized that the pressure exerted on everybody by this strange man was unbearable. To Herr von Tschirschky, during his tenure of office as Secretary of State, belongs the merit of finally bringing the unendurable situation to a head. On being questioned by me, he declared that he considered it impossible that Herr von Holstein should remain longer at his post ; he was unsettling the whole Foreign Office, seeking to eliminate him, the Secretary of State, entirely, and creating all kinds of obstacles, likewise, for the chancellor. Thereupon I ordered Herr von Tschirschky to take steps for the dismissal of Herr von Holstein ; this duly occurred, with the approval of the chancellor, after the latter had recovered from the serious break-down in health which he had suffered meanwhile. Herr von Holstein showed what manner of man he really was by going, immediately after his dismissal, to Herr Harden and placing himself at the latter's disposal for the campaign against the Emperor.

§ 2

The year 1901 gave Count Bülow plentiful opportunities to assert himself in our relations with England. He still believed strongly in the Bismarckian theory of having " two irons in the fire "—i.e. in making friendly argeements with another country while always remaining on good terms with Russia— in which he received support from the many professing adherents of Bismarck.

From the midst of the jubilee celebration of the 200th coronation anniversary, I was called to the death-bed of my grandmother, Queen Victoria, by a dispatch announcing to me her serious condition. I hurriedly made the journey with my uncle, the Duke of Connaught, who was in Berlin as the Queen's representative at the festivities—he was the favourite son of the Queen and my particular friend and also a son-in-law of Prince Frederick Charles. I was cordially received in London by the then Prince of Wales and the royal family. As my carriage drove at a trot from the railway station, a plainly dressed man stepped forward from the closely packed crowd standing there in absolute silence, to the side of the carriage, bared his head, and said : " Thank you, Kaiser ! " The Prince of Wales, later Edward VII, added : " That is what they all think and they will never forget this visit of yours." Nevertheless, they did forget it, and quickly.

After the Queen had quietly breathed her last in my arms, the curtain fell for me upon many memories of childhood. Her death signified the close of an epoch in English history and in Germany's relations with England. I now got into touch, as far as possible, with prominent personages and noted everywhere a thoroughly sympathetic, friendly spirit, which made no secret of the wish for good relations with Germany. At the farewell banquet, impromptu speeches were made by King Edward VII and myself which were cordial in tone and contents, and did not fail to make an impression on their hearers. After the meal, the English Ambassador at Berlin clasped my hand and said that my speech had touched all his fellow-countrymen's hearts, because what I said was sincere and simple, as was fitting for Englishmen ; that the speech must at once be made public, because it would have an effect throughout the country, which was grateful for my coming ; and that this would be useful to the relations between the two countries. I answered that it was a matter for the British Government and the King to decide, that personally I had no objection to the speech being made public. Nevertheless, it was not made public, and the British people never learned of my words, which were the sincere expression of my thoughts and sentiments. In another talk later on with me at Berlin, the same ambassador deeply regretted this, but was unable to say what the reason was for the omission.

In concluding my remarks on my stay in England I cannot pass over the fact that a portion of the German Press was unfortunately lacking both in tactful appreciation of the grief of the English royal family and people, as well as of the obligations which my family relationship and political considerations imposed upon me.

After my return home I was able to report to the chancellor on the good impression I had received,

and particularly that opinion in England was
apparently in favour of an understanding and of
closer relations with Germany. Bülow expressed
himself as satisfied with the results of the journey,
after we had talked at length about it at Homburg
and consulted as to how the situation so created
should be put to use. I suggested that we should
unquestionably come to a good agreement, if an
alliance—which I preferred—could not be secured.
In any event, a firm agreement would suffice, I said,
and would suit the English ; an alliance might develop from it eventually.

§ 3

The opportunity for such an alliance came with
unexpected promptness. While I was at Homburg
vor der Höhe in the spring of 1901, Count Metternich,
who was with me as representative of the Foreign
Office, brought me a notification from Berlin that
Mr. Chamberlain had inquired there as to whether
Germany was prepared for an alliance with England.
I immediately asked : " Against whom ? "—for it
was evident that if England so suddenly offered to
make an alliance in the midst of peace, she needed
the German army, which made it worth while to
find out against whom the army was needed and for
what reason German troops were to fight, at England's behest, by her side. Thereupon the answer
came from London that they were needed against

Russia, for Russia was a menace both to India and to Constantinople.

The first thing I did was to call London's attention to the old traditional brotherhood-in-arms between the German and the Russian armies, and the close family ties between the reigning dynasties of the two countries; in addition, I pointed out the dangers of a war on two fronts, in the event of France coming in on the side of Russia, and also the fact that we had acted jointly with France and Russia in the Far East (Shimonoseki, 1895) and that there was no reason to unloose a conflict with Russia at this time, when we were in the midst of peace; that the numerical superiority of the Russian army on a peace footing was very great and that the eastern frontier of Prussia was seriously threatened by the grouping of the Russian forces; that England would not be in a position to protect our eastern province from a Russian attack, since her fleet could accomplish little in the Baltic and would be unable to sail into the Black Sea; that, in case of our making common cause against Russia, Germany would be the only one who would be in great danger, quite independently of the possibility of France's entry into the fight. Chamberlain then informed us that a firm alliance was intended, by which England would naturally bind herself to come to our aid.

I had also pointed out that the validity of an alliance could only be assured when the English Parliament had given its approval of it, for the ministry might be driven from office by the will of the nation as expressed in Parliament, whereby the signature of the ministry might be rendered null and void and the alliance invalidated, and that for the time being we could look upon Mr. Chamberlain's suggestion merely as a purely personal project of his own.

To this Chamberlain replied that he would get backing from Parliament in due time and would find a way to win the Unionists over to his idea; that all now needed was the signature of Berlin. Matters did not progress so far as that, because Parliament was not to be won over, and Chamberlain's " plan " therefore came to nothing. Soon afterwards England concluded her alliance with Japan (Hayashi). The Russo-Japanese War broke out, in which Japan—owing to the fact that it fitted in with her schemes—played the role of pawn in England's interests, which role had originally been reserved for Germany. By this war Russia was thrown from the East back to the West, where she might concern herself again with the Balkans, Constantinople and India—a result clearly to Japan's advantage—leaving Japan with a free hand in Korea and China.

§ 4

In 1905 occurred my journey to Tangier, undertaken much against my will. It came about as follows. Towards the end of March I intended, as in the previous year, to take a Mediterranean trip for the sake of my health, for which I proposed to avail myself of some ship sailing empty from Cuxhaven to Naples. The *Hamburg* was detailed by Ballin for this purpose. At his suggestion that I should take along some other guests, seeing that the steamer was quite empty, I invited a number of gentlemen, among whom were Privy Councillor Althoff, Admiral Mensing, Count Pückler, Ambassador von Varnbuhler, Professor Schiemann and Admiral Hollmann.

Soon after the proposed trip became known Bülow informed me that there was a strong desire at Lisbon that I should call there and pay the Portuguese Court a visit. To this I agreed. As the date of departure approached, Bülow expressed the additional wish that I should also call at Tangier and, by visiting that Moroccan port, strengthen the position of the Sultan of Morocco in relation to the French. This I declined to do, for it seemed to me that the Morocco question was too full of explosive matter, and I feared that such a visit would work out disadvantageously rather than beneficially. But Bülow returned to the attack, without, however, persuading me of the necessity or advisability of the visit.

During the journey I had several talks with Freiherr von Schoen, who accompanied me as representative of the Foreign Office, as to the advisability of the visit. We agreed that it would be better to drop it. I telegraphed this decision to the chancellor from Lisbon. Bülow replied emphatically that I must take into consideration the view of the

German people and of the Reichstag, which had become interested in the project, and that it was necessary that I should call at Tangier.

I gave in, with a heavy heart, for I feared that this visit, in view of the situation in Paris, might be construed as a provocation and give rise to an inclination in London to support France in case of war. I suspected that Delcassé wished to make Morocco a pretext for war, and I feared that he might make use of the Tangier visit for this purpose.

The visit took place, after much difficulty had been experienced in the open roadstead of Tangier, and it met with a certain amount of friendly participation by Italian and Southern French anarchists, rogues and adventurers. A number of Spaniards congregated amid waving banners on a small square uttering loud cries; these, according to a police official who accompanied us, were an assembly of Spanish anarchists.

The first I learned of the consequences of my Tangier visit was when I arrived at Gibraltar and was formally and frigidly received by the English, in marked contrast to my cordial reception the year before. What I had foreseen was justified by the facts. Embitterment and anger reigned in Paris, and Delcassé tried to rouse the nation to war; the only reason that he did not succeed was that both the Minister for War and the Minister of the Navy declared that France was not yet ready. The fact that my fears were justified was also corroborated later by the conversation between Delcassé and the

editor of *Le Gaulois*, in which the minister informed
an astonished world that in the event of war England
would have sided with France. Thus, even as far
back as that, I ran the risk, through the forced visit
to Tangier, of being blamed for the unchaining of a
world war. To think and act constitutionally is
often a difficult task for a ruler, upon whom, in
every case, responsibility is finally saddled.

In October, 1905, the Paris *Matin* reported that
Delcassé had declared, in the council of ministers,
that England had offered, in the event of war, to
land 100,000 men in Holstein and to seize the Kaiser
Wilhelm Canal. This English offer was repeated
once again, later on, with the suggestion that it be
affirmed in writing. The well-known Jaurès—who
was murdered in accordance with the political views
of Isvolsky upon the outbreak of war in 1914—knew
beforehand of the statements by Delcassé published
in the *Matin*.

The downfall of Delcassé and the accession of
Rouvier to his post are to be ascribed partially to the
influence of the Prince of Monaco. During the
regatta week at Kiel the prince had assured himself, by talks with me, the Imperial Chancellor and
Government officials, of the sincerity of our desire
to compromise with France for the purpose of enabling
us to live at peace with each other. He stood well
with the ambassador, Prince Radolin, and worked
actively towards a *rapprochement* between the two
countries. The Prince of Monaco himself was of
the opinion that Delcassé was a menace to the main-

tenance of peace and hoped that he would soon fall and be replaced by Rouvier, who was a prudent politician and thoroughly inclined to arrive at an understanding with Germany. The prince said that he was on good terms with Rouvier personally and would willingly place himself at the disposal of the German Ambassador as a go-between.

Then came Delcassé's fall, and Rouvier became minister. At once I caused the initiation of the measures wherein I could count upon the support of the Prince of Monaco. The chancellor was instructed to prepare a *rapprochement* with France, and I particularly told Prince Radolin, who received his instructions personally in Berlin, to make good use of the Rouvier regime for the purpose of eliminating all possibilities of conflict between the two countries. I added that the reports of the Prince of Monaco, with whom he was well acquainted, would be useful to him in relations with Rouvier. Prince Radolin proceeded with zeal and pleasure to the accomplishment of his task.

At first the negotiations went well, so much so that I began to hope that the important goal would be attained and the evil impression caused by the Tangier visit effaced by an understanding. In the meantime, the negotiations concerning Morocco were continued ; they were concluded, after endless trouble, by the summoning of the Algeciras Conference, based upon the circular Note of Prince Bülow, which pointed out that the Most-Favoured-Nation Clause (No. 17) of the Madrid Convention

should remain in force, and that the reforms in
Morocco, for which France alone was working, should
be carried out, in so far as necessary, only in agreement with the signatory powers of the Madrid Conference. These events, which riveted general attention, relegated the special negotiations with Rouvier
to the background.

§ 5

With regard to domestic policy, I had agreed with
the chancellor that his main task was to be the
restoration of order in the relations between the
parties in the Reichstag, which had got into a bad
way under Hohenlohe, and, above all, to rally the
Conservatives—who had been won over to the Opposition by the post-Bismarckians—once more to the
support of the Government. The chancellor accomplished this task with great patience and tenacity.
He finally formed the famous " Block " which arose
from the great electoral defeat of the Socialists.

The Conservative Party had many members who
had direct relations with the Court and also with me
personally, so that it was easier for this party than
for any other to become informed as to my plans
in political and other matters, and to discuss my
ideas with me before they took shape in projects
for laws. I have not the impression that this was
done to the extent that was possible. I might perhaps have come into agreement with the gentlemen,
through informal conversations, on the question

of the building of the Central Canal—opposed, as is well known, by the Conservatives—as well as in the less important matters of the construction of the Cathedral and the Berlin Opera House, in which I was deeply interested for the sake of the Church and of art.

I am saying nothing new if I remark that it was by no means easy to deal with the members of the Conservative Party. Through their past services to the State they had acquired great experience and independence of judgment and had thus formed firm political convictions, to which they held faithfully and in a genuinely conservative manner. From their ranks great statesmen, eminent ministers, a brilliant officer corps, a model body of officials, had largely been produced. Therefore, the consciousness of their own merit was not without justification; in addition, their loyalty to their King was unshakable. The King and the country both owed them gratitude. Their weakness lay in the fact that they were occasionally too conservative—that is, they recognized too late the demands of the time, and began by opposing progress, although it might be progress advantageous to themselves. One may understand this in view of their past, but the fact remains that it worked to the detriment of their relations with me, especially during my reign, when the development of the empire, particularly of industry and commerce, pushed rapidly forward, and I desired—and was compelled—to place no obstacles in the way of that development, but to promote it.

When I say that it was not always easy, for the
reasons adduced, to deal with the Conservatives, I
am well aware that the same is maintained about
me. Perhaps this is because I stood close to the
Conservatives on account of my traditions ; but I was
not a Conservative from the party point of view. I
was, and am indeed, in favour of progressive Conservatism, which preserves what is vital, rejects what
is outworn and accepts that portion of the new
which is useful.

Let me add that, in discussions, I was able to
endure the truth—even when it was uncomfortable
and bitter—better than people are aware, provided
that it was told to me tactfully.

So that, when it is maintained that I and the
Conservatives did not get on well in dealings with
each other, the same reason was at the root of the
difficulty on both sides. It would have been better
to have sought oftener for an understanding with me
in private conversation, for which I was always
ready. With regard to the canal question, on which
we could not agree, who were better qualified than
the Conservatives to understand and appreciate the
fact that I have never subscribed to the pretty
couplet : "*Unser Konig absolut, wenn er unseren
Willen tut.*"? ["Absolute our King may be, if he does
what we decree."] For, had I acted according to that
principle—a very comfortable one for me—the Conservatives, in view of their belief in a strong king
who really governs, would logically have been forced
to oppose me. Surely the Conservatives must have

respected me for having matched their honourable axiom of manly pride before the thrones of kings with mine of kingly pride before the throne of the Conservative Party, just as I did with regard to all other parties. In any event, the occasional differences with the Conservative Party and with individual Conservatives cannot make me forget the services rendered by men of this very party to the House of Hohenzollern, the Prussian State and the German Empire.

Well, Bülow finally did the great trick of bringing Conservatives and Liberals together, thus securing a big majority for the parties siding with the Government. In doing so the great abilities of the chancellor, his skill, statesmanship, and shrewd knowledge of men, shone forth most brilliantly. The great service rendered by him in achieving this success won him thorough appreciation and gratitude from his country and from myself, and, in addition, an increase of my trust in him. The boundless delight of the people of Berlin in the defeat of the Social Democrats at the polls led to the nocturnal demonstration, which I shall never forget, in front of my palace, in the course of which my automobile had to force a way for itself, little by little, amid a cheering crowd of many thousands surrounding it. The Lustgarten was packed with a great multitude of people, at whose tumultuous request the Empress and I had to appear on the balcony in order to receive their homage.

§ 6

The chancellor was present at the visit of King Edward VII to Kiel. Among the many guests was the former Chief Court Marshal of the Empress Frederick, Count Seckendorff, long acquainted through his many visits to England with Edward VII, who reposed great trust in the count. This gentleman, at the behest of Bülow, with whom he was friendly, arranged an interview between the King and the chancellor.

It took place on board the English royal yacht after a breakfast to which I and the chancellor were invited. Both sat for a long time together over their cigars. Afterwards Bülow reported to me what had transpired at the interview. In discussing the possible conclusion of an alliance between Germany and England, the King, he told me, had stated that such a thing was not at all necessary in the case of our two countries, seeing that there was no real cause for enmity or strife between them. This refusal to make an alliance was a plain indication of the English policy of encirclement, which soon made itself clearly and disagreeably felt at the Algeciras Conference. The pro-French and anti-German attitude of England, which was then openly revealed, was due to special orders from King Edward VII, who had sent Sir D. Mackenzie Wallace to Algeciras as his " supervising representative," equipped with personal instructions.

From hints given by the latter to his friends it

turned out that it was the King's wish that Germany should be strongly opposed and France supported at every opportunity. When it was pointed out to him that it might be possible, after all, to take up later with Germany this or that question and perhaps come to an understanding, he replied that an Anglo-Russian agreement was the paramount objective; once that were assured an " arrangement " might be made with Germany also. The English " arrangement " consisted in the encirclement of Germany.

The relations between myself and the chancellor remained trustful and friendly throughout this period. He was present repeatedly at the Kiel regatta. Among other matters which demanded his attention here he found opportunity to confer with the Prince of Monaco and a number of influential Frenchmen, who were guests aboard the prince's yacht, among whom doubtless the most eminent was Monsieur Jules Roche, the leading expert on European budgets, and a great admirer of Goethe, of whose *Faust* he always carried a copy in his pocket.

In April, 1906, came the unfortunate collapse in the Reichstag of the overworked chancellor. As soon as I received the news, I hurried there and was glad that Privy Councillor Renvers could give me encouraging news as to Bülow's condition. While the prince was recuperating during the summer at Norderney, I went to the island on a torpedo boat from Heligoland, where I had been inspecting, and surprised the chancellor and his wife at their villa.

I

I spent the day in chatting with him ; he had already recovered his health to an encouraging degree and was bronzed by the sea air and sunshine.

In the late autumn of 1907 the Empress and I paid a visit to Windsor, at the invitation of King Edward VII. We were most cordially received by the English royal family and the visit passed quite harmoniously. After this visit I went for a rest to Highcliffe Castle, belonging to General Stuart-Wortley, situated on the south coast of England, opposite the Needles.

Before my departure for England, the chancellor, who was greatly pleased at the English invitation, had some long talks with me as to the best means of securing a better footing with England, and suggested to me a number of his desires and projects to serve as guides in my conversations with Englishmen. During my visit I had frequent occasion to discuss the subjects agreed upon and conduct conversations as desired by the chancellor. Cipher telegrams containing my reports on these conversations went regularly to Berlin, and I repeatedly received approving replies from the chancellor. I used to show these after the evening meal to my intimates who accompanied me on my visit, among whom were the Chief Court Marshal, Count Eulenburg and Prince Max Egon Fürstenberg ; they read them and rejoiced with me at the harmonious understanding between me and the chancellor. After my return from England, I made a general report to the chancellor, whereupon he expressed to me his thanks for my having personally troubled myself so much and worked so hard towards improving the relations between the two countries.

A year later came the incident of the so-called " interview " published in the *Daily Telegraph*. Its object was the improvement of German-English relations. I had sent the draft submitted to me to the chancellor for examination, through the representative of the Foreign Office, Herr von Zenisch. I had called attention, by means of notes, to certain portions which, in my opinion, should be eliminated. When the matter was enquired into at my request, it was found that through a series of mistakes on the part of the Foreign Office this was not done.

A storm broke loose in the Press. The chancellor spoke in the Reichstag, but did not defend the Kaiser, who was the object of attack, to the extent that I expected, declaring, on the other hand, that he wished to prevent in future the tendency towards personal politics which had become apparent in the last few years. The Conservative Party took upon itself to address an open letter to the King through the newspapers, the contents of which are known.

During these proceedings, I was staying first at Eckartsau, with Franz Ferdinand, heir to the Austrian throne, and later with Kaiser Franz Joseph at Vienna, both of whom disapproved of the chancellor's conduct. From Vienna I went to Donaueschingen to visit Prince Fürstenberg, to whom the Press saw fit to address the demand that he, being an honest, upright man, should tell the Emperor the truth for once. When we talked over the whole matter, the prince advised me to get together at the Foreign Office the dispatches from Highcliffe in 1907, together with the answers to them, and have these laid before the Reichstag.

During this whole affair I underwent great mental anguish, which was heightened by the sudden death before my eyes of the intimate friend of my youth, Count Hülsen-Haeseler, chief of the military cabinet. The faithful, self-sacrificing friendship, and care of the prince and his family were most welcome to me in these bitter days; while letters and demonstrations from the empire, part of which sided with me and severely censured the chancellor, were a consolation to me during that period.

After my return the chancellor appeared, lectured me on my political sins, and asked me to sign the well-known document which was afterwards communicated to the Press. I signed it in silence and in silence I endured the attacks of the Press against myself and the Crown.

By his conduct, the chancellor struck a serious blow at the firm confidence and sincere friendship which had hitherto bound me to him. Undoubtedly Prince Bülow thought that by handling the matter as he did both in the Reichstag and with me personally, he could best serve me and the cause, especially as public excitement was running very high at that time. In this I could not agree with him, all the more so since his actions towards me in the *Daily Telegraph* affair stood out in too sharp contrast to

the complaisance and recognition which he had
previously manifested towards me. I had become
so accustomed to the amiability of the prince that I
found the treatment now accorded me incompre-
hensible. The relationship between Emperor and
chancellor, excellent and amicable up to that time,
was, at all events, disturbed. I gave up personal
relations with the chancellor and confined myself
to official dealings. After consultation with the
minister of the royal household and the chief of the
cabinet, I resolved to follow Prince Fürstenberg's
advice as to getting together the Highcliffe dispatches,
and charged the Foreign Office with this task. It
failed of accomplishment because the dispatches in
question were not to be found.

Towards the end of the winter the chancellor
requested an audience with me. I walked up and
down with him in the picture gallery of the palace,
between the portraits of my ancestors and the paint-
ings of the battles of the Seven Years' War, of the
proclamation of the empire at Versailles, and was
amazed when the chancellor harked back to the
events of the autumn of 1908 and undertook to ex-
plain his attitude. Thereupon I took occasion to talk
with him about the entire past. This frank conversation and the explanations of the prince, which
satisfied me, released the tension between us.
The result was that he remained in office. The
chancellor requested that I should dine with him
that evening, as I had so often done before, in order
to show the outer world that all was again well.

I did so. A pleasant evening, enlivened by the visibly delighted princess with charming amiability, and by the prince with his usual lively, witty talk, closed that memorable day. Alluding to the prince's audience with me, a wag wrote later in a newspaper, parodying a famous line: " The tear flows, Germania has me again."

By this reconciliation I also wished to show that I was in the habit of sacrificing my own sensitiveness to the good of the cause. Despite Prince Bülow's attitude towards me in the Reichstag, which was calculated to give me pain, I naturally never forgot his eminent gifts as a statesman and his distinguished services to the Fatherland. He succeeded, by his skill, in avoiding a world war at several moments of crisis, during the period indeed, when I, together with Tirpitz, was building our protecting fleet. That was a great achievement.

A serious epilogue to the above mentioned audience was provided by the Conservatives. The civil cabinet informed the party leaders of the chancellor's audience and what happened there, with the request that the party should now take back its " Open Letter." This request—which was made solely in the interest of the Crown, not of myself personally—was declined by the party. Not until 1916, when the war was under way, did we get into touch again, through a delegate of the party, at Great General Headquarters.

Just as the Conservatives did not do enough out of respect for the Crown to satisfy me, so also the

Liberals of the Left, the Democrats and the Socialists, distinguished themselves by an outburst of fury, which became, in their partisan Press, a veritable orgy, in which loud demands were made for the limitation of autocratic, despotic inclinations, etc. This agitation lasted the whole winter, without hindrance or objection from high government circles. Only after the chancellor's audience with me did it stop.

Later, a coolness gradually arose between the chancellor and the political parties. The Conservatives drew away from the Liberals; rifts appeared in the Block. Centre and Socialists—but, above all, the chancellor himself—finally brought about its collapse at Spa, as Count Hertling repeatedly explained to me later. He was proud to have worked energetically towards causing Bülow's downfall.

When matters had reached an impossible pass, the chancellor drew the proper conclusions and recommended to me the choice of Herr von Bethmann as the fifth chancellor of the empire. After careful consultations, I decided to acquiesce in the wish of Prince Bülow, to grant his request for retirement, and to summon the man recommended by him as his successor.

V

BETHMANN

§ 1

FROM my youth I had been well acquainted with
Herr von Bethmann-Hollweg. When I was on
active service for the first time in 1877, as lieutenant
in the 6th Company of the First Infantry Guard
Regiment, it was once quartered at Hohenfinow,
the home of old Herr von Bethmann, father of the
chancellor. I was attracted by the pleasant family
circle there, which was presided over by Frau von
Bethmann, a most worthy, amiable, and refined
lady, born of Swiss nationality. Often, as prince
and later as Emperor, I went to Hohenfinow, to
visit the old gentleman, and I was received on
each occasion by the young head of the rural district administration ; at that time neither of us
imagined that he would become Imperial Chancellor
under me.

From these visits sprang up, little by little, an
intimate relationship, which served steadily to
increase my esteem for Bethmann's diligence, ability,
and nobility of character—qualities much to my
liking, which clung to him throughout his career.

As Chief President and as Imperial Secretary of
State for the Interior Bethmann gave a good account

of himself, and, while occupying the last-named post, made his appearance successfully before the Reichstag.

Co-operation with the chancellor was easy for me. With Bethmann I kept up my custom of daily visits, whenever possible, and while walking in the garden of the chancellor's palace discussed fully with him questions of politics, events of the day, special bills and occurrences, and received reports from him. It was a pleasure, too, for me to visit the chancellor's home, for Bethmann's spouse was the very model of a genuine German wife, one whose simple distinction earned the esteem of every visitor, while her winning kindness of heart spread around her an atmosphere of cordiality. During the Bethmann regime the custom of holding small evening receptions, instituted by Prince Bülow and most enjoyable to me, was continued, and this enabled me to retain an informal association with men of all circles and walks of life.

In the journeys which the chancellor had to make in order to introduce himself, he won esteem everywhere by his distinguished calm and sincere methods of expression. Such foreign countries as were not hostile to us considered him a factor making for political stability and peace, to the maintenance and strengthening of which he devoted his most zealous efforts. This was entirely to my liking.

In foreign politics he busied himself from the start with the position of England in relation to Germany, and with the " encirclement " policy of

King Edward VII, which had become more and more evident after Reval, and was a source of worry to Bethmann. This was likewise true of France's growing enmity and desire for revenge, and the unreliability of Russia. During his regime as chancellor it became clear that Italy was no longer to be reckoned upon militarily; the work of Barrère in that country made " extra tours " a chronic necessity.

Upon assuming office, Herr von Bethmann found the situation with regard to France cleared up to such an extent that the German-French Morocco Agreement had been signed on February 9, 1909. By recognizing thereby the political predominance of France in Morocco, Prince Bülow had put the finishing touch to the German political retreat from Morocco. The standpoint which had determined the trip to Tangier, and, in addition, the Algeciras Conference, was thereby definitely abandoned. The great satisfaction of the French Government at this victory was expressed in a manner unwelcome to us by the conferring of the Cross of the Legion of Honour upon Prince Radolin and Herr von Schoen.

On the same day, King Edward VII, with Queen Alexandra, made his first official visit to the German Emperor and his wife at their capital city of Berlin— eight years after his accession to the throne ! Berlin received the exalted gentleman with rejoicing (! !) and showed no signs of dissatisfaction at his unfriendly policy.

The King did not look well ; he was tired and aged, and suffered, moreover, from a severe attack

of catarrh. Nevertheless, he accepted the invitation
of the municipal authorities of Berlin to an informal
tea at the City Hall. From his description, which
was corroborated by Berlin gentlemen, the function
must have been satisfactory to both parties.

I informed my uncle of the signing of the German-
French Morocco Agreement and the news seemed
to please him. When I added : " I hope this agreement will be a stepping stone to a better understanding between the two countries," the King nodded
his head approvingly and said " May that be so ! "
If the King had co-operated towards this, my project would probably not have failed. Nevertheless,
for the time being, the visit of their English Majesties
engendered a more friendly atmosphere, which
greeted Herr von Bethmann upon his assuming
office.

§ 2

During his term as chancellor Herr von Bethmann
had plenty of foreign problems to handle in connexion with the well-known events of 1909–14.
Concerning this period a mass of material has been
published in different quarters, for instance in the
book, " Causes of the World War," by Secretary of
State von Jagow. In the " Belgian Documents,"
the attitude of the German Government in the various
complications is described from a neutral standpoint. I had based this attitude on the following
axiom : " Caution on the one hand, on the other,

support of our Austro-Hungarian allies whenever
there is a plain threat against their position as a
world Power, combined with counsels of moderation
in action. Efforts in the role of ' honest broker '
everywhere, activity as a go-between wherever peace
seems endangered. Firm assertion of our own interests."

In view of the " encirclement " ambitions of our
opponents, we were at the same time, for the sake
of self-preservation, in duty bound to work steadily
towards building up our army and navy for purposes of defence, on account of the central location
of Germany and her open, unprotected frontiers.
This period of history is well described in Stege-
mann's book, and Heeferich and Friedjung also
depict the pre-war days interestingly.

The death of the " encircler," Edward VII—of
whom it was once said, in a report of the Belgian
Embassy at Berlin, that " the peace of Europe was
never in such danger as when the King of England
concerned himself with its maintenance "—called me
to London, where I shared with my close relations,
the members of the English royal family, the mourning into which the passing of the King had thrown
the dynasty and the nation. The entire royal
family received me at the railway station as a token
of their gratitude for the deference to family ties
shown by my coming.

King George drove with me to Westminster
Hall, where the gorgeously decorated coffin reposed
upon a towering catafalque, guarded by Household

troops, troops of the line, and detachments from the Indian and Colonial contingents, all in the traditional attitude of mourning—heads bowed, hands crossed over the butts and hilts of their reversed arms. The old, grey hall, covered by its great Gothic wooden ceiling, towered imposingly over the catafalque, lighted merely by a few rays of the sun filtering through the narrow windows. One ray flooded the magnificent coffin of the King, surmounted by the English crown, and made marvellous play with the colours of the precious stones adorning it. Past the catafalque countless throngs of men, women and children of all classes of the nation, passed in silence, many with hands folded, to bid a reverent farewell to him who had been so popular as a ruler. A most impressive picture, in its marvellous mediæval setting!

I went up to the catafalque, with King George, placed a cross upon it, and offered a silent prayer, after which my right hand and that of my royal cousin found each other quite unconsciously on our part, and met in a firm clasp. This made a deep impression on those who witnessed it, to such an extent that, in the evening, one of my relations said to me : " Your handshake with our King is all over London, the people are deeply impressed by it, and take it as a good omen for the future." " That is the sincerest wish of my heart," I replied.

As I rode through London behind the coffin of my uncle I was a witness of the tremendous and impressive demonstration of grief on the part of

the vast multitude—estimated at several millions—
on streets, balconies and roofs, every one of whom
was clad in black, every man of whom stood with
bared head, among all of whom reigned perfect order
and absolute stillness. Upon this sombre, solemn
background the files of British soldiers stood out all
the more gorgeously. In splendid array marched
the battalions of the Guards : Grenadiers, Scots
Guards, Coldstreams, Irish Guards—in their per-
fectly-fitting tunics, white leather belts and heavy
bearskin headgear ; all picked troops of superb
appearance and admirable martial bearing, a joy
to any man with the heart of a soldier, and all the
troops lining the path of the funeral cortège stood
in the attitude of mourning already described.

During my stay I resided, at the special desire
of King George, in Buckingham Palace. The widow
of the dead King, Queen Alexandra, received me
with moving and charming kindness and talked
much with me about bygone days ; my recollections
stretched back to my childhood, when I, while still a
little boy, had been present at the wedding of my
dead uncle.

The King gave a banquet to the many princely
guests and their suites, as well as to the representatives of foreign nations, at which Monsieur Pichon
was present. He was introduced to me and, in
conversation with him, I told him of the wishes
communicated to me by the Imperial Chancellor
regarding our interests in Morocco and other
political matters, which Monsieur Pichon readily

agreed to carry out. All other reports of this conversation which have emanated from various quarters belong to the domain of fancy.

§ 3

Although the period between 1909 and 1914 demanded extraordinary attention to foreign events, interior development was, nevertheless, zealously promoted, and efforts were made to meet the rapidly increasing demands of commerce, transportation, agriculture and industry. Unfortunately, endeavours in this direction were made much more difficult by the discord which existed among political parties.

The chancellor wished to accomplish everything possible of accomplishment, but his inclination to get to the bottom of problems and his desire to deal only with what was, from his meticulously critical standpoint, thoroughly matured, tended in the course of time to hamper progress. It was difficult to get him to make decisions before he was thoroughly convinced of their absolute freedom from objection. This made working with him tiresome and aroused in those not in close touch with him the impression of vacillation, whereas, in reality, it was merely over-conscientiousness carried too far.

In addition, the chancellor eventually developed an increasingly strong inclination towards domination; in discussions this tended to make him obstinate and caused him to lay down the law as dogmatically as a school teacher to those who differed from him This brought him many enemies and often made things difficult for me. A boyhood friend of the chancellor, to whom I once spoke about this, replied, with a smile, that it had been so with him even at school; there Herr von Bethmann had so constantly taught and school-mastered his fellow students, of whom my informant was one, that finally his classmates had nicknamed him " the governess." He added that this trait was a misfortune for Bethmann, but that it had so grown into his very being that he would never be able to get rid of it.

An example of this is found in Bethmann's relations with Herr von Kiderlen, whom he desired to have as secretary of State, despite my emphatic objections. Herr von Kiderlen was an able worker and a man of strong character, who always sought to assert his independence. He had been in office about a year when Herr von Bethmann came to me one day, complained of Kiderlen's obstinacy and insubordination, and asked me to appeal to his conscience. I declined, with the observation that the chancellor had chosen Kiderlen against my wishes and must now manage to get along with him; that the maintenance of discipline at the Foreign Office was a duty devolving upon the chancellor, in which I had no desire to interfere.

Meanwhile, Bethmann's inadequacy as chancellor became evident. Deep down in his heart he was a pacifist and was obsessed with the aberration of arriving at an understanding with England.

I can perfectly well understand that a man of pacifist inclinations should act thus in the hope of thereby avoiding a war. His object was entirely in accord with my policy. The ways and means whereby Bethmann sought to achieve it were, in my opinion, unsuitable. Nevertheless, I backed his endeavours, but I certainly did not believe that real success would result. It became even more apparent, while he was chancellor, that he was remote from political realities. Yet he always knew everything better than anybody else. Owing to his over-estimation of his own powers he stuck unswervingly to his ideas, even when things turned out differently from what he had expected.

His reports were always admirably prepared, brilliant in form, and, hence, impressive and attractive. In this there was an element of danger. In his opinion there was always but one solution—the one which he proposed. The apparent solidity and thoroughness of his reports and suggestions, the illuminating treatment from every angle of the matters reported upon, the references to experts, to foreign and native statesmen and diplomats, etc., easily led to the impression that the Bethmann solution was solely worthy of consideration. In spite of these thorough preparations, he made mistake after mistake.

Thus he had an actual share in our misfortune. When I returned from my Norwegian trip in 1914 he did not, it is true, place his resignation in my hands, but he admitted that his political calculations

J

had gone wrong. Nevertheless, I left him in office, even after his Reichstag speech and the English declaration of war on August 4, 1914, because I considered it most serious to change the highest official in the empire at the most critical moment in German history. The unanimous attitude of the nation in the face of the challenge from the Entente might have been impaired by such action.

Moreover, both the chancellor and the chief of the civil cabinet maintained that they had the working classes behind them. I was loth to deprive the working classes, who behaved in an exemplary manner in 1914, of the statesman whom, I was told, they trusted.

This theory, constantly repeated to me by the chief of the civil cabinet and the representative of the Foreign Office, that Bethmann alone had the support of the working classes, was finally further supplemented by reports to me that in foreign countries the chancellor enjoyed the confidence which was necessary to the conclusion of peace. Thus it came about that Bethmann remained in office, until, finally, the Crown Prince made the well-known investigation among the party leaders which showed that the above-mentioned theory was mistaken. This mistake was made all the clearer to me when I read, at the time of Bethmann's dismissal—to which other factors also contributed—the most unfavourable opinions of him, especially in the Social Democratic and Democratic Press.

I do not wish to blame Bethmann with these

frank remarks, nor to exonerate others ; but, when such important matters are discussed, personal considerations must be ignored. I never doubted Bethmann's noble sentiments.

§ 4

May I be allowed to say a few words here concerning the reform in the Prussian franchise, since the handling of this by Herr von Bethmann is characteristic of his policy of vacillation. Following the brilliant summer campaign came the hard, severe winter of 1914–15 with its trench-fighting that brought military movements to a standstill. The extraordinary achievements of all the troops and the spirit which I had found among officers and men, both at the front and in the hospitals, made such a profound impression on me that I resolved to provide something in the political domain for the tried, magnificent " Nation in Arms " when it returned home, which should prove that I recognized what it had done and wished to give the nation joy. I often touched upon this theme in conversations and suggested reforms in the Prussian franchise ; " The man," said I, " who, after a struggle like this, returned home with the Iron Cross—perhaps of both classes—must no longer be ' classified ' at the polls."

At this juncture a memorial was submitted to me by Herr von Loebell which proposed a reform in the Prussian franchise on similar grounds. The concise, clear and convincing treatment of the subject pleased me so much that I had the memorial—which took up, in its original form, only general points of view without going into detail—read by a number of gentlemen, and I was pleased to find that it met the approval of all whom I questioned concerning it.

I had my thanks expressed to Herr von Loebell through the chief of the cabinet, von Valentini, and caused Loebell to work out the matter in detail, and make suggestions. This was done in the spring of 1915. The memorial was very thorough and dealt with a number of possible schemes for the franchise, without advising any one system. It was approved by me, and sent by the chief of the cabinet to the chancellor, with the command that it should be discussed in the course of the year by the ministers, and that their vote on it—with possibly, also, some suggestions from them—be laid before me. The Franchise Law, of course, was not to be proposed until after the conclusion of peace.

Immediately after that I went to Pless. The battle of Gorlice—Tarnow, with its smashing victory over the enemy, brought on the Galician-Polish campaign, which resulted in the re-conquest of Lemberg, Przemysl and the capture of Warsaw, Ivangorod, Modlin (Novogeorgievsk), Brest-Litovsk, etc., and completely engaged my attention. The matter of the *Lusitania*, too, cast its shadow over events, and Italy severed her alliance with us. So it is not to be wondered at that the subject of the franchise was pushed into the background.

The next winter and the summer of 1916, likewise, with their fighting on all fronts, the terrible battle of the Somme, and the brilliant Rumanian autumn and winter campaign, took me to all kinds of places on the western and eastern fronts, even as far as Nish—where the first memorable meeting with the Bulgarian Tsar took place—and Orsova, so that I had no opportunity to take up the matter of franchise reform with the care that its importance demanded.

In the spring of 1917 I asked the chancellor to draw up an announcement of the reform, to be made to the nation at Easter, for I assumed that the ministers had long since discussed it. The chancellor drew up the text of the proclamation at Homburg in agreement with the chief of the cabinet and myself; he proposed that the method of voting be left open for the time being, as he was not yet quite sure about this. The Easter proclamation appeared; it was based, as in the previous treatment of the matter, on the idea that the reform was not to be introduced until after the conclusion of peace, seeing that most of the voters were away facing the enemy.

Party and Press, by recriminations and strife, did what they could to postpone the accomplishment of my purpose by bringing up the question of the Prussian Reichstag franchise, and by the demand for the introduction of the Franchise Bill while the war was still in progress. Thus the question embarked upon its well-known and not very pleasant course, which dragged itself out on account of the interminable negotiations in the Landtag. It was not until after the retirement of Herr von Bethmann that I learned through Loebell that the memorial of 1915 had never been submitted to the ministers but had lain untouched, for a year and a half, in a desk-drawer; that the chancellor, influenced by the desires expressed in the country, had dropped the various schemes proposed and concentrated upon the general (Reichstag) franchise, of the eventual introduction of which he was, doubtless, inwardly convinced.

In any event, the original basic idea was thoroughly bungled through Bethmann's dilatoriness and Party strife. What I wanted was to present of my own free will a gift of honour to my victorious army on its triumphal return home, to my " Nation in Arms," my brave Prussians, with whom I had stood before the enemy.

One of the results of Bethmann's marked inclination towards control was that the Secretary of State for Foreign Affairs became, under him, a mere helper, so much so that the Foreign Office was almost affiliated with the office of the chancellor—a state of affairs that made itself felt most especially in the use made of the Press department. Bethmann likewise decidedly asserted his independence in his relations with me. Basing himself upon the fact that, constitutionally, the chancellor alone is responsible for foreign policy, he ruled as he pleased. The Foreign Office was allowed to tell me only what the chancellor wished, so that it sometimes happened that I was not informed at all concerning important occurrences.

The fact that this was possible is to be laid at the door of the constitution of the empire; and this is the right place to say a word concerning the relations between the Emperor and the chancellor. In what follows I do not refer particularly to my relations with Herr von Bethmann, but, quite impersonally, to the difficulties which are caused by the Imperial Constitution in the relationship of the German Emperor to the Imperial Chancellors.

I wish to call attention to the following points :—

1. According to the constitution of the empire, the chancellor is the director and representative of the foreign policy of the empire, for which he assumes full responsibility; he has this policy, after he has reported on it to the Emperor, carried out by the Foreign Office, which is subordinated to him.

2. The Emperor has influence on foreign policy only in so far as the chancellor grants it to him.

3. The Emperor can bring his influence to bear through discussions, information, suggestions, proposals, reports and impressions received by him on his travels, which then rank as supplemental to the political reports of the ambassadors or ministers to the countries which he has personally visited.

4. The chancellor *may* act pursuant to such action by the Emperor, and may make it the basis of his decisions, whenever he is in agreement with the Emperor's point of view. Otherwise he is supposed to maintain *his own* point of view and carry it out (*vide* Kruger dispatch).

5. According to the constitution, the Emperor has no means of compelling the chancellor or the Foreign Office to accept his views. He cannot cause the chancellor to adopt a policy for which the latter feels that he cannot assume responsibility. Should the Emperor stick to his view, the chancellor can offer his resignation or demand that he be relieved of his post.

6. On the other hand, the Emperor has no constitutional means of hindering the chancellor or the Foreign Office from carrying out a policy which he thinks doubtful or mistaken. All he can do, if the chancellor insists, is to make a change in the chancellorship.

7. Every change of chancellors, however, is a serious matter, deeply affecting the life of the nation, and hence, at a time of political complications and high tension, an extremely serious step, an *ultima ratio* which is all the more daring in that the number of men qualified to fill this abnormally difficult post is very small.

The position of the Imperial Chancellor, which was based on the towering personality of Prince Bismarck, had assumed a serious preponderance in view of the constantly increasing number of posts under the empire, over all of which the chancellor was placed as chief and responsible head. If this be borne in mind, it is absolutely impossible that anybody should still hold the Emperor alone responsible for everything, as was done formerly, especially towards the end of the war and after the war, by critical know-alls and carping revolutionists, both at home and in the Entente countries. That, quite apart from every personal consideration, is a proof of complete ignorance of the earlier constitution of the German Empire.

§ 5

The visit of the Tsar to Potsdam in November, 1910, passed off to the satisfaction of all concerned, and was utilized by the chancellor and Herr von Kiderlen to get into touch with the newly-appointed Minister for Foreign Affairs, Sazonoff, whom the Tsar had brought with him. Apparently, the Russian ruler enjoyed himself among us; he took an active part in the hunt arranged in his honour, and proved himself an enthusiastic huntsman. The result of the conferences between the two statesmen seemed to promise well for the future; after they had exchanged views, both harboured the hope of the establishment of favourable relations between the two countries.

During my visit to Corfu in the spring, the Melissori troubles began, which riveted attention upon

Greek affairs. The authorities at Corfu were well informed as to the constant smuggling of arms from Italy into Albania by way of Valona, and there was a feeling in Greek circles that machinations across the Adriatic, as well as in Montenegro, were not without responsibility for what was happening. It was also felt that the new Turkish Government had not been wise in its handling of the Albanians, who were very sensitive and suspicious ; that the former Sultan, Abdul Hamid, had fully realized this and had understood admirably how to manage the Albanians and to keep them quiet. Nevertheless, there was no fear that more serious complications would ensue.

At the beginning of 1911 I received a most cordial invitation from King George of England to be present at the unveiling of the statue of Queen Victoria, the grandmother of both of us. Therefore I went to London in the middle of May with the Empress and our daughter. The reception on the part of the English royal family and the people of London was cordial.

The unveiling festivities were well arranged and very magnificent. The big space in front of Buckingham Palace was surrounded by grand stands, which were filled to overflowing with invited guests. In front of them were files of soldiers of all arms and all regiments of the British Army, in full parade uniform, the cavalry and artillery being on foot. All the colours of the troops were arrayed at the foot of the statue.

The royal family, with their guests and their suites, were grouped round the statue. King George made a dedication speech which had a good effect, and in the course of this he made mention of the German Imperial couple.

Then, amid salutes and greetings, the statue was unveiled; the Queen, in marble, seated upon a throne, and surmounted by a golden figure of Victory became visible. It was an impressive moment. Afterwards the troops marched past, the Guards in the van, then the Highlanders—who, with their gaily-coloured, becoming costume, gave an especially picturesque touch to the military spectacle— then the remainder of the soldiers. The march past was carried out on the circular space, with all the troops constantly wheeling; the outer wings had to step out, the inner to hold back, a most difficult task for troops. The evolution was carried out brilliantly; not one man made a mistake. The Duke of Connaught, who was responsible for the military arrangements, deservedly won unanimous applause.

The remainder of our stay in England was devoted to excursions; we also enjoyed the hospitality of noble English families, at whose homes there was opportunity to hold intercourse with many members of English society.

Special enjoyment in the domain of art was provided by the King for his guests by a theatrical performance at Drury Lane Theatre. A well-known English play, " Money," was performed by a

company consisting of the leading actors and actresses
of London, especially assembled for the occasion.
As a surprise, a curtain, painted by a lady for use
at this particular performance—on which was depicted
King George and myself, life-size, on horseback, riding
towards each other and exchanging military salutes
—fell between the acts. The picture was executed
with much dash, and was enthusiastically acclaimed
by the audience.

The playing of the actors and actresses in
" Money " was veritably masterly, for all concerned
interpreted their roles, even the smallest, to perfection.
It was, in fact, a classic production.

On another day I attended at Olympia to watch
British Army and Navy sports, which included
admirable individual feats on foot and on horseback, as well as evolutions by bodies of troops in
close formation.

In describing the unveiling of the Queen Victoria
statue and the funeral of King Edward VII, I have
concerned myself purposely with the externals and
pomp that are characteristic of such occasions in
England. They show that in a country under parliamentary rule—a so-called " democratic " country—
more importance is attached to pageants of almost
mediæval magnificence than is the case in the young
German Empire.

The French actions in Morocco, which were no
longer such as could be reconciled with the Algeciras
Agreement, had once more engaged the attention of
the diplomats. For this reason the chancellor had

requested me to ascertain, as soon as opportunity offered, what King George thought about the situation.

I therefore asked him if he considered that the French methods were still in accordance with the Algeciras Agreement. The King remarked that the Agreement, to tell the truth, was no longer in force, and that the best thing to do would be to forget it; that the French, fundamentally, were doing nothing different in Morocco from what the English had previously done in Egypt; that, therefore, England would place no obstacles in the path of the French, and would follow their own course; that the only thing to do was to recognize the *fait accompli* of the occupation of Morocco and make arrangements for commercial protection with France.

The visit passed off well, to the very end, and the inhabitants of London, of all social strata, expressed their goodwill every time the guests of their King showed themselves.

Thus, the German Imperial couple was enabled to return home with the best of impressions. When I informed the chancellor of these, he expressed great satisfaction. From the remarks of King George he drew the inference that England considered the Algeciras Agreement no longer valid and would not place any obstacles in the way of the French occupation of Morocco.

From this arose the policy followed by him and the Foreign Office which led to the Agadir incident, the last and equally unsuccessful attempt to maintain

our influence in Morocco. The situation became
more serious during the Kiel Regatta week. The
Foreign Office informed me of its intention to send
the *Panther* to Agadir. I gave expression to strong
misgivings as to this step but had to drop them in
view of the urgent representations of the Foreign
Office.

§ 6

In the first half of 1912 occurred the mission of
Sir Ernest Cassel with a verbal note in which England
offered to remain neutral in case of an " unprovoked "
attack upon Germany, provided that Germany
agreed to limit her naval construction programme
and to drop her new Naval Bill—the latter being
darkly hinted at. Owing to our favourable reply
to this Lord Haldane was entrusted with the negotiations and sent to Berlin. The negotiations finally
fell through owing to the increasingly uncompromising attitude of England. Sir Edward Grey finally
disavowed Lord Haldane and withdrew his own
verbal note, because he was afraid of offending the
French by a German-English agreement and of jeopardizing the Anglo-French-Russian understanding.

Here are the details of the matter :

On the morning of January 29, 1912, Herr Ballin
was announced to me at the palace in Berlin and
asked for an audience. I assumed that it was a case
of a belated birthday greeting, therefore I was not a
little astonished when Ballin, after a short speech

of congratulation, said that he had come as an emissary of Sir Ernest Cassel, who had just arrived in Berlin on a special mission and wished to be received.

I asked whether it was a political matter, and why, if so, the meeting had not been arranged through the English Ambassador. Ballin's answer was to the effect that, from hints dropped by Cassel, he knew the matter to be of great importance and the explanation for Cassel's acting without the intervention of the ambassador was, that the earnest desire had been expressed in London that the official diplomatic representatives, both English and German, should not be apprised of the affair.

I declared that I was ready to receive Cassel at once, but added that, should his mission have to do with political questions, I should immediately summon the chancellor, since I was a constitutional monarch and not in a position to deal with the representative of a foreign Power apart from the chancellor.

Ballin fetched Cassel, who handed me a document which, he stated, had been prepared with the " approval and knowledge of the English Government." I read the short note through, and was not a little surprised to see that I was holding in my hand a formal offer of neutrality in case Germany became involved in future warlike complications, conditional upon certain limitations in the carrying out of our programme of naval construction, which were to be the subject of mutual conferences and agreements. Walking with Ballin into the next room I handed over the document for him to read.

After he had done so, both of us exclaimed in the same breath : " A verbal note ! "

It was plainly apparent that this " verbal note " was aimed at the forthcoming addition to our Naval Law and designed in some way to delay and frustrate it. No matter how the matter was interpreted, I found myself confronted with a peculiar situation, which equally amazed Ballin. It reminded me of the situation at Cronberg-Friedrichshof in 1908, when I was obliged to decline the demand, made to me personally by the English under-secretary, Hardinge, that we should forgo our proposed naval construction.

Now, an intimate business friend of Edward VII appears, without previous announcement through official diplomatic channels, before the German Emperor, with a " verbal note " inspired by the English Government, with explicit instructions to evade all the diplomatic officials of both countries ! He hands over an offer from the English Government to maintain neutrality in future warlike complications provided certain agreements regarding limitation of naval construction are made. And this is done by England, the mother of " constitutionalism ! " When I pointed this out to Ballin, he exclaimed : " Holy constitutionalism ! What has become of you ? This is ' personal politics ' with a vengeance ! "

I agreed with Ballin to send at once for Herr von Bethmann, in order that he might learn what was transpiring and decide what was to be done in this peculiar situation.

Bethmann was called up on the telephone and

soon arrived. At first the situation aroused in him likewise a certain degree of astonishment; it was interesting to watch the play of expression on his face as he was told about the matter. The chancellor suggested that, for the proper settlement of the business, Grand Admiral von Tirpitz should also be summoned; he also recommended that a reply be drawn up in English, in the same manner and form as the note delivered by Cassel, and that it be handed to Sir Ernest, who wished to return home that night. English was chosen because there was fear of obscurity and misunderstanding if the note were translated in London. The chancellor asked me to draw up the note, as I was best acquainted with English. After some objection I had to agree to be the writer of the reply.

The following scene now took place:

I sat at the writing-table in the adjutant's room, the other gentlemen stood around me. I would read a sentence from the note aloud and sketch out an answer, which was, in turn, read aloud. Then criticisms were made from right and left: one thought the sentence too complaisant, another too abrupt; it was thereupon remodelled, recast, improved and polished. The chancellor particularly subjected my grammar and style to much torture, owing to his habit of probing things philosophically, and to his methods of profound thoroughness, which caused him to be most particular with every word, in order that, having been studied from every angle, it should afford nobody cause for criticism later on.

K

After hours of work the note was finally finished and, having been passed a couple of times from hand to hand and then read aloud by me half a dozen times more, it was signed.

When our group broke up the chancellor asked Sir Ernest who was to be expected from England to conduct the negotiations. Cassel replied that it would certainly be a minister, which one he did not know—perhaps Mr. Winston Churchill, Minister for the Navy, since the question was a naval one. Then the chancellor arranged further with him that the unofficial method should be retained, and that Ballin should undertake to transmit all news regarding the matter which should emanate from England.

Sir Ernest expressed his lively gratitude for his cordial reception and his satisfaction at the tenor of our reply. Later, Ballin informed me from his hotel that Cassel had expressed himself as completely satisfied at the successful outcome of his mission, and that he would report to his Government the good impression made upon him.

When I thereupon conferred on the matter with Admiral von Tirpitz, we both agreed that the Naval Bill was in danger, and that we must be very careful.

In perfect secrecy the material which Admiral von Tirpitz was to present at the negotiations was collected; it consisted of a short historical sketch of the development of the fleet and of the increasingly difficult tasks devolving upon it; the Naval Law and its aims, nature, enactment and extension;

finally, the contemplated Naval Bill, its meaning and the method of putting it through.

The chancellor asked that the main negotiations should be conducted at the palace in my presence. In addition, I agreed with Admiral von Tirpitz that he should speak in English, as far as possible, and that I, in case of difficult technical expressions, would interpret.

Until England made known the name of the negotiator, our time was spent in speculation on the matter, and Ballin informed us of combinations in connexion with which a number of names, even that of Grey, came up.

At last the news arrived, through Ballin, that Haldane—the Minister for War, previously a lawyer—had been entrusted with the conduct of the negotiations and would soon arrive. General amazement! Just imagine, *mutatis mutandis*, if Germany had sent her Minister for War (at that time von Heeringen) to London, instead of Admiral von Tirpitz, for the discussion of a naval matter!

When this point was discussed with Bethmann and Tirpitz a number of theories were advanced; the chancellor said that Haldane was known in England as a student of Goethe and as a man versed in German philosophy and well acquainted with the German language, so that his choice was a polite compliment towards us. Tirpitz observed that Haldane had formerly spent some time in Berlin and worked with General von Einem at the Ministry of War, and hence knew the state of affairs in Germany.

I suggested that this was all very well, but that
the choice of Haldane showed that England looked
upon the question as a purely political one, seeing that
he had but a superficial knowledge of naval affairs;
that the whole matter was probably directed against
Germany's naval policy in general and the new
Naval Bill in particular; that it would be well,
therefore, not to forget this, in order that the matter
might not develop into a foreign assault upon our
right of self-determination as to the strength of our
defensive measures.

Haldane arrived and was received as an Imperial
guest. Ballin, who accompanied him, solved the
riddle of Haldane's choice on the basis of information received by him from England.

He said that when Cassel returned to London,
reported on his reception, and handed over the
German reply, the impression made was so favourable
that no further doubt was entertained there as to
the satisfactory course of the negotiations and their
conclusion in the form of an agreement; that thereupon a keen dispute had arisen among ministers—
especially between Churchill and Grey—as to who
should go to Berlin, in the event of the achievement
of the object of making Germany abandon the
further development of her fleet, and affix his name
to this great historical document. Churchill considered himself the right man for the job, seeing
that he was the head of the navy, but Grey and
Asquith would not allow their colleague to reap the
glory. Thus, for a time, Grey stood in the fore-

ground—another proof that some political purpose rather than the number of ships was the leading factor. After a while, however, it was decided that it was more fitting to Grey's personal and official importance that he should appear only at the termination of the negotiations, to affix his name to the agreement, and—as it was put in the information transmitted from England to Ballin—" to get his dinner from the Emperor and to come in for his part of the festivities and fireworks," which, in good German, means to enjoy the " Bengal light illumination."

As it had been decided that, in any event, Churchill was not to get this, it was necessary to choose somebody for the negotiations who was in close accord with Asquith and Grey and who, possessing their complete confidence, was willing to conduct the negotiations as far as the beginning of the " fireworks " ; one, moreover, who was already known at Berlin and not a stranger to Germany. Churchill certainly qualified to this extent, for he had attended the Imperial manœuvres in Silesia and Würtemberg on several occasions as a guest of the Emperor. Ballin guaranteed the reliability of his source of information in London.

Before the negotiations began I once more pointed out to Secretary of State von Tirpitz that Haldane, in spite of his being Minister for War, had probably prepared himself for his task and was sure to have received careful instructions from the English Admiralty, where the influence of Fisher was paramount.

In his "Handbook for English Naval Officers," Fisher had stated, among other precepts well worthy of being remembered, one which is characteristic of the admiral, his department, and its spirit, which runs, word for word, as follows : "If you tell a lie, stick to it." Moreover, I pointed out to Tirpitz that the amazing adaptability of the Anglo-Saxons, which fitted them to occupy positions that had no relation to their previous life and training, must not be overlooked. Furthermore, that in England the interest in the navy was generally so intense that almost every educated man to a certain degree was an expert on naval questions.

In the course of the negotiations Haldane proved himself admirably well informed and a skilful, tenacious debater ; his brilliant qualities as a lawyer came well to the fore. The conversation lasted several hours and resulted not only in a general clarifying of the question, but in a preliminary agreement as to the postponement of time-limits for ship construction, etc. The details concerning it are recorded in documents at the Imperial Naval Office. Tirpitz was splendid.

After some further conferences—at which, likewise, Ballin was present—Haldane returned to England. Ballin informed me that Haldane had expressed himself to him as entirely satisfied with the outcome of his mission, and had stated that the first draft of the agreement would be sent to us in the course of a week or two.

Time passed; the date appointed for the introduction of the Naval Bill approached. Tirpitz suggested that in the event of the agreement being previously concluded, the Naval Bill should be altered accordingly; otherwise, that it be introduced without alteration.

At last we received, not the draft of the agreement, but a document asking all manner of questions and expressing a desire for all sorts of data, a reply to which required many consultations and much reflection. Little by little the suspicion grew in me that the English were not in earnest with regard to the agreement, for question followed question and details, which had nothing directly to do with the agreement, were sought. England withdrew more and more from her promises, and no draft of the agreement came to hand.

In Berlin a great agitation on the part of the Foreign Office and from other quarters, both qualified and unqualified, set in against the Naval Bill, Tirpitz and myself. The chancellor who hoped to achieve the agreement and affix his name to a document which would free Germany from " encirclement " and bring her into a regular and better relationship with England, also pronounced in favour of dropping the Naval Bill. That would simply have meant allowing a foreign Power to exercise enormous influence in matters of German national defence and in the event of a war being forced upon us, thereby jeopardizing the national right of self-determination and our readiness for battle. Had we permitted this, it would have amounted to our consenting to

England—Germany's principal foe—granting us whatever she wished, after securing her own interests, without our receiving the guarantee of any equivalent concession.

In this confused state of affairs differences of opinion and disputes arose, which, especially in those circles that really knew little about the navy, were conducted with much violence and not always in a practical manner. All through that winter—which was such a difficult one for him and me—Admiral von Tirpitz fought his fight like a genuine patriotic officer; he thoroughly realized the situation and with clear vision saw through his opponents and, to the limit of his ability, supported me with complete conviction. All the Government officials agreed that no foreign country could be allowed any voice in helping us to decide what we had or had not to do towards insuring our protection.

The hope of bringing about the agreement grew ever fainter; England showed continually lessening interest and eliminated part after part of importance from her original verbal note. And so it came about that Admiral von Tirpitz and I realized that the whole proposal was merely a " political manœuvre."

The fight over the Naval Bill grew steadily hotter. I happened at this time to meet at Cuxhaven the President of the Hamburg Senate, Dr. von Burchard, whom I respected greatly, because he was the very model of an aristocratic citizen of a Hanseatic city, and had often been consulted by me in political matters. I described to him the entire

course of the affair and the disputes in Berlin as to
the introduction or non-introduction of the bill;
I then asked him to tell me, with his usual complete frankness, what he thought was the right
thing to do in the national interest, because I greatly
desired to hear an objective opinion, uninfluenced
by the rival camps of Berlin.

Dr. Burchard replied, in his clear, keen, pointed,
convincing manner, that it was my duty towards
the people and the Fatherland to stick to the bill;
that whosoever spoke against its introduction was
committing a sin against them; that whatever we
thought necessary to our defence must be unconditionally brought into being; that, above all else,
we must never permit a foreign country to have
the presumption to interfere with us; that the
English offer was a feint to make us drop the Naval
Bill; that, in no circumstances, must this be allowed;
that the German nation would not understand why
its right of self-determination had been sacrificed;
that the bill must unquestionably be introduced;
that he would work in its favour in the Federal
Council (as indeed he did, in a brilliant, compelling
speech) and in other ways also press its acceptance
in Berlin; that the English would naturally resort
to abuse, but that this was immaterial, seeing that
they had been doing so for a long time; that
they certainly would not go to war for such a
cause; that Admiral von Tirpitz was merely doing
his duty and fulfilling his obligations and that
I should support him in every way; that the

chancellor must abandon opposition to the measure, or otherwise he would run the risk of finally forfeiting public esteem on account of being " pro-English."

Thus spoke the representative of the great commercial city, which was threatened above all others in the event of war with England. The genuine Hanseatic spirit inspired his words.

Strangely enough, Dr. Burchard's opinion concerning the English offer has recently been corroborated to me in Holland by a Dutchman who heard from Englishmen at that time the English point of view. I and Tirpitz guessed aright : the offer of neutrality *was* a political manœuvre.

Soon news came from Ballin that the matter also was not going well in England; that, according to the information he received, a dispute had arisen concerning the agreement; that there was dissatisfaction with Haldane, who, it was said, had allowed himself to be cheated by Tirpitz ! This was plain evidence of the indignation felt because Tirpitz had not walked into the trap and simply let the bill drop, and that Haldane had been unable to serve up the bill to the English Cabinet on a platter at tea-time. It is useless to say that there was " cheating " on Germany's part, but the reproach levelled at Haldane justifies the suspicion that his instructions were that *he* should seek to " cheat " the Germans. Since his fellow-countrymen thought that the reverse was true, one can but thank Admiral von Tirpitz most sincerely for having correctly asserted the German standpoint to the benefit of our Fatherland.

Towards the end of March the fight concerning the bill became so violent that, finally, on the 22nd, as I stepped out of the vault in the Charlottenburg Park, the chancellor asked me for his dismissal. After long consultation, and after I had told him Dr. Burchard's view, the chancellor withdrew his request.

When, some time afterwards, I paid a visit to Herr von Bethmann in his garden, I found him quite overcome and holding in his hand a message from London. It contained the entire disavowal of the verbal note delivered by Cassel, the withdrawal of the offer of neutrality as well as of every other offer, and, at the end, the advice that I should dismiss Herr von Bethmann from the Imperial Chancellorship, seeing that he enjoyed to a marked degree the confidence of the British Government! Tears of anger shone in the eyes of the chancellor, thus badly deceived in his hopes. The praise accorded to him by a foreign Government, with which Germany and he had just had such painful experiences, hurt him deeply. For the second time he offered me his resignation. I did not accept it, but sought to console him. I then ordered that the ambassador in London should be asked how under any conditions he could have accepted and forwarded such a message.

The chancellor was now in favour of the bill; but it was honourably proposed with the limitation which it had been decided to impose upon it in the event of the conclusion of the agreement. In England, on the other hand, the full naval construction programme was carried out.

This "Haldane episode" is characteristic of England's policy. The whole manœuvre, conceived on a large scale, was engineered for the sole purpose of hampering the development of the German fleet: while, simultaneously, in America—which had an almost negligible merchant fleet; in France—whose navy was superior in numbers to the German; in Italy; in Russia—which also had ships built abroad —vast construction programmes were carried out without eliciting one word of protest from England. Germany, wedged in between France and Russia, certainly had, at least, to be sufficiently prepared to defend herself on the water against those nations.

For this purpose our naval construction programme was absolutely necessary; it was never aimed against the English fleet, which was four or five times stronger than ours and assured England's superiority and security. No sensible man in Germany ever dreamed of attempting to equal its strength. We needed our fleet for coast defence and the protection of our commerce; the lesser means of defence, such as U-boats, torpedo-boats and mines, are not sufficient for the purpose. Moreover, the coast batteries on the Baltic were so antiquated and miserably equipped that they could have been razed within forty-eight hours by the

massed fire of the heavy guns of modern battleships.
Thus, our Baltic coast was practically defenceless.
To protect it the fleet was necessary.

The Skager Rak (Jutland) battle proved what that
fleet meant and what it was worth. That battle
would have meant annihilation for England if the
Reichstag, up to 1900, had not refused all proposals
for strengthening the navy. Those twelve lost years
were destined never to be retrieved.

Before we take our leave of Haldane, I wish to
touch upon another episode in his activities. In
1906 he came to Berlin with the permission of the
German Government, to inform himself concerning
the conditions of Prussian defence, recruiting, General
Staff, etc. He busied himself at the Ministry for
War, where the minister, General von Einem, personally gave him information. After about two or
three weeks' work there he returned, well satisfied,
to England.

When, after the outbreak of the world war, the
" pro-German " Haldane, the friend of Goethe, was
boycotted and treated with such hostility that he
could no longer show himself in public, he had a
defence written of his term of office as Minister for
War by the well-known littérateur and journalist,
Mr. Begbie, entitled " Vindication of Great Britain."
Therein his services towards the formation of a
regular General Staff, and the preparation of the
British Army for the world war are placed in a bright
light ; emphasis is laid on the skill with which he
utilized the permission obtained from the Prussian

War Ministry to secure information in Germany upon military matters on which to reorganize the British Army and General Staff, to the minutest detail, on the German model, in readiness for the coming war against his erstwhile German hosts.

Here we see the sly, adroit lawyer, who, sheltered under the hospitality of a foreign country, studies its military arrangements in order to forge weapons against it out of the material and knowledge thus acquired. Quite characteristically the book is dedicated to King Edward VII, whose intimate, emissary and tool Haldane was. In those days Berlin saw in Haldane's mission that *rapprochement* with England towards which Germans were always bending their efforts; in reality, however, it was a "reconnoitring expedition" under the very roof of the German cousin. England showed her gratitude by the world war, which Haldane helped to prepare. In this case Haldane "cheated" the Germans!

That is the history of the Haldane mission. Later it was summarily maintained by all sorts of ignorant dabblers in politics belonging to the Press and the general public, that the promising *rapprochement* with England through Haldane had been wrecked by the obstinacy of the Emperor and Admiral von Tirpitz, and by their clinging to the Naval Bill against the wishes of all "sensible counsellors."

§ 7

At that time the question of the establishment of an independent Albanian state and the Powers' choice of a head for it, was also brought to my attention. A number of candidates lusting for a crown had already presented themselves before the tribunal of the Powers, without securing acceptance ; a number of candidates, considered by the Powers, were declined by the Albanians. I looked upon the matter in itself with indifference, and was of the opinion that—as in the case of every " creation of a nation "—the greatest possible attention should be paid to historical development, to geographical peculiarities and the customs of the people.

In this curious country there has never been a united nation under one ruler and one dynasty. In valleys, encircled and cut off by high mountain ranges, to a considerable degree the Albanian tribes live separated from each other. Their political system is not unlike the clan system of the Scotch. Christians and Mohammedans are represented in about equal proportions.

The custom of " vendetta " is an ancient one, sanctioned by tradition, which is no less true of robbery and cattle-stealing. Agriculture is still in a backward stage of development, farming is in its infancy, the implements used therein date from before the Flood.

The head-man of the clan dispenses justice in the open, under the village tree, as it used to be done

once upon a time among the ancient Germans.
Every man is armed and most are excellent shots.
Whenever the head-man of the clan turns up in
some hamlet, while touring on horseback through his
territory, the inhabitants expect a blessing from him
in the form of jingling coins, which sometimes are
scattered about by him from the saddle. This, of
course, is particularly customary at the commencement of a new Government's term of office, and
great is the dissatisfaction when distribution of
largesse does not happen.

Up to the time of the Balkan War many Albanians
entered the Turkish service, where they were greatly
prized and rose to high importance on account of
their diligence, keen intelligence and tenacious energy.
They supplied the Turkish administration with a
large number of officials, and with a certain percen-
tage of the diplomatic corps and the army. The
young Albanian nobles were proud to serve in a
splendid company of palace guards of the Sultan,
which scarcely had an equal for size, martial appearance and manly beauty. These were in a way rela-
tives of the Sultan, for the latter used to have noble
Albanian women of the principal clans in his harem,
in order that he—protected by blood-brotherhood—
might be safe from the vendettas of the clans, and,
also, that he might find out everything calculated
to influence the feelings of the Albanian chieftains.
The desires of the Albanians which reached him
by this road—for instance, as to supplies of arms
and ammunition, schoolhouses, building of high-

ways, etc.—were thereupon granted in an inconspicuous manner. Thus by means of "family ties" the Sultan was enabled to keep the usually turbulent Albanians quiet and loyal.

With this knowledge of the state of affairs as a foundation, I sought to bring my influence to bear towards the appointment, if possible, of a Mohammedan—perhaps an Egyptian—not forgetting that he should have a well-lined purse, which is an absolute necessity in Albania. My advice was not heeded by the "Areopagus of the Powers," whose members were not bothering themselves with the interests of the Albanians, but seeking, first of all, for pretexts and opportunities for fishing in the troubled Albanian waters, in such a way as to benefit their own countries.

I was not at all pleased, therefore, when the choice fell upon Prince William of Wied. I esteemed him as a distinguished, knightly man of lofty sentiments, but considered him unfitted for the post. The prince knew altogether too little about Balkan affairs to undertake this thorny task with hope of success. It was particularly unpleasant to me that a German prince should make a fool of himself there, as it was apparent from the start that the Entente would place all kinds of obstacles in his path. Upon being questioned by the prince—my cousin—I told him all my doubts, laying stress upon the difficulties awaiting him, and advised him urgently to decline. I could not command him, since the Prince of Wied, as head of the family, had the final word in the matter.

L

After the prince's acceptance of the candidature offered him by the Powers, I received him in the presence of the chancellor. A certain irresolution in the bearing of the prince, who contemplated his new task with anything but enthusiasm, strengthened me and the chancellor in our resolve to try hard once more to dissuade the young candidate from ascending the recently-invented Albanian " throne " ; but in vain. The ambitious, mystically excited wife of the prince saw in Albania the fulfilment of her wishes, and " Ce que femme veut, Dieu le veut " [" What woman wishes, God wishes "].

Carmen Sylva* also worked towards his acceptance ; she went so far, indeed, as to publish an article in the newspapers headed " Fairyland wants its Prince."

So even the best-meant warnings were useless. I had further strongly advised the prince not to go to Albania before the financial question was settled, as the reasons which had led me to suggest the selection of a rich ruler now came to the fore. The prince was not very wealthy and the Powers had to supply him with a " dotation," concerning the amount of which and the method of payment by instalments, an unpleasant quarrel arose. At length a part payment was made.

Danger lurked for the new prince and his eventual government in the person of Essad Pasha, an unreliable, intriguing, greedy soldier of fortune, who himself had designs on the Albanian throne and

* The Queen of Rumania.

held sway over a certain number of armed adherents.
From the start he was an opponent of the prince
and plotted secretly with Italy, which was not favourably inclined towards the Prince of Wied. Now it
would have been quite natural and a matter of course
if the new ruler had taken with him in his suite men
from Germany whom he knew and who were faithful to him. But he did not. An Englishman and
an Italian were attached to his person as " secretaries," and they had nothing better to do than to
work against his interests, to give him bad advice,
and to intrigue against him.

While the Prince of Wied was making his preparations there appeared an excellently written pamphlet by an Austrian General Staff Officer, dealing
with his travels in Albania. The officer described
in a vivacious and clear style, the geographical and
climatic drawbacks, the population and customs, the
general poverty and backwardness of the country.

He pointed out that in no circumstances must a
future ruler reside on the coast, but must show himself to the inhabitants and travel about the
country. Owing to the primitive means of transportation, he went on, the lord of the land must sit
all day on horseback and ride through his domain,
having at his saddle-bow the famous " bag of sequins "
mentioned in all Oriental tales and legends, in order
to sway public opinion in his favour, in the places
visited, by the expected shower of gold. The ruler
must be sure, the author continued, to bind some
of the clans of the region closely to himself, so as to

have at his beck and call an armed force for asserting his will and overcoming any opponents wishing to rebel, since this was the only way to maintain his power, in view of the utter lack of " army " or " troops " in the European sense of the words !

This meant that the ruler of Albania must lead at first a nomadic life, on horseback, and, in addition, provide himself with a wandering camp, with tents and other accessories, and the necessary horses. Plenty of men adapted to this sort of life might have been found in the prince's squadron of the Third Guard Uhlan Regiment, as many of his men, who were very fond of him, had declared that they were ready to accompany him as volunteers. They certainly would have served him better and have been more useful to him than the course he adopted in preparing to take over the overlordship of Albania, without knowledge of the country.

I advised my cousin urgently to study this pamphlet and to follow its recommendations, especially with regard to his residence. I suggested that he should fix this at some point as far as possible from the warships of the Powers, in order that he might not be forced to act under their pressure and thereby arouse the suspicion among the Albanians that their ruler needed these ships for protection against his subjects. Did the prince ever read the pamphlet ? At all events, the course subsequently adopted by him was contrary to its advice and the advice given him by me.

The prince and his wife journeyed to Albania

and matters turned out as I had foreseen. According to reports describing the arrival of the sovereign couple, the princess, although she was a German, addressed the assembled Albanians from her balcony in French, as they understood no German! The " Court " remained at Durazzo under the guns of the foreign ships. The prince did not travel on horseback through the land, nor did he scatter gold sequins about—not even from his balcony on the day of his arrival—nor did he push Essad out of the way. So the adventure ended as one might have imagined it would.

I have gone into some detail in describing my attitude towards the question of the choice of the ruler of Albania because false rumours have been circulated from every possible quarter with the purpose of imputing to me motives which were utterly foreign to me. In this matter, too, I gave honest advice when questioned, based on sound knowledge of mankind.

§ 8

The year 1912 also witnessed the meeting with the Tsar at Baltic Port, whither I repaired on board my yacht at the invitation of Nicholas II. Our two yachts anchored side by side, so that visiting from ship to ship was easy. The Tsar, his children and his entire entourage vied with each other in evidences of goodwill and hospitality. The Russian and German escorting squadrons were inspected, turn and turn about, by the Tsar and myself together, and we took our meals either at the Tsar's table or mine.

We spent one morning on land near Baltic Port. The 85th ("Viborg") Infantry Regiment, whose commander I was, had been drawn up in a field and was inspected first in parade formation, then in company and battalion exercises, which were carried out in as satisfactory a manner as was the parade with which the evolutions were brought to a close.

The regiment, composed of four battalions, made an excellent impression. It was in field equipment— brown-grey blouses and caps—and the latter, worn by all jauntily cocked over one ear, gave to the sun- burnt, martial faces of the strong young soldiers a bold air which brought joy to the heart of every soldier who gazed upon them.

In the course of the brilliant and uncommonly amiable reception which I met with on this occasion, I received no hint of the Balkan alliance, concluded a short time before.

It was my last visit to Russia before the out- break of the war.

VI

MY CO-WORKERS IN THE ADMINISTRATION

§ 1

IT behoves me to remark that I found particular pleasure in working with His Excellency von Stephan and in dealing with him. He was a man of the old school, who fitted in so well with me that he always grasped my ideas and suggestions and afterwards carried them out with energy and power, owing to his firm belief in them. A man of iron energy and unflagging capacity for work and joyousness; endowed, moreover, with refreshing humour, quick to perceive new possibilities, never at a loss for expedients, well versed in political and technical matters, he seemed to have been born especially for creative co-operation. I trusted him implicitly and my trust in him was never betrayed. I learned much from my association with this stimulating, shrewd counsellor.

The Post Office Department reached an unimagined degree of excellence and aroused the admiration of the whole world. The great invention of the telephone was utilized to the limit, applied extensively to the public service, and developed so as to facilitate its general use.

In the domain of building also, Stephan brought about a decided improvement, which received my approval and support.

All great State building projects depended on the vote of the investigating " Academy of Building," which, at that time, was a slow-moving, cumbrous and backward body. I had already had experiences of my own with it. The " White Drawing-room," originally merely provisional, had been put up without much attention to style—it had been intended at first for an Indian masquerade, a " Lalla Rookh " festival, in honour of the Grand Duchess Charlotte, daughter of Frederick William III and her husband, later Tsar Nicholas I. An investigation instituted at my order showed the material to be spurious and inferior; the structure was in the worst possible state of decay and in danger of collapse; a new one was needed.

With the co-operation and collaboration of the Empress Frederick, projects and plans were made, and, finally, a big model was provided by Building Councillor Ihne—the " modern Schlüter," as the Empress Frederick used to call him—which won unanimous approval. Only the Building Academy opposed wearisome objections, stating that the " White Drawing-room " required no alterations and ought to be preserved " in its old historical beauty."

When the new structure was completed, however, it met with the entire approval of the gentlemen who formerly had been so critical.

Herr von Stephan was also at loggerheads with the Academy of Building. He wanted to alter many post offices, or build entirely new ones, especially in the big cities, but, in view of the fearful slowness and devotion to red tape of the aforesaid official body, he either had no answer at all, or received refusals, when he brought these matters to its attention. There the rule of thumb was supreme. Herr von Stephan was of the opinion that, in its buildings as well as in other directions, the youthful German Empire must give an impression of power, and that the Imperial Post Offices must be built accordingly; he believed that they should harmonize with the general style of the towns where they were located, or, at least, conform to the style of their oldest and most important buildings. Nor could I do otherwise than agree with such a view.

At last there came an open rupture with the Academy. His Excellency von Stephan lost patience and informed me that he had freed his office, and the buildings erected by it, from the supervision of the Academy; that he had even formed a committee from among his own architects and officials for supervising purposes; and that all he asked of me was to subject the more important plans for buildings to a final inspection. I willingly agreed.

Stephan was an enthusiastic huntsman, so that I had additional opportunities, while on the Court hunts, to enjoy association with this refreshing, unchanging, faithful official and counsellor.

§ 2

Among the ministers whom I particularly esteemed, His Excellency Miquel took first place. He it was who, as my Minister of Finance, put through for Prussia the great reform which placed the country on a sound basis and helped it towards prosperity. Intercourse with this astute political expert gave me great pleasure, and a wealth of knowledge and stimulus.

The degree to which Miquel was versed in almost every subject was astounding. In conversation he was brisk, humorous and keen in elucidating and arguing a point, in addition to which a strong historical bent ran, like a red thread, through his quotations. In history and ancient languages he was marvellously well equipped, so that, in his reports, he was often able to hark back to the times of the Romans and quote from his store of knowledge—not out of Büchmann*—Latin quotations in support of his arguments. On account of his brilliant dialectics, even when he was instructing, he was never tiresome, but would hold his hearers spell-bound to the very end.

It was His Excellency Miquel who incited me to favour the great canal projects and supported me when the Prussian Conservatives opposed the Central (Rhine—Weser—Elbe) Canal and brought about the failure of the plan to build it. He lent strength to the King and made the latter decide not to give up this fight until victory was won. He knew, as I did, what

* A German philologist who compiled a well-known book of quotations.

blessings the canals in Holland and the splendid network of waterways in France had brought to those countries and what a relief they were to the increasingly hard-pressed railways.   In the world war we might have had a splendid, East-to-West artery of transportation for ammunition, wounded, siege material, supplies and the like, which would have made it possible, by thus relieving the railways, for the latter to transport troops on an even greater scale.   This would, moreover, have lessened the shortage of coal.   In peace time also, for which the canal was primarily destined, it would have been most beneficial.

Minister von Miquel was a most ardent enthusiast for the Imperial German idea and the German Empire of the Hohenzollerns ; I lent an attentive ear to his spirited handling of this theme.   He was a man who, clinging to the old tradition, thought in a great German, Imperial way ; he was fully alive to the requirements and demands of the new era, and rightly appreciated their value.

§ 3

From the start I concerned myself with the completion of the railway system.   From the reports relating to national defence and the complaints of the General Staff, as well as from personal observation, I knew of the absolutely incredible neglect suffered by East Prussia in the matter of railways.   The state of affairs was absolutely dangerous, in view of the steady, though gradual, reinforcement of the Russian troops facing our frontier, and the development of the Russian railway system.

During the last years of his reign Emperor William the Great had commanded Field Marshal Moltke to report on the situation, for even then, under the influence of France, the Russian armies were being posted ever more conspicuously on the Eastern frontier of Prussia, arousing apprehension as to the possibility of irruptions of great masses of Russian cavalry into Prussia, Posen and Silesia. Quartermaster-General Count Waldersee and I were present at the reading of this report. From it came the decision to shift Prussian troops eastward and to push forward the completion of the neglected railway system.

The measures ordained by Emperor William I and begun by him required time, particularly as the new railway bridges over the Vistula and Nogat had to be built by the military authorities in the teeth of strong official opposition (Maybach). As the railways were considered a " national pocket-book " there was a desire to build only " paying " lines, which raised prejudice against any outlay for purely military lines designed for the defence of the Fatherland ; it diminished the fine surplus fund on which such great store was laid.

Not until my reign were the plans of Emperor William I brought to realization. Anyone taking up a railway map of 1888 will be amazed at the lack of railway connexions in the east, particularly in East Prussia, and still more so if he compare it with a 1914 map, showing the development in the intervening years. If we had retained the old system we should have lost our eastern territory in 1914.

Unquestionably Minister von Maybach rendered valuable services in the promotion and development of the railway system. He had to take into account the wishes and demands of the rapidly-developing industrial sections of Western Germany; in doing this he naturally considered military requirements also, as far as he could. But, during his regime, Eastern Germany was very badly treated wth regard to railway lines, bridges, and rolling-stock. Had mobilization occurred at that time it would have been necessary to transfer hundreds of locomotives to the East in order to maintain schedules capable of meeting even part of the requirements of the General Staff. The only means of communication with the East were the two antiquated trestle bridges at Dirschau and Marienburg. The General Staff became insistent, and quarrels arose between it and Maybach.

Not until Minister Thielen came into office was there a change, occasioned by his self-sacrificing work, for which thanks are due him. Realizing correctly what the military requirements were, he expedited the completion of the eastern railways. Thielen was an able, diligent, thoroughly reliable official of the Old Prussian type, faithful to me and enjoying my high esteem. In common with Miquel he stood faithfully by the side of his sovereign in the fight for the Central Canal. Characteristic of him were the words which he uttered in my presence, before

a big assembly of people, at the opening of the Elbe–
Trave Canal : " The Central Canal must and will be
built." Relations between him and myself remained
harmonious until his retirement.

Despite the railway construction work in the
western part of Germany, in that region likewise,
from the point of view of mobilization and deployment of troops, there were serious gaps in the network of railways which had long needed attention.
The Rhine, as far up as Mainz, was crossed by but
one railway bridge ; the Main could be crossed only
at Frankfort. For a long time the General Staff
had been demanding that these conditions should be
remedied. Fortunately, general traffic moved in
the same direction ; for instance, if a traveller coming
from the west wished to reach one of the watering-
places in the Taunus Mountains, or some place on
the railway along the right bank of the Rhine, he
had to go as far as Frankfort and then return in
the same direction whence he had come, although,
at Mainz, he had been almost opposite Wiesbaden.

Minister Budde was the man chosen for the accomplishment of this work. As chief of the Railway
Department of the General Staff he had long since
attracted my attention by his extraordinary capacity
for work, his energy and his promptness in making
decisions. He had often reported to me on the gaps
in our railway system which would hamper quick
deployment of troops on two fronts, and always
pointed out the preparations being made by Russia
and France, which, in the interests of national

defence, we were in duty bound to meet with preparations of equal scope.

Of course, the first consideration in railway construction had been the improvement and facilitation of industry and commerce, but it had not been able to meet the immeasurably increased demands of these, because the great network of canals designed to relieve the railways was not in existence. The war on two fronts, which threatened us more and more—and for which our railways were, militarily speaking, not yet adequate, partly owing to financial and technical reasons—made it necessary that more careful attention should be paid to military requirements. Russia was building, with French billions, an enormous network of railways against us, while, in France, the railways destined to facilitate the deployment of forces against Germany were being indefatigably extended by the completion of three- and four-track lines—things as yet totally unknown in Germany.

Minister Budde set to work without delay. The second great railway bridge over the Rhine at Mainz was constructed, likewise the bridge over the Main at Kostheim and the necessary switches and loops for establishing communication with Wiesbaden and the line along the right bank of the Rhine. The triangle at Biebrich—Mosbach was also completed. Budde's talents found brilliant scope in the organization and training of the railway employees, whose numbers had grown until they formed a large army, and in his far-sighted care for his subordinates.

I respected this vigorous, active man with all my heart and deeply regretted that a treacherous ailment put an end to his career in the very midst of his work.

In His Excellency von Breitenbach I acquired a new and valuable aide and co-worker in my railway plans. In the course of years he developed into a personage of high eminence. Distinguished and obliging, of comprehensive attainments, keen political insight, great capacity for work, and untiring industry, he stood in close relationship to me.

His co-operation with the General Staff in military matters was due to his thorough belief in the necessity for strengthening our means of defence against possible hostile attacks. Plans were made for the construction of three new Rhine bridges—named respectively, after the Crown Prince, Hindenburg and Ludendorff—at Rüdesheim, Neuwied and the Loreley, which were not completed until during the war. In the east, there were great extensions of railway stations, while bridges and new lines were built, some of them while the war was in progress.

Other important works carried out by Breitenbach in the west were :—the great railway bridge at Cologne, to replace the old trestle bridge ; a new bridge by the Beyen Tower for freight traffic, and new railways in the Eifel Mountains. At my special suggestion, a through line was built from Giessen to Wiesbaden, which included reconstruction of the stations at Homburg and Wiesbaden and the building of a loop around Frankfort and Höchst. In addition, trains were provided with through cars from Flushing to the Taunus.

To show that it is impossible to please everybody I wish to observe in passing that we were violently attacked by the hotel proprietors of Frankfort, who were naturally not at all pleased at this elimination of Frankfort and of the previously existing necessity for passengers to change trains there; they lost thereby many customers who were formerly compelled to spend a night in some Frankfort hotel. Particularly strong opposition against the loop line round Höchst was raised by this section of the community.

The battle concerning the Central Canal was decided at length in favour of my plans. Under Breitenbach's direction its construction was pushed forward by sections with great energy. Those portions of this canal which it has been possible to place in operation have fully realized expectations.

During this period, too, the extraordinarily difficult extension and deepening of the Kaiser Wilhelm Canal—almost equivalent to building an entirely new waterway—was brought to completion, as was also the great Emden sea-lock. These were remarkable achievements which aroused the admiration of the world; the locks built at that time surpassed in size those of the Panama Canal. The difficult tasks were brilliantly and thoroughly completed by the responsible officials in charge; where the work of construction was in the hands of the Empire, it was

M

mostly carried out with the supervising co-operation
of the Prussian Ministry of Transportation.

I often went to Breitenbach's home, where, thanks
to him, I had opportunities for interesting talks on
commercial-political and economic subjects with a
highly intelligent circle, and of meeting a number of
eminent men and discussing important questions.
The plans and sketches of all the larger railway
stations, locks and bridges were submitted to me
before the work of building or rebuilding was begun,
and reports concerning them were made to me.

I have intentionally gone into detail in this
matter in order to show, firstly, how a monarch can
and must influence the development of his realm by
personal participation; secondly, how, if he makes his
selections quite independently of party reasons, he
can place able men at the head of the various departments; thirdly, how, by the honest co-operation
of these men with the sovereign—whose complete
confidence they enjoy—brilliant results can be
achieved. Everything that we did together was
honest and above board; nothing mattered but the
welfare and development of the Fatherland, its
strengthening and equipment for competition in the
world-market.

§ 4

As was natural, I had close and enduring relations,
in the regular course of events, with the Ministry of
Public Worship and Instruction. Herr von Gossler

and Herr von Trott may certainly be considered its most important and prominent controllers, and in this ministry a co-worker almost without equal, a man of genius, indeed, arose in the person of Minister Director Althoff.

I had been made acquainted by my own experiences at school with the dark side of the high school system of education. The predominantly philological character of the training which prevailed throughout the whole educational system, indeed, led to a certain one-sidedness.

When I was at the Cassel High School (1874–77), I had observed that, although there was great enthusiasm for 1870–71 and the new Empire among the boys, there was, nevertheless, a distinct lack of the right conception of the German idea—*Civis Germanus sum* ("I am a German citizen ")—which I impressed later upon my people at the laying of the foundation-stone of the Saalburg. To create such sentiments and awaken them in the rising generation and to lay the foundations of them firmly in the young hearts was a task somewhat beyond the powers of the teaching staff in view of the fossilized, antiquated, philological curriculum.

There was great neglect in the department of German history, which is exactly the study through which young hearts may be made to glow, through which the love of one's native country, its future and greatness, may be aroused. But little was taught of more recent history, covering the years from 1815. Young philologists were produced, but no German citizens qualified for practical co-operation in building up the flourishing young Empire.

In other words, *no youths who were consciously German* were being turned out. In a small reading club composed of my classmates I often tried to inculcate the idea of the Greater Germany, in order to eliminate parochial and similar conceptions which hampered the German idea. Admiral Werner's " Book of the German Fleet " was one of the few works by means of which the living feeling for the German Empire could be fanned into flame.

Another thing that struck me, in addition to the one-sidedness of the methods of education, was the tendency among youths in those days, when planning their careers, to turn their attention towards becoming Government officials and to consider the profession of lawyer or judge the most worthy goal.

This was doubtless due to the fact that the conditions obtaining in the Prussia of olden days still had their effect in the youthful German Empire. As long as the State consisted, so to speak, of government and administration, this tendency among German youths in the shaping of their lives was understandable and justified ; living as we were in a country of officials, the right road for a young man to select was the service of the State. British youths of that time, self-reliant and robustly developed by sports, were already talking of colonial conquests, of expeditions to explore untrodden regions of the earth, of extension of British commerce ; they were trying, as pioneers of their country, to make Great Britain still greater and stronger, by practical independent action, not as paid hirelings of the State. But England had long been a world-Empire when we were still but a land of officials; the youth of Britain therefore had better opportunity to seek more remote and important goals than those of Germany.

Now that Germany had entered into world economics and world politics, however, as a by no means negligible factor, the aspirations of German youth should have undergone a more prompt transformation. For this reason, during the later years of my reign, I used to compare with a heavy heart the proud young Britons, who had learned much less Latin and Greek than was required among us, with the children of Germany, pale from overstudy. To be sure, there were even then enterprising men in Germany—brilliant names can be cited among them— but the conception of serving the Fatherland by travelling not along a definite, officially certified road, but by independent competition, had not yet become sufficiently general. I, therefore, held the English up as an example, for it seems to me better to take the good where one finds it, without prejudice, than to go through the world wearing blinkers.

With these considerations as a basis I won *School Reform* for my German youths against desperate opposition from the philologists, inside and outside the ministry and educationist circles. Unfortunately, the reform did not take the shape which I hoped, and did not lead to the results which I had expected.

The Germanic idea in all its splendour was first

revealed and preached to the astonished German people by Chamberlain, in his " Foundations of the Nineteenth Century." But—as is proved by the collapse of the German people—this was in vain. Certainly there was much singing of " *Deutschland über alles,*" but Germans, obeying the commands of their enemies, allowed the Emperor to fall and the empire to be broken in pieces ; placing themselves under the orders of Russian criminals vastly inferior to them in culture, they stabbed their own army in the back while it was still fighting valiantly.

Had Germans of all classes and conditions been educated to feel joy and pride in their Fatherland, such a degradation of a great nation would have been unimaginable. This degradation—which, it must be admitted, occurred under remarkable, extremely trying circumstances—is all the more difficult to understand in view of the fact that the youth of Germany, although it was impaired in health by overstudy, and not so toughened by sports as the English, achieved brilliant feats in the world war such as were nowhere equalled before.

The years 1914–18 revealed what might have been made out of the German people had it only developed its admirable qualities in the right direction. The 4th of August, 1914, the heroes of Langemark, countless splendid figures from all classes, rise from the chaos of the long war, to show what the German can do when he throws away Philistinism, and devotes himself to a great cause, with the enthusiasm which so seldom completely reveals itself in him.

May the German people never forget these incarnations of its better self, may it emulate them with its full strength, by inculcating in itself the true German spirit !

§ 5

In the post of Minister of Justice I found His Excellency Friedberg, the intimate, faithful friend of my father, whom I had known from my youth, when he was a welcome guest in the home of my parents. This simple, affable man enjoyed with me the same consideration which had been shown him by my parents.

In later years I had frequent and welcome dealings with His Excellency Beseler, who also enabled me at his house to hear informal discussions of many an interesting legal problem by prominent lawyers, and to come into touch with legal luminaries. I felt no particular inclination towards the lawyers in themselves—for, to my taste, pedantry, remoteness from actualities and doctrinaire learning often assert themselves altogether too much in the domain of the law—but the compilation of the " Citizens' Law Book " interested me greatly. I was present at sessions dealing with it and was proud that this fundamentally German work should have been brought to completion in my reign.

On one of my visits to England, while staying with Lord Haldane, I met the Lord Chief Justice of England and asked that great jurist what he thought of the administration and interpretation of the law in Germany. His answer was to this effect: " You pronounce judgment too much according to the letter of the law, we according to the spirit and content of the law."

I have often pointed out how unfortunate it was that we have not been able to introduce in police cases—connected with traffic, streets, etc.—the prompt procedure of the English Police Court. In such cases punishment is there meted out the very next day, whereas, in Germany, what with the collection of evidence and examination of witnesses, months often elapse, until, finally, some insignificant sentence is pronounced long after the case has been forgotten. I should also have liked to introduce into Germany the heavy penalties which are customary in England for libels published in the Press.

I had worked for a while when I was still a prince, with Minister of Finance Scholz, and taken part in sessions wherein figured that famous man, His Excellency Meinecke. Meinecke was under-secretary of State in the Finance Ministry and, as finances were an important factor everywhere, had therefore much to do with other ministries. He had achieved a certain degree of fame because he—as he thought—was always able smilingly to find the best way out of a tight corner.

Scholz was capable and faithful to his duty, but he did not succeed in making the dry subject of taxes and the like particularly interesting and pleasant to me, nor was there any change in this state of affairs until the versatile Miquel took charge of the Finance Ministry. When Miquel reported to me concerning Prussian financial reform, he suggested three plans : one modest, ône medium, one ambitious. To the delight of the minister, I decided, without hesitation, for the third. Both the monarch and the minister were filled with satisfaction when the reform was carried out.

The Minister of the Interior, Herr von Puttkamer, had been forced to retire during the Ninety-Nine Days, to the great sorrow of him who was then Crown Prince. He was an able, tried Old Prussian official ; one of those Pomeranians of the old school, filled with loyalty to the King—a nobleman through and through. Rumour had it that the Empress Frederick had driven him from office by a plot, but this is not true. The Empress, with her inclination to English Liberalism, doubtless did not like the old-time Prussian Conservative, yet she was not at all to blame for his going. Prince Bismarck pushed him aside, perhaps out of consideration for the Empress Frederick.

I was deeply interested in forestry and its improvement along practical lines, especially as new gold reserves could be created for the State from re-afforestation.

Next to Herr von Podbielski the ablest Minister of Agriculture and Forests was Freiherr von Schorlemer. Just as Herr von Podbielski exerted his efforts towards the creation of great stretches of forests in the east, in order to temper the East wind by a compact forest zone and thus improve our climate, and, at the same time, provide a natural protection against Russian attacks, so Herr von Schorlemer opened up the eastern forest reservations by the extensive construction of roads and, by thus facilitating the transportation of wood, greatly helped Germany to make headway in the competition against imported wood from Russia.

Both ministers sought, in co-operation with me, to improve our splendid Prussian forestry personnel, to better their conditions of living, and to help towards promotions in their ranks—all of which these officials, zealous in their work and faithful to their King, fully deserved. The influx of large sums into the State's pocket-book depended, indeed, on the honesty, industry and reliability of these men.

I expected much towards the restoration of the Fatherland from the statesmanlike shrewdness and ability of Herr von Schorlemer, who was always quite conscious of the goal at which he was aiming.*

I learned much about forestry from Head Foresters Freiherr von Hövel (Joachimsthal, Schorfheide), and Freiherr Speck von Sternburg (Szittkohmen, Rominten), on my many hunting expeditions with these excellent huntsmen and administrators.

Let me say a word here regarding a curiosity in the Russian method of preserving wild game. The Tsar, who had heard a great deal about the fine antlers of the stags at Rominten, wished to have some of the

---

* His recent death, which snatched him away in the midst of beneficial labours, is a serious loss to the Fatherland.

same kind at Spala, in Poland. Freiherr von Sternburg was sent to the hunting lodge there one summer
in order to give advice regarding this project.

He was received very cordially by a general, who
had charge of the hunting and lived at the lodge.
Sternburg noticed that all the apartments, even those
not in actual use, were always kept heated. When
he spoke of the enormous waste of wood this
occasioned, the general shrugged his shoulders and
remarked that one never could tell, the Tsar might
put in an appearance any day. A gamekeeper, who
was a German, was assigned to Sternburg, as the
general did not know his way about the reservation
and was quite ignorant of game-feeding.

In the course of his tours about the place, Sternburg observed a number of spots that could be
turned into pastures or where good feeding-places
could be installed. He drew attention to the need of
such arrangements, as he had also noticed that the
deer had to a considerable extent already begun to
shed their horns, thereby causing much damage to the
trees.

The gamekeeper shook his head sadly, and remarked that he had already reported all this, but in
vain ; the hay for the deer had to be brought by rail
from the Black Sea and the shipments sometimes
either did not arrive at all, or were so greatly delayed
that they arrived spoiled. Nothing could be done to
alter this, continued the gamekeeper, for too many
people made a good thing out of this transportation of
hay, which was paid for at huge prices.

He also told how—after he had called attention to the many splinters of wood found in the intestines of the deer, in order to prove that they were insufficiently fed and that feeding-places must be provided—a committee of veterinary surgeons had been brought from St. Petersburg in order to investigate the matter. The said committee lived and ate for weeks in Spala at the Tsar's expense, shot many deer, examined them, and held meetings; and the upshot of it all was a report that the animals had wood in their stomachs, which proved that they could live on wood, hence feeding-places would be superfluous and the hay from the Black Sea would suffice to supplement the wood. There the matter remained, in spite of Sternburg's visit !

When I heard this yarn, I involuntarily thought of an anecdote which Prince Bülow especially delighted to tell in connexion with his sojourn at St. Petersburg. While there, he had attended the salon of Madame Durnovo, where society often used to gather. One day a prominent general was complaining to the hostess that he had been trapped in a money matter, which had brought him much unpleasantness from " above." Apparently he wished by his mournful description to arouse sympathy for his bad luck, but Madame Durnovo retorted in her rough manner : " Mon cher général, quand on fait des sâletés, il faut qu'elles réussissent ! " [" My dear general, when you play dirty tricks it is necessary that they be successful ! "]

Herr von Podbielski, after I had chosen him and

declined a number of other candidates, did excellent work as secretary of State in the Imperial Postal Department, treading worthily in the footsteps of Stephan. Very practical; endowed with keen instincts and a great knowledge of business; well versed and clever in financial matters, of innate administrative talent, and, at the same time, quick to fight; caustically witty; a good speaker and debater, he worked with zeal and skill, often as a pioneer, particularly in matters of world-postal service, wireless telegraphy, etc. This former colonel in the Ziethen Hussars made for himself in the service of his Fatherland a name which will never be forgotten.

An amusing contrast to his career is that of a Russian hussar officer under Nicholas I. This Tsar, being full of anger against the Holy Synod, had driven away the man at its head. Shortly afterwards he inspected the regiment of Hussar Body-Guards, commanded by Colonel Count Protassoff. The immense satisfaction of the Tsar at the splendid appearance and manœuvring of the fine regiment found expression in the words, amazing alike to the commander and his men: " Thou hast manœuvred thy regiment magnificently, and as a token of my satisfaction, I name thee Procurator of the Holy Synod, which thou must put into good shape for me ! "

Mention must be made here, also, of another excellent and worthy man, Minister Möller. He came like Hintzpeter, from Bielefeld, and was bound to my old teacher by lasting ties of friendship. In

the legislature he was one of the leaders of the
National Liberals, by whom he was highly esteemed,
as he was in the Reichstag generally, on account
of his upright, distinguished Westphalian charac-
teristics and his great experience in the commercial-
political sphere.

When Imperial Chancellor Bülow suggested Möller
to me as minister I remarked that he was a party man
and a member of the Reichstag. The chancellor said
that the National Liberals would be pleased at
Möller's appointment. I observed that the State
Ministry of the Prussian King could not and must not
be a party ministry, but must stand aloof from the
parties and in entire independence of them ; that I
esteemed Möller personally very much, but, should he
become a minister, every member of the legislature
would have the ambition to become one likewise ;
that, through Möller's appointment, the ambitions of
the other parties to obtain ministerial chairs would also
be aroused and nobody could foresee the consequences ;
that, moreover, Möller would be greatly missed in the
Reichstag, from which I did not wish to take him on
account of his influence with all parties.

Despite these objections and my advice against it,
Bülow adhered to his idea. Möller became minister,
and, as such, stood very well with me, but what I had
prophesied occurred comparatively soon : Minister
Möller was obliged to retire through circumstances
partially connected with the inner workings of his
party.

VII

SCIENCE AND ART

§ 1

THE broad and many-sided field the care of which devolved upon the Ministry of Public Worship and Instruction—embracing art, science, research, medical matters, etc.—always aroused my lively interest and enlisted my efforts in its behalf.

Special pleasure was afforded me by the development of the technical high school. The growing importance of technical matters drew increasing numbers of the ablest youths to institutions of learning of this description, and the achievements of the teachers and of the young engineers who graduated there constantly brought new laurels to the German name.

Among the teachers at Charlottenburg one of the most prominent and best-known all over the world was Professor Dr. Slaby. Until his death he had constant dealings with me and, by means of captivating discourses, kept me informed concerning the newest inventions. These were given not only in his laboratory, but also in the quiet hunting lodge in the forests of Brandenburg, where I, together with the Empress, surrounded by a few intimates, used to listen eagerly to Slaby's words. Slaby was

also personally dear to me and provided me with
much enjoyment by his simple, clear views on
every possible topic in this world, which he could
always express in the most stimulating and enthral-
ling manner. Slaby meant much to me and I felt
grateful affection for him up to the time of his
death.

Influenced by the achievements of the technical
high schools and of such men as Slaby, Intze, etc.,
I resolved to grant the high schools the same privilege of representation in the Prussian Upper House
as was enjoyed by the universities. The universities,
however, protested vehemently against this to the
Minister of Public Worship and Instruction and
there ensued a violent struggle against the classical-
scientific arrogance of the savants, until I finally
enforced my will by a decree. Slaby received the
news from me by telegraph while he was delivering
a lecture in his laboratory, and gave it to the students,
who burst into wild cheers. The technical high
schools have shown themselves worthy of the honour
conferred upon them.

In view of the increasingly strenuous fight for
the world's market and its outlets, it became
necessary in order to utilize the wisdom of the leaders
of German science in this direction, to provide them
with greater freedom, quiet, possibilities for working, and materials. Many savants of importance
were hampered in research work by their activities
as teachers, so that the only time they had available
for research was in their vacations. This condition

of affairs resulted in overwork and overstrain, and had to be stopped.

Attention was turned first to improvements in the sphere of chemistry. Minister von Trott and Director of the Ministry Althoff, having grasped the state of affairs with clear understanding, made possible for me the establishment of the " Kaiser Wilhelm Society " and drew up the statutes governing it. In the short time of its existence it has achieved brilliant results and at its general meetings afforded me opportunities to become acquainted with eminent men in all branches of knowledge, with whom I thereafter entered into regular intercourse. I also visited their laboratories, where I could follow the progress of their labours. New laboratories were founded, others were subsidized from the contributions of the Senate and members of the organization.

I was proud of this creation of mine, for it proved a boon to the Fatherland, and the inventions due to the research of its members benefited the entire nation. It was a peace-time achievement with a great and most promising future, which, under the guidance of Herr von Trott, was in most excellent hands ; unfortunately, the war robbed me of this joy, along with all others. Nowadays I have to do without the intercourse with the men of learning of my society and that is a cruel blow to me. May it continue to live and labour for the benefit of research and the good of the Fatherland !

I had to face a severe fight to get Professor Harnack summoned to Berlin. The theologians of

N

the Right and the " orthodox " section protested
vehemently. After I had again obtained full information from Hintzpeter and he had closed his
opinion with the words that it would be most regrettable for Berlin and Prussia if I backed down, I
insisted upon the summoning of Harnack, and summoned he was.

Nowadays it is impossible to understand the
opposition to him. What a man Harnack is ! What
an authoritative position he has won for himself in
the thinking world ! What benefit, what knowledge,
has intercourse with this fiery intellect brought to
me ! What wonders he has achieved, as head of
the Royal Library and Dean of the Senate of the
Kaiser Wilhelm Society, where he, the theologian,
delivered most learned and most substantial discourses on the sciences, research, inventions. I
shall always look back with pleasure on the labours
and personality of Harnack.

Professor Erich Schmidt, of the University of
Berlin, was also a friend of mine and was often at my
home ; I owe many an enjoyable evening to the
learned discourses of this savant.

Professor Schiemann enjoyed my particular confidence. An upright man, a native of the Baltic
Provinces, a champion of the Germanic idea against
Slavic arrogance, a clear-sighted politician and brilliant historian and writer, Schiemann was constantly
asked by me for advice on political and historical
questions. To him I owe much good counsel, especially regarding the East. He was frequently at my

home and often accompanied me on journeys—as, for instance, to Tangier—and he heard from me in our talks much important confidential matter on political questions, not then known to others. His unshakable capacity for keeping his mouth shut justified my trust in him. It was a source of satisfaction to me, after the liberation of the Baltic Provinces, to appoint this tried man curator of the University of Dorpat.

How well he and I agreed in our political views regarding Russia is illustrated by the following incident : After the Peace of Portsmouth between Russia and Japan, brought about by me in conjunction with President Roosevelt in 1905, there was much official (Foreign Office) and unofficial puzzling of heads at Berlin as to what political line Russia would take. In general it was thought that Russia, angered at her defeat, would lean towards the West—and hence towards Germany—in order to find there new connexions and strength to help her to strike a blow for revenge against Japan and for the reconquest of her lost territory and prestige.

My opinion was quite different, but I could not make the official world share it. I emphasized the following points : that the Russians were both Asiatics and Slavs; as the first, they would be inclined to favour Japan, in spite of their defeat; as the second, they would prefer to ally themselves with those who had proved themselves strong. Hence I thought that, after a while, in spite of the Björkö Agreement, Russia would join with Japan, not Germany, and

turn later against Germany. On account of these
" fantastic " ideas, I was actually ridiculed, officially
and unofficially.

I summoned Schiemann and questioned him on
this subject, without revealing to him what I thought
about it. I was much pleased when his answer
agreed absolutely with my views. For a long time
when this weighty matter of foreign politics came
up in discussions, Schiemann and I stood almost
alone.

The event justified us. The so-called " Russian
experts " of Berlin, as well as the official world, were
mistaken.

§ 2

During the very first years of my reign there was
occasion for much important building work.

First, there was the question of erecting a worthy
monument over the tomb of my grandparents. As
the old mausoleum at Charlottenburg was inadequate, it was necessary to erect an addition. Unfortunately, the so-called " Extra Construction
Fund " left by Emperor William the Great for such
" extra construction " had been used for another
purpose during the Ninety-Nine Days. Hence I was
obliged to burden the Crown revenues with unfore-
seen building expense. The mausoleum of my
parents at Marly was erected by the Empress
Frederick, according to her own sketches and designs,
and for this, too, I had to provide the funds.

A thorough examination of the royal palaces—including those in the provinces—had revealed, particularly at the palace in Berlin, such deplorable conditions in sanitation, comfort, etc., that there could be no further delay in remedying the defects. In the course of my thirty years' reign I restored these palaces to good condition. I worked in accordance with carefully prepared budgets, examined, corrected and supervised by myself with the help of architects (such as Ihne), and of artists, with due regard for the traditions of my ancestors; although all this work gave me much trouble and tried my patience, it also provided me with a great deal of enjoyment. In restoring the Berlin Palace, the Empress Frederick, with her sound judgment and sure, keen eye for the proper style, helped materially in offsetting the harm and neglect dating from bygone days. My mother's expression of her point of view ought surely to be of general interest : " Any style is good so long as it is pure." Ihne used to call the eclecticism of the 'nineties " a peu près style " (the " Almost Style "). The restoration of the picture gallery, the last work of Herr Ihne—who died, unfortunately, all too soon—was not completed until during the first half of the war. The palace of my forefathers, erected at much pains and a source of pride to me, was later bombarded, stormed, sacked and devastated by revolutionary hordes.

These artistic building enterprises, as well as the restoration of the White Drawing-room previously referred to, belong to the representative duties devolving upon every government, be it absolute, constitutional or democratic in form. They afford a criterion of the national culture and are a means of encouraging artists and, through them, the development of art.

During my vacations I busied myself with archæology and was active in excavation work. Here I kept one basic idea in view : to discover the roots from which Ancient Greek art developed and to find— or erect—a bridge in the endeavour to establish the cultural influence of the East on the West. It appeared to me that Assyriology was important, as from it might be expected an elucidation and vitalization of the Old Testament, and, hence, of the Holy Scriptures. I, therefore, accepted with pleasure the offer of the presidency of the German Oriental Society and devoted myself to the study of its work, which I promoted to the best of my ability, never missing one of its public lectures on the results of its explorations. I had much to do with those at the head of it and caused detailed reports to be made to me of the excavations at Nineveh, Assur and Babylon, in Egypt and in Syria, for the protection and facilitation of which I often personally brought influence to bear on the Turkish Government.

Professor Delitzsch, a member of the society, gave his well-known and much-attacked lecture on " Babel and Bible," which, unfortunately, fell upon the ears of a public as yet too ignorant and unprepared, and led to many misinterpretations, some of them in Church circles.

I strove hard to clear up the matter. I realized that the importance of Assyriology, then enlisting the efforts of many prominent men, including both Catholic and Protestant clergymen, was not yet understood and appreciated by the general public; therefore I arranged that my trusted friend and brilliant theatre director, Count Hülsen-Haeseler, should produce the play " Assurbanipal," after long preparation, under the auspices of the German Oriental Society. Assyriologists of all countries were invited to the dress rehearsal; in the boxes, commingled indiscriminately, were professors, Protestant and Catholic clergymen, Jews and Christians. Many expressed to me their thanks for having shown, by this performance, how far research work had already progressed and for having, at the same time, revealed more clearly to the general public the importance of Assyriology.

My sojourn at Corfu likewise afforded me the pleasure of serving archæology and of busying myself personally with excavation work. The accidental discovery of a relievo head of a Gorgon near the town of Corfu led me to take personal charge of the work. I called to my aid the experienced excavator and expert in Greek antiques, Professor Dörpfeld, who took over the direction of the excavation operations. This savant, who was as enthusiastic as I for the ancient Hellenic world, became, in the course of time, a faithful friend of mine and an invaluable source of instruction in questions relative to architecture, styles, etc., among the ancient Greeks and Achæans.

It was a joy to hear Dörpfeld read and elucidate the old Homeric poems, and, by means of a map and by following the hints and descriptions of the poet, to establish the locality of the old Achæan settlements which were destroyed later by the Doric migration. It appeared that the names of the old places had often been transferred to new sites by the dispossessed inhabitants. This made the identification of the locality more difficult. Nevertheless, Dörpfeld had rediscovered the locality of a whole series of them, with the help of his Homer, which he carried in his hand like a Baedeker—hitting upon them by following the minute geographical descriptions given by the poet.

This interested me so much that I took a trip by water, with the Empress, in the company of Dörpfeld, so that I might put the matter to the test. We went to Leukas (Ithaca) and visited, one after another, the places made famous by the "Odyssey," while Dörpfeld read from his Homer the descriptive text referring to each. I was amazed and had to admit that the region and the description tallied exactly.

The excavations begun by me in Corfu under Dörpfeld's direction had valuable archæological results, in that they produced evidence of an extremely remote epoch of the earliest Doric art. The relievo of the Gorgon has given rise already to many theories—probable and improbable—combined, unfortunately, with a good deal of superfluous acrimonious discussion. From all this it seems to me that one of the piers for the bridge between Asia and Europe, sought by me, is assuming shape.

I sent reports regularly to the Archæological Society and I also brought the well-known Professor Caro from Athens to work with me. I was busy with preparations for lectures to be delivered before the society during the winter of 1914–15, with searching discussions on many disputed questions, which I hoped to bring towards a solution *sine ira et studio*. It was a pleasure to me to be visited frequently, at Corfu, by English and American archæologists, former pupils of Dörpfeld, who helped zealously in throwing light on the difficult problems which were so often presented to us. They were at work in Asia Minor, and I was deeply interested in hearing what importance they attached—as a result of their discoveries—to Asiatic influence on early Greek art, and how readily they recognized a connexion with the East in the finds made at Corfu. In 1914, Professor Duhn, of Heidelberg, visited the excavations at Corfu and after thorough investigation gave his support to the views held by Dörpfeld and myself. I shall write in another place of the result of my Corfu excavations.

That was the kind of subject which, in the spring of 1914, occupied the thoughts of the German Emperor who, " lusting for robbery and conquest," is accused of having bloodthirstily brought on the world war.

While I was exploring and discussing Gorgons, Doric columns and Homer, mobilization was being effected against us in Russia and the Caucasus! And the Tsar, at the beginning of the year, when asked about his plans, had replied : " Je resterai chez moi cette année, parce que nous aurons la guerre ! " [" I shall stay at home this year, because we shall have war."]

VIII

MY RELATIONS WITH THE CHURCH

§ 1

MUCH has been written and talked about my relations with the Church. Even while I was yet a prince, and a student at Bonn, I realized the harmful influence of the *Kulturkampf* in its last phase. The antagonism caused by the religious rift was such that on one occasion, for example, while on a hunting expedition, I was directly boycotted by members of leading noble Rhenish-Westphalian families of the Rhineland who belonged to the Ultramontane Party. Even so far back as that, I resolved in the interests of national welfare to work with a view to creating a *modus vivendi* that would make it possible for people professing the two creeds to live peacefully with each other. The *Kulturkampf*, as such, had come to an end before the commencement of my reign.

I strove patiently and earnestly to be on good terms with the prelates, and I was on very friendly terms indeed with several, particularly Cardinal Kopp, Archbishop Simar, Dr. Schulte, Prince-Bishop Bertram, Bishop Thiel, and, last but not least, Archbishop Faulhaber and Cardinal von Hartmann. These men were all far above the average and ornaments to the episcopate, who gave proof during the war of their patriotic devotion to Emperor and empire. This is evidence that I had succeeded in clearing away the mists of the *Kulturkampf* and enabling my Catholic subjects to rejoice with others in the empire, in accordance with the motto : *Suum cuique* [To each his own].

I was bound particularly closely all my life to Cardinal Kopp, Prince-Bishop of Breslau. He always served me loyally, so that my relationships with him were most trustful. His mediation in dealings with the Vatican, where he stood in high honour, were of great value to me, although he championed the German point of view absolutely.

Probably little is known by the general public of the friendly, [trustful relationship that existed between me and Pope Leo XIII. A prelate who was in his confidence told me later, that I had won the confidence of the Pope on my first visit by the absolute frankness which I showed towards him, and with which I told him things that others deliberately kept from his ears.

Receptions by the Pope were conducted with tremendous pomp. Swiss and Noble Guards, in brilliant uniforms, servants, chamberlains, and ecclesiastical dignitaries, were present in large numbers— representation in miniature of the might of the Roman Catholic Church.

After I had traversed the courts, halls and drawing-rooms, in which all these men were arrayed, I seated myself opposite the Pope himself, in his little, one-windowed study. This distinguished man, with the fine, noble-featured old face, whose eyes gazed piercingly at his visitor, made a deep impression upon me. We discussed many topical subjects. I was greatly pleased that the Pope spoke appreciatively and gratefully of the position occupied by the Catholic religion and its adherents in Germany, and by his assurance that, for his part, he would do all he could towards inducing the German Catholics to yield to no other Germans in loyalty and love for their Fatherland.

Pope Leo XIII gave evidence of friendliness towards me whenever he could. For instance, on one of my visits to Rome, he accorded the honour of a special audience to my suite and servants ; he sent Prince-Bishop Kopp as Papal Delegate on the occasion of the consecration by me of the portal which I had had added to the cathedral at Metz, and was so kind as to inform me of the elevation of Archbishop Fischer of Cologne to the Cardinalate, to celebrate that occasion.

On the occasion of the Papal Jubilee in 1903, to celebrate the twenty-fifth anniversary of his accession to the Papacy, I sent a special mission to convey my congratulations to the Pope, at the head of which was Freiherr von Loe, for many years intimately acquainted with him.

Not long after that—and only a few months before his death—I paid my third and last visit to the Pope. Though he was very weak, this man of ninety-three years came up to me, holding both his hands outstretched. Concerning this visit, which was characterized by great cordiality on both sides, I immediately jotted down some notes, which recently came into my possession again.

Among other things, the Pope said that he could not but give his full approval to the principles on which I governed; that he had followed with interest my methods of governance and recognised with pleasure that I had built up my rule on a firm foundation of Christianity; that such lofty religious principles underlay it, that it behoved him to ask the blessing of Heaven upon myself, my dynasty and the German Empire, and to grant me his apostolic benediction.

It was of interest to me that the Pope said on this occasion that Germany must become the sword of the Catholic Church. I remarked that the old Roman Empire of the German nation no longer existed, and that conditions had changed. But he adhered to his words.

The Pope then went on to say that he must thank me once more for my unflagging attention to the welfare of my Catholic subjects; that he had heard of this from so many sources that he was glad to tell me personally how grateful both he and the German Catholics were for this attention to their interests; that he could assure me that my Catholic subjects would stand by me, in good and bad times, with absolute fidelity. " Ils resteront absolument et infailliblement fidèles." ["They will remain absolutely and infallibly faithful."]

I rejoiced greatly at these words of appreciation from such an exalted source. I answered that I considered it to be the duty of a Christian sovereign to care for his subjects to the best of his ability, irrespective of creed; that I could assure him that, during my reign, everybody could profess his religion without interference and fulfil his duties towards his ecclesiastical overlord; that this was a fundamental principle of my life, from which I should not swerve.

Because I showed my Catholic fellow-countrymen from the very beginning that I wished to allow them complete freedom in the exercise of their religion, a quieter spirit was engendered in the land, and the aftermath of the *Kulturkampf* gradually disappeared. But I did not conceal from myself the fact that, despite all politeness and friendliness, the prelates—with the sole exception of Cardinal Kopp—still continued to look upon me as the Emperor, and I was compelled to take into account that, in the Catholic south and west, this idea would never be completely dispelled. Grateful acknowledgment has repeatedly been made to me that during my reign the Catholics were as well off as they could possibly desire; but the unalterably uncompromising attitude of the Church to mixed marriages and that of the Centre Party in politics, were sure indication that the anti-heretical tendency still existed beneath the peaceful surface.

This made my desire for the firm union of the Protestant Churches, first in Prussia, then in Germany, and finally in all Europe, all the more intense. My endeavours, in conjunction with the chief ecclesiastical councillor, the general superintendent, etc., to find means of effecting this union, were most earnest. I hailed the Eisenach Conference with joy and followed its proceedings with interest. I assembled all the general superintendents for the consecration of the church at Jerusalem and was also able to greet invited deputations from Sweden, Norway, etc. I did the same on the occasion of the consecration of the Berlin Cathedral, where, among many other deputations, the Church of England was represented by the Bishop of Ripon (W. Boyd Carpenter), the pastor of Queen Victoria of England and equally prominent as writer and preacher.

I worked towards compromise, closer relations and union on every possible occasion, yet nothing definite resulted. Though Church union in Prussia has been a success, in other parts of the Fatherland Lutherans and Reformists remained strictly separate. Many state rulers kept sharp watch over their rights in relation to religion, and, owing to this, were hostile to a closer union of the different creeds within their territory.

Despite my endeavours, therefore, the German Protestant Church was not able to unite and make common cause against the elements hostile to it. Only through the emergency brought on by the revolution was this made possible. On Ascension Day, 1922, to my great joy, the German Evangelical

Church Union was solemnly formed at the Schloss Church at Wittenberg.

During the first years of my military service at Potsdam I had felt deeply the inadequacy of the sermons, which often dealt only with dry dogmatic matter and paid too little attention to the personality of Christ. In Bonn I became acquainted with Dr. Dryander, who made an impression on me which has endured to this day. His sermons were free from dogma, the personality of Christ was their pivotal point, and " practical Christianity " was brought right into the foreground.

Later I brought him to Berlin and soon had him appointed to a post at the cathedral and in my palace. Dryander was by my side for years, until long after the 9th of November [1918], standing close to me spiritually, and affording me spiritual consolation. We often talked on religious matters and threshed out thoroughly the tasks and the general future of the Protestant Church. The views of Dryander—mild, yet powerful, clear and of truly evangelical strength—made him a pillar and an ornament of his Church, and a faithful co-worker with the Emperor, to whom, in the interests of the Church and its development, he was closely bound.

Since the 9th of November, Dr. Dryander has also been exposed to persecutions, but he has held his ground courageously ; the hopes, beliefs and trust of his King are with him and the Evangelical Church. The Church must again spiritually raise

o

the broken nation in accordance with the gospel of
"*Ein' feste Burg ist unser Gott.*"

I cannot allow to pass without mention the influence exerted by the work—translated at my
instigation—of the English missionary, Bernard Lucas,
entitled "Conversations with Christ," as well as
the sermons on Jesus by Pastor Schneller [Jeru-
salem] and the collections of sermons called "The
Old God Still Lives" and "From Deep Trouble"
by Consistorial-Councillor Conrad. These brought
us much inspiration and comfort by their vital
ability to hold absorbedly both readers and hearers.

The fact that I could deal with religious and
Church questions with complete objectivity *sine ira
et studio* is due to my excellent teacher, Professor
Dr. Hintzpeter, a Westphalian Calvinist. He caused
his pupil to grow up and live with the Bible, eliminating, at the same time, all dogmatic and polemical
questions. Because of this tuition, polemics in
religion have remained alien to me, and such autocratic expressions as "orthodox" are repulsive to
me. As to my own religious convictions, I set them
forth some years ago in a letter to my friend, Admiral
Hollmann, which was made public at the time and
part of which is reproduced at the end of this chapter.

I was enabled to bring joy to the hearts of my
Catholic subjects when I presented to the German
Catholics of Jerusalem the plot of ground known as
the "Dormition," acquired by me from the Sultan
in 1898 as a result of my sojourn in the Holy City.
The worthy, faithful Father Peter Schmitz, repre-

sentative of the Catholic Society in Jerusalem, expressed to me on the spot at the dedication ceremony the heartfelt thanks of the German Catholics in eloquent words.

When I conferred with him as to future building operations and as to the selection of persons to occupy the place, the old expert on Jerusalem advised me to select none of the orders of monks there, as all were more or less mixed up in the intrigues and quarrels concerning the " *loci sacri* " [sacred spots]. After my return, a delegation of the German Knights of Malta, under Count Praschma, appeared before me to express their gratitude. The design for the church, skilfully adapted to the local style by a very talented Cologne architect, was submitted to me. After the completion of the church I decided that the monks of Beuron should control the " Dormition " ; they took possession in 1906, taking over at the same time the monastery built next to the new Church of St. Mary.

For many years I was on friendly terms with the Benedictine monks of the Beuron congregation, with whose Arch-abbot, Wolter, I had become acquainted at Sigmaringen. In mediæval times the order always stood well with the German Emperors, of whom scarcely one, in connexion with his journeys to Rome, failed to visit the magnificently situated Monte Cassino. When the Benedictine monks asked permission to establish a settlement on the Rhine, I had the splendid Romanesque Abbey of Maria Laach—unused at the time—turned over to them.

The order, which counts among its members excellent artists, including Father Desiderius, has brought new glory to the abbey—which had fallen into neglect and decay—by magnificent interior decorations. Often have I visited Maria Laach and rejoiced in the progress of its restoration, as well as in conversations with the intelligent abbots, and in the hearty, simple reception on the part of the faithful brethren.

When I visited the monastery of Monte Cassino, I became acquainted with a man of extraordinary mental gifts and comprehensive culture, in the person of Arch-abbot Monsignor Krug, who had travelled a great deal about the world. He could express himself with equal fluency in German—his mother-tongue—Italian, English, and French. In his address to King Victor Emmanuel of Italy and myself, he pointed out that nearly all the German Emperors, as well as the Lombard kings before them, had paid visits to Monte Cassino. He presented me with a magnificent collection of copies of documents of the time of the Emperor Frederick II, taken from the library of the order, and I reciprocated by presenting him with the works of Frederick the Great.

Agriculture flourishes in the environs of the monasteries maintained by the Benedictine Order. It is carried on by the lay brothers with all the latest improvements, to the benefit of the backward peasantry of the region. In the country and town communities of the order, church singing and organ-playing are zealously cultivated by the monks, who have attained a high degree of artistic skill.

The art of the goldsmith also flourishes among them, and art embroidery among the Benedictine nuns.

I commissioned full size reproductions of the *Labarum* [standard] of the Emperor Constantine the Great, designed in accordance with the researches made by Mgr. Wilpert; one I presented to the Pope, another to my Palace Chapel at Berlin. The latter was stolen from the chapel by the mob during the days of the revolution. The metal work was executed entirely by the monks, the embroidery by nuns of the order, both excellently. One of the establishments of the nuns of this order is the Convent of Saint Hildegard, above Rüdesheim, which I visited in 1917.

§ 2

My letter to Admiral Hollmann was written owing to the excitement aroused by the lecture entitled "Babel and Bible," delivered by Professor Delitzsch before the German Oriental Society, of which Admiral Hollmann was one of the board of managers. The first part of the letter, which deals primarily with Professor Delitzsch's statements, has been omitted from the following reprint of the letter:

February 15th, 1903.

My dear Hollmann :

.   .   .   .

.   .   .   .

I should now like to return once again to my own standpoint regarding the doctrine or view of revelation, as I have often set it forth to you, my dear Hollmann, and others. I distinguish between two different kinds of revelation : a progressive, to a certain extent historical revelation, and a purely religious one, paving the way to the future coming of the Messiah.

Of the first, this is to be said : there is not the smallest doubt in my mind that God constantly reveals Himself to the human race created by Him. He has " breathed His breath into mankind," or, in other words, given it a part of Himself—a soul. He follows the development of the human race with a father's love and interest ; for the purpose of leading it forward and benefiting it, he " reveals " Himself in some great savant, or priest, or king, be they heathens, Jews or Christians.

Hammurabi was one of these, likewise Moses, Abraham, Charlemagne, Luther, Shakespeare, Goethe, Kant, Emperor William the Great. These men were selected by Him and made worthy, by His grace, of achieving for their people splendid and imperishable things, both in the spiritual and the physical domain, in accordance with His will. How often did my grandfather clearly emphasize that he was but an instrument in the hand of the Lord !

The works of great minds are gifts of God to the peoples of the earth, in order that they may improve themselves on these models and grope forward, by means of them, through the confusion of that which is still unexplored here below. God has certainly revealed Himself in different ways, to different peoples, according to their standing and degree of culture, and He is still doing it now. For, just as when we contemplate it, we are overcome most by the greatness and majesty of the splendour of creation, and are amazed at the greatness of God as revealed therein, so also may we, in contemplating whatever is great or splendid in the works of a man or a people, recognize therein with gratitude the splendour of the revelation of God. He works directly upon us and among us!

The second kind of revelation, the more religious kind, is that which leads to the coming of the Lord. It is introduced from Abraham onwards, slowly but with foresight, all-wise and all-knowing; without it mankind would have been doomed.

And now begins the most astounding influence, the revelation of God. The tribe of Abraham, and the people descended from it, consider the holiest thing of all, unescapable in its logical consequences, to be the belief in one God. This belief they must have and cultivate. Scattered by the captivity in Egypt, the separate parts are welded together by Moses for the second time, and still they try to maintain their " monotheism." The direct intervention of God is what brings regeneration to this people.

And thus it goes through the centuries, until the Messiah announced and foreshadowed by the Prophets and Psalmists shall at last appear. The greatest revelation of God in the world! For He Himself appeared in the body of His Son; Christ is God, God in human form. He saved us, He inspires us, we are led to follow Him, we feel His fire burning within us, His pity strengthening us, His dissatisfaction destroying us, but, also, His intercession saving us. Sure of victory, building solely upon His word, we go through work, scorn, grief, misery and death, for in Him we have the revealed word of God—and God never lies.

That is my view of this question. The Word, especially for us of the Evangelical faith, has become everything on account of Luther; and Delitzsch, as a good theologian, should not forget that our great Luther taught us to sing and believe : " *Das Wort sie sollen lassen stehn.*" [" The Word, they must allow to stand."]

It is self-evident that the Old Testament contains a great deal which is of purely human historical character and not " God's revealed Word." These sections are essentially historical descriptions of all kinds of events which occurred in the life of the people of Israel in the spheres of politics, religion, morals, and spiritual life.

For instance, the giving out of the Law on Mount Sinai can be looked upon only in a symbolical sense as having been inspired by God, since Moses had to turn to a revival of laws perhaps known of old (possibly drawn from the Code of Hammurabi), in order to bring coherence and solidarity to the constitution of his people, which was loose and little capable of resistance. Here the historian may perhaps find a connexion, either in sense or words, with the laws of Hammurabi, the friend of Abraham, which may be logically right ; but this can never affect the *fact* that God had inspired Moses to act thus, and, to that extent, had revealed Himself to the people of Israel.

My view, therefore, is that our good professor should rather avoid introducing and treating of religion as such in his lectures before our Association, but that he may continue, unhindered, to describe whatever brings the religion, customs, etc., of the Babylonians, etc., into relation with the Old Testament.

So far as I am concerned, I am led by the above to the following conclusion :

(*a*) I believe in one God only.

(*b*) In order to teach Him, we men need a *Form*, especially for our children.

(*c*) This *Form* has been, up to now, the Old Testament, as we know it to-day. This Form will be essentially changed by research, inscriptions and excavations ; but that will cause no harm, nor will the fact that much of the halo of the Chosen People will, thereby, disappear, cause any harm. The kernel and content remain always the same : God and His influence.

Religion was never an outcome of Science, but something flowing from the heart and being of man, through his relations with God.

With heartiest thanks and many greetings, I remain always

Your Sincere friend,
(signed) WILHELM I.R.

IX

THE ARMY AND NAVY

§ 1

MY close relations with the army are a matter of common knowledge. In this respect I conformed to the traditions of my family. Prussia's kings did not chase cosmopolitan mirages, but realized that the welfare of their land could only be assured by means of a real power, protecting industry and commerce. If, in a number of utterances, I admonished my people to " keep their powder dry " and " their sword sharp," the warning was addressed alike to friend and foe. I wished our foes to pause and think a long time before they dared to engage with us. I wished to cultivate a manly spirit in the German people ; I wished to make sure that when the hour struck for us to defend the fruits of our industry against an enemy's lust of conquest, it should find a strong race.

In view of this I attached high value to the educational duty of the army. General compulsory military service has a social influence upon men in the mass equalled by nothing else. It brings together rich and poor, some of the soil and some of the city ; it brings acquaintanceship and mutual understanding to young people whose roads, otherwise, would lead them far apart; the knowledge that they are serving one idea unites them.

Think what we made out of our young men! Pale town boys were transformed into erect, healthy, sport-hardened men; limbs grown stiff through labour were made adroit and pliable.

I stepped direct from brigade-commander to King—to repeat the well-known words of King Frederick William III. Up to that point I had climbed the steps of an officer's career. I still think with pleasure of my pride when, on the 2nd of May, 1869, during the spring parade, I first stood in the ranks before my grandfather. Relations with the individual man have always seemed valuable to me, and, therefore, during my military service, I particularly treasured the appointments where I could cultivate such relations. My experiences as commander of a company, a squadron and a battery, or as head of a regiment, are unforgettable to me.

I felt at home among my soldiers. In them I placed unlimited trust. The painful experiences of the autumn of 1918 have not diminished this trust. I do not forget that a section of the German people, after four years of unprecedented achievements and priva-tions, had become too ill to withstand corruption by foes within and without. Moreover, the best of the Germans lay under the green sod; the others were thrown into such consternation by the events of the revolution—which had been considered an impos-sibility—that they could not spur themselves to further action.

Compulsory military service was the best school for the physical and moral toughening of our people. It created for us free men who knew their own value. From these an excellent corps of non-commissioned officers was formed; from the latter, in turn, we drew our Government officials, the like of whom, in ability, incorruptibility and fidelity to duty, no other nation on earth can show.

It is from these very elements nowadays that I receive evidences of loyalty, every one of which does me good. My old 2nd Company of the First Infantry Guard Regiment has shared, through good and evil days, the vicissitudes of its old captain. I saw them for the last time in 1913, in close formation—still 125 strong—under that excellent sergeant, Hartmann, on the occasion of the celebration of the twenty-fifth anniversary of my accession to the throne.

In view of its proud duty as an educator and leader of the nation in arms, the officer corps occupied a particularly important position in the German Empire. The method of replacement, which, by adoption of the officers' vote, had been lodged in the hands of the various bodies of officers themselves, guaranteed the necessary homogeneity. Harmful outcroppings of the caste idea were merely sporadic; wherever they made themselves felt they were instantly rooted out.

I entered much and willingly into relations with the various officer corps and felt a comrade among them. True, the materialistic spirit of our age had not passed over the officer corps without leaving traces ;

but, on the whole, it must be admitted that nowhere else were self-discipline, simplicity and fidelity to duty cultivated to such an extent as among the officers.

A weeding-out process, such as existed in no other profession, allowed only the ablest and best to reach positions of influence. The commanding generals were men of a high degree of attainment and ability and—what is even more important—men of character. It is a difficult matter to single out individuals for special mention from among them.

Though the man in the ranks at the front was always particularly close to my heart, I must, nevertheless, give special prominence to the General Staff as a school for the officer corps. I have already remarked that Field Marshal Count Moltke had known how, by careful training, to build up men who were not only up to requirements, technically speaking, but also qualified for action demanding willingness to assume responsibility, independence of judgment, and far-sightedness. " To be more than you seem " is written in the preface to the " Pocket Manual for the General Staff Office." Field Marshal Count Moltke laid the foundations for this training ; and his successors—Count Waldersee, that great genius, Count Schlieffen, and General von Moltke—built upon them. The result was the General Staff, which accomplished unprecedented feats in the world war that aroused admiration throughout the world.

I soon realized that the greatest possible improvement of our highly-developed technical department was absolutely necessary and would save precious blood. Wherever possible, I worked towards the perfection of our armament and sought to place machinery in the service of our army.

Among new creations the very first place is taken by the heavy artillery of the army in the field. In bringing this into being I was obliged to overcome much opposition—particularly, strange to relate, in the ranks of the artillery itself. It is to me a source of great satisfaction that I put this matter through. I laid the foundation for the carrying out of operations on a large scale, and it was long before our foes could catch up with us in this direction.

Mention must also be made of the machine-gun, which developed from modest beginnings to being the backbone of the infantry's fighting powers; the replacement of the rifle by the machine-gun multiplied the firing-power of the infantry while, at the same time, diminishing its losses.

Nor can I pass over without mention the introduction of the movable field-kitchen, which I had seen for the first time at some manœuvres of the Russian army. It was of the greatest value in maintaining the fighting efficiency of the army, since the possibility of getting sufficient nourishment kept our troops fresh and healthy.

All human work remains unfinished. Nevertheless, it may be said, without exaggeration, that the German army, which marched to battle in 1914, was an instrument of warfare without equal.

§ 2

Whereas, at my accession to the throne, I had found the army in a condition which merely required development upon the foundations already laid, the navy, on the other hand, was only in the first stage of development.

After the failure of all the attempts of Admiral Hollmann to move the recalcitrant Reichstag to adopt a progressive, systematic strengthening of German sea-power—largely due to the cheap catchwords of Deputy Richter and the lack of understanding of the Liberals of the Left, who were fooled by them—the admiral requested me to retire him. Deeply moved, I acceded to his request ; for this plain, loyal man, the son of a genuine Berlin bourgeois family, had become dear to me through his upright character, his devotion to duty and his attachment to me. My friendship with him, based upon this estimate, lasted for many years up to the moment of the admiral's sudden death. It often led me to visit this faithful man, endowed with fine Berlin wit, at his home, and there to associate with him as head of the German Oriental Society, as well as to see him at my own home, in a small circle of intimates, or to take him with me as a valued travelling companion. He was one of the most faithful of my faithful friends, always the same in his disinterestedness, never asking anything for himself. Happy the city which can produce such citizens ! I preserve a grateful memory of this tried and trusted friend.

Admiral Tirpitz succeeded Hollmann. In his very first reports, which laid the foundation of the first Naval Law, he showed himself thoroughly in accord with me in the belief that the sanction of the Reichstag for the building of warships was not to be gained by the old form of procedure. As I have already pointed out, the Opposition was not to be convinced; the tone of the debates conducted by Richter was unworthy of the importance of the subject; for instance, the gunboat obtained in the Reichstag by the Poles under Herr von Koscielsky, was jokingly dubbed *Koscielska.* Ridicule was the weapon used, although the future of the Fatherland was in question.

It was necessary that the representative of the navy should have a solid phalanx behind him, both among the ministers of State and in the Reichstag, and that it should energetically support him and the cause from absolute conviction. Therefore, there was need to communicate to the Reichstag members—still rather ignorant in naval matters—the details of the great work. Moreover, a great movement had to be engineered among the people, among the, as yet indifferent, " general public," to arouse its interest and enthusiasm for the navy, in order that pressure from the people itself might be brought to bear upon the Reichstag. To this end an energetic propaganda was necessary, through a well-organized and well-directed Press, as well as through eminent men of science at the universities and technical high schools.

There was need of a complete change in the whole method of handling the matter in the Reichstag.

There must be no more bickerings over individual ships and docks. Unless it was a matter of new formations, no arguments arose over the strength of the army in making up the military budget. In like manner the arrangements for the navy must be settled by law once and for all, and its right of existence recognized and protected. The units composing it must no longer be matter for debate. Moreover, not only the officer corps but that of non-commissioned officers must be strengthened and trained in order to be ready for service on the new ships. At the beginning of my reign, sixty to eighty cadets, at the most, were enrolled every year; in the last few years before the war several hundreds sought admission annually. Twelve precious years, never to be retrieved, were lost by the failure of the Reichstag; it is even more difficult to create a navy overnight than an army.

The goal to be striven for was implied in the law, which expressed the " idea of risk "; the aim was to cause even the strongest hostile fleet to think seriously before it came to blows with the German fleet, in view of the heavy losses that were to be feared in a battle, losses which might place the foe in danger of becoming too weak for other tasks. The " idea of risk " was brilliantly vindicated in the Skager Rak (Jutland) battle; the enemy, in spite of his immense superiority, dared not risk a second battle. Trafalgar was already dim ; its laurels must not be completely lost.

The total number of units (ships) in commission—

P

it was principally a matter of ships-of-the-line—was taken as a basis for the Naval Law, although these, with the exception of the four ships of the " Brandenburg " class, were little better than old iron.

In view of the numbers involved, the Naval Law was looked upon by many laymen as a naval increase. In reality, however, this was a false view, inasmuch as the so-called existing fleet was absolutely no longer a fleet. It was slowly dying of old age—as Hollmann said when he retired ; included in it were almost the oldest ships still in service in all Europe.

While the Naval Law was gradually coming into form lively building operations set in, launchings were reported in the Press, and there was joy among those under the dominion of the *rage du nombre* at the growing number of ships. But when it was made clear to them that as soon as the new ships were ready, the old ones must immediately be eliminated, so that the total number of ships of fighting value would, as a matter of fact, at first, not be increased, they were greatly disillusioned. Had the necessary ships been built in time during the wasted twelve years, the Naval Law would have found a quite different, usable nucleus already in existence ; but, as matters then stood, it was really a question of the complete rebuilding of the entire German fleet. The large number of ships—to which those that had to be eliminated were added—was a fallacy. The English made a mistake, therefore, when they merely took into account the number of ships—though that fitted in well with the propaganda against Germany—

and paid no attention to age or type; thus they arrived at a total that was far too high, and, by such misleading methods, artificially nourished the so-called apprehension at the growth of the German navy.

Admiral Tirpitz now went ahead with the programme approved by me. With iron energy and merciless sacrifice of his health and strength, he soon was able to inject efficiency and power into the handling of the naval question. After the drafting of the Naval Law, he went, at my command, to Friedrichsruh, the residence of Prince Bismarck, in order to convince the latter of the necessity for a German navy.

The Press worked zealously towards the introduction of the Naval Law, and political economists, experts on commerce and politics, etc., placed their pens at the service of the great national cause; the necessity for a navy by now had become widely realized.

In the meantime the English, too, helped—though quite unconsciously—towards bettering the chance of the Naval Law's acceptance. The Boer War had broken out and had aroused among the German people much sympathy for the little country and great indignation against England's violent assault upon it. When the news came, therefore, of the utterly unjustified capture of two German steamers on the East African coast by English warships, the indignation became general.

The news of the stopping of the second steamer

happened to be received by Secretary of State von Bülow at the very moment when Tirpitz and I were with him.   As soon as Bülow had read the dispatch aloud, I quoted the old English proverb : " It's an ill wind that blows nobody good," and Tirpitz exclaimed : " Now we have the wind we need for bringing our ship into port.   The Naval Law will go through.   Your Majesty must present a medal to the captain of the English ship in gratitude for having put through the Naval Law."

The Imperial Chancellor ordered up champagne and the three of us drank joyously to the new law, its acceptance and the future German fleet, not forgetting to express our thanks to the English Navy, which had proved so helpful to us.

Many years later, on my return journey from Lowther Castle where I had been hunting with Lord Lonsdale, I was invited to dine with Lord Rosebery, the great Liberal statesman and former Minister for Foreign Affairs—also known because of his researches in the history of Napoleon—at his beautiful country seat of Dalmeny Park, situated close to the sea, not far from the great Forth Bridge.   Among the guests was General Sir Ian Hamilton (a Scotsman)—well known on account of his part in the Boer War, and with whom I had become acquainted when he was a guest at the Imperial German manœuvres—the Lord Provost of Edinburgh, and an English naval captain who was commander of the naval station there.

The latter sat next to Admiral Freiherr von Senden, directly across the table from me, and

attracted my attention by the obvious embarrassment which he manifested in his conversation, conducted in a low voice, with the admiral. After
dinner Admiral von Senden introduced the captain
to me, whereat the Englishman's embarrassment
caused him to behave even more awkwardly than
before, and aroused my attention because of his
pale face and the worried look in his eyes.

After the conversation, which turned on various
maritime topics, had come to an end, I asked Freiherr
von Senden what was the matter with the man ; the
admiral laughed and replied, that during the meal
he had elicited from his neighbour that he was
the commander of the ship which had captured the
two German steamers in the Boer War, and that he
had been afraid that I might find this out. Senden
had thereupon told him that he was entirely mistaken ; that, had His Majesty learned who he was, he
could rest assured that he would have been very
well treated and thanked into the bargain.

" Thanked ? What for ? " queried the Englishman.

" For having made the passage of the Naval Law
so much easier for the Emperor ! "

One of the prime considerations in the passage of
the Naval Law—as also for all later additions, and,
in general, for the whole question of warship construction—was the question whether the German
shipbuilding industry would be in a position to keep
pace with the naval programme ; whether, in fact,
it would be able to carry it out at all. Here, too,

Admiral von Tirpitz worked with tireless energy. Encouraged and fired with enthusiasm by him, the German shipbuilding yards went at the great problem, filled with German audacity, and solved it with positively brilliant results, greatly out-distancing their foreign competitors. The admirable technical endowment of the German engineers, as well as the better education of the German working-classes, contributed in full measure towards this achievement.

Consultations, conferences, reports to me, service trips to all shipbuilding yards, were the daily bread of the indefatigable Tirpitz. But the tremendous trouble and work were richly rewarded. The people woke up, began to have a thought for the value of the colonies (raw materials provided by ourselves without foreign middlemen!) and for commercial relations, and to feel interest in commerce, navigation, shipping, etc.

At length, the derisive Opposition stopped cracking its jokes. Tirpitz, always ready for battle, wielded a sharp blade in fighting, never joked and allowed nobody to joke with him, so that his opponents no longer felt like laughing. Things went particularly badly with Deputy Richter, when Tirpitz brilliantly snubbed and silenced him by quoting a patriotic saying, dating from the 'forties, of old Harkort—whose district Richter represented—concerning the need for a German fleet. Now it was the turn of the other side of the Reichstag to laugh.

And so the great day dawned. The Naval Law was passed, after much fighting and talking, by a great majority. The strength of the German Navy was assured; naval construction was to be accomplished.

By means of construction and of keeping an increased number of ships in service, a fleet soon sprang into being. In order to manœuvre, lead and train its personnel, a new book of regulations and signal code were needed. At the beginning of my reign these had been planned merely for one division—four ships—for at that time a larger number of units never operated together in the German Navy—i.e. a larger number was not in commission. And even these were out of service by the autumn, so that, in winter, there was (with the exception of cruisers in foreign waters) absolutely no German Navy. All the care expended during the summer season on the training of crews, officers, non-commissioned officers, engine-room crews and stokers, as well as on rigging and upkeep of ships, was as good as wasted when the ships were withdrawn from service in the autumn; and, when spring came and they were put back into commission, everything had to be started at the beginning again. The result was that any degree of continuity in training and of coherence among the crews with relation to each other and their ships—of " ship " spirit, in short—could not be maintained. This was only secured on board the vessels stationed in foreign waters. Therefore, after the necessary heating equipment, etc., had been put in, I ordered that ships were to be kept in service through the winter also, which was a veritable boon to the development of the fleet.

In view of the shortage of ships-of-the-line, and in order to obtain the necessary number of units needed by the new regulations, Admiral von Tirpitz had already formed into divisions every type of vessel available, including gunboats and dispatch boats, and carried out evolutions with them, so that, when the replacement of line ships began to take place, the foundations for the new regulations had already been laid. The latter were then constantly developed, with the greatest energy, by all the officials concerned, and pace kept with the growth of the fleet.

Hard work was done on the development of that important weapon, the torpedo-boat. At that time we were filled with joyful pride that a German torpedo-boat division was the first united torpedo squadron that ever crossed the North Sea. It sailed, under the command of my brother, Prince Henry, to take part in the celebration of Queen Victoria's Jubilee (1887).

The development of Heligoland and its fortifications as a point of support for small cruisers and torpedo-boats—and later on, for U-boats—was also taken in hand, after the necessary protective work for preserving the island had been constructed by the State—in connexion with which work the Empire and Prussia fought like cat and dog.

On account of the growth of the fleet, it, became necessary to widen the Kaiser Wilhelm Canal. After a hard struggle, we caused the new locks to be built of the largest possible size, capable of meeting the development of " Dreadnoughts " for a long time to come. There the far-sighted policy of the admiral was brilliantly vindicated.

This was unexpectedly corroborated by a foreigner. Colonel Goethals, the builder of the Panama Canal, requested, through the United States Government, permission to inspect the Kaiser Wilhelm Canal and its new locks. Permission was most willingly granted. After a meal with me, at which Admiral von Tirpitz was present, the admiral questioned the American engineer—who was enthusiastic over our construction work—concerning the measurements of the Panama locks, whereupon it transpired that they were much smaller than those of the Kaiser Wilhelm Canal. To my astonished question as to how that could be possible, Goethals replied that the Navy Department, upon inquiry by him, had given those measurements for ships-of-the-line. Admiral von Tirpitz then remarked that these dimensions would be far from adequate for the future, and that as the newer type of Dreadnoughts and super-Dreadnoughts would not be able to go through the locks, consequently the canal would soon be useless for American and other big battleships. The colonel agreed, and remarked that this was already true of the newest ships under construction, and he congratulated His Excellency upon having had the courage to demand and put through the big locks of the Kaiser Wilhelm Canal, which he had looked upon with admiration and envy.

In like manner the very inadequate and antiquated Imperial docks (" the old tinker's shops," as Tirpitz called them) were rebuilt and developed into model modern plants; also, the arrangements for the workers were developed so as to further the welfare of the latter along the most approved lines. Only those who, like myself, have followed and seen with their own eyes from the very beginning the origin and development of all these factors necessary to the building up—nay, the creation anew—of the fleet, can form anything like a proper idea of the enormous achievement of Admiral von Tirpitz and his entire corps of assistants.

The office of the Imperial Naval Department was also a new creation. The old *Oberkommando* was eliminated when it was divided into the two main branches of Admiralty Staff and Imperial Naval Department. Both of these (as in the army) were directly under the Supreme War Commander-in-Chief; this meant that there was no longer any official between the Emperor and his navy.

§ 3

When Admiral Fisher evolved an entirely new type of ship for England in the shape of the *Dreadnought*—thereby surprising the world as much as if he had launched a sudden assault upon it—and thought that he had thus given England, once for all, an unapproachable naval superiority which the rest of the Powers could never meet, there was naturally

great excitement in all naval circles. The idea
certainly did not originate with Fisher, but came—
in the form of an appeal to shipbuilders of the whole
world—from the famous Italian engineer Cuniberti,
who had made public a sketch in Fred Jane's " Illustrated Naval Atlas." At the first conference regarding the introduction of the " Dreadnought " type of
big fighting ship by England, I at once agreed with
Admiral von Tirpitz that it had robbed all pre-
Dreadnoughts of their value and consigned them to
the scrap-heap, especially the German ships, which it
had been necessary—on account of the measurements
of our old locks—to keep considerably smaller than the
ships of other navies, the English in particular.

Thereupon Admiral von Tirpitz remarked that, as
soon as the other nations had followed Fisher's
example, this would also apply to the English fleet
itself; that England had robbed her enormous pre-
Dreadnought force—upon which her great superiority
was based—of its fighting value, and that would
necessitate her building an entirely new fleet of big
fighting ships, in competition with the entire world,
which would do likewise; that this would be
exceedingly costly ; that England, in order to maintain
her notorious " two-power standard," would have to
exert herself to such an extent that she would look
with more disfavour than ever on new warships built
by other nations towards whom she was unfriendly,
and begin to raise objections ; that this would be
especially true if we commenced to build, but would
be in vain, for with the existing types of ships in our

fleet we could not expect to fight against big battle-ships, so were forced, *nolens volens*, to follow England along this road.

The war fully confirmed Admiral Tirpitz's opinion. Every one of our ships not in the big fighting-ship class had to be retired from service.

When the first German big fighting ship was placed in service there was a loud outcry in the land of the British. The conviction gradually dawned that Fisher and his shipbuilders had counted absolutely on the belief that Germany would not be able to build any big fighting ships. The disappointment, therefore, was all the greater. Why such an assumption was arrived at is beyond comprehension, for even at that time German shipbuilders had already built the great ocean greyhounds—far surpassing our warships-of-the-line in tonnage—which had occasioned painfully noticeable competition with the English steamship lines. Our big fighting ships, despite their small number, showed themselves, at the Skager Rak (Jutland) battle, not merely equal to their English opponents, but superior to them both in seaworthiness and power to stand gunfire.

The building of U-boats, unfortunately, could not be pushed forward before the war to an extent commensurate with my desires. On the other hand, it was necessary not to overburden the naval budget during the carrying out of the Naval Law ; moreover, most important of all, it was necessary to collect further data from experiments.

Tirpitz believed that the types with which other

nations were experimenting were too small, and fit only for coast defence; that Germany must build sea-going submarines capable of navigating the open sea; that this necessitated a larger type, which, however, must first be systematically developed. This took a long time and required careful experiments with models.

The result was that, at first, in 1914, there were only a small number of seaworthy submarines in readiness. Even so, greater pressure might have been brought to bear upon England, with the available submarines, had the chancellor been less concerned not to provoke England.

The number and efficiency of the submarines rose rapidly in the course of the war. In considering numbers, however, one must always remember that, in war-time, U-boats are to be reckoned as follows: one-third of the total in active service, one-third on the outward or return journey, one-third undergoing repairs. The achievements of the U-boats aroused the admiration of the entire world and won the ardent gratitude of the Fatherland.

§ 4

Admiral von Tirpitz's tremendous success in creating the commercial colony of Tsing-tao must never be forgotten. Here he gave proof once more of his brilliant all-round talent for administration and organization. Out of a place that was previously almost unknown and entirely without importance, these talents of his created a commercial centre which, within a few years, showed a turn-over of between 50 and 60 millions.

His dealings with members of the Reichstag, the Press, and big industrial and world-commercial concerns, gradually increased the admiral's interest in politics, particularly in relation to foreign affairs, which were always bound up with the utilization of ships. The clear world-vision acquired by him as a travelled sailor, well acquainted with foreign parts, qualified Tirpitz to make quick decisions, which his fiery temperament wished to see promptly translated into action.

The opposition and dilatoriness of officialdom greatly irritated him. A certain tendency to distrust, perhaps strengthened by many trying experiences, often led him to harbour suspicion—sometimes justified, sometimes not—against individuals. This created a strong tinge of reserve in Tirpitz's character and " hampered the joyful workings of the heart " in others. He was also capable of bringing to bear with great decision new views on a subject, when, after renewed reflection or study of new facts, he had found occasion to alter his previous point of view. This made working with him not always exactly agreeable or easy. The tremendous results of his achievements, of which he was justly proud, gave him a consciousness of the force of his personality which sometimes made itself apparent even to his friends.

During the war Tirpitz's tendency to interpose in political matters got the upper hand of him to such an extent that it eventually led to differences of opinion that finally caused his retirement. Von Bethmann, the Imperial Chancellor, demanded the dismissal of the Admiral-in-Chief, with the observation that the Imperial Secretaries of State were his subordinates and that political policy must be conducted by himself alone.

It was with a heavy heart that I acquiesced in the departure of this energetic, strong-willed man, who had carried out my plans with genius, and who was indefatigable as a co-worker. Tirpitz may always rest assured of my Imperial gratitude. If only this source of strength might soon stand again by the side of the unfortunate German Fatherland in its misery and distress! Tirpitz can do and dares to do what many others do not dare. The saying of the poet most certainly applies to Admiral von Tirpitz: " The greatest blessing to the children of earth is, after all, personality ! "

The criticism which the admiral felt constrained to level at me in his book—which is well worth reading—cannot, in the slightest, change my opinion of him.

X

THE OUTBREAK OF WAR

§ 1

AFTER the arrival of the news of the assassination of my friend, the Archduke Franz Ferdinand, I abandoned the visit to Kiel for the regatta week and went back home, as I intended to go to Vienna for the funeral. I was, however, asked from there to give up this plan. Later I heard that one of the reasons for this was consideration for my personal safety, to which, naturally, I would have paid no attention.

Greatly worried on account of the turn which affairs might now take, I decided to give up my intended journey to Norway and remain at home. The Imperial Chancellor and the Foreign Office held a contrary view to mine and wished me to undertake the journey, as they considered it would have a quieting effect on all Europe. For a long time I argued against leaving my country at a time when the future appeared so unsettled, but Imperial Chancellor von Bethmann told me in short and concise terms, that if I were now to abandon my plans for the trip, which were already widely known, it would make the situation appear more serious than it really was at that moment, and might possibly lead to an outbreak of war for which I might be held responsible; that the whole world was merely waiting to be put out of suspense by the news that, in spite of the situation, I had quietly gone on my trip.

I thereupon consulted the Chief of the General Staff, and, when he also proved to be calm and unworried regarding the state of affairs and himself asked for summer leave of absence to go to Carlsbad, I decided, though with a heavy heart, upon my departure.

The much-discussed, so-called Potsdam Crown Council of July 5th in reality never took place. It is a malevolent invention. Naturally, before my departure, I received as my custom was, some of the ministers individually, in order to hear from them reports concerning their departments. There was no council of ministers, nor was there talk of war preparations at a single one of these conferences.

My fleet was cruising as usual in the Norwegian fjords, while I was on my summer vacation trip. During my stay at Balholm I received but meagre news from the Foreign Office and was obliged to rely principally on the Norwegian newspapers, from which I received the impression that the situation was growing worse. I telegraphed repeatedly to the chancellor and the Foreign Office that I considered it advisable to return home, but was asked each time not to interrupt my journey.

When I learned that the English fleet had not dispersed after the review at Spithead but had remained concentrated, I telegraphed again to Berlin

Q

that I considered my return to be necessary. My opinion was not shared there.

When, after that, however, I learned from the Norwegian newspapers—*not from Berlin*—of the Austrian ultimatum to Serbia, and, immediately after, of the Serbian Note to Austria, I started upon my return journey without further ado and commanded the fleet to repair to Wilhelmshaven. Upon my departure I learned from a Norwegian source that it was rumoured that a part of the English fleet had left secretly for Norway in order to capture me (though peace still reigned) ! It is significant that Sir Edward Goschen, the English Ambassador, was informed, on July 26th at the Foreign Office, that my return journey —undertaken on my own initiative—was to be regretted, as it might cause agitating rumours.

Upon my arrival at Potsdam I found the chancellor and the Foreign Office in conflict with the Chief of the General Staff ; General von Moltke was of the opinion that war was certain to break out, whereas the other two stuck firmly to their view that things would not get to such a bad pass, that there would be some way of avoiding war, provided I did not order mobilization. This dispute was steadily maintained. Not until General von Moltke announced that the Russians had set fire to their frontier posts, torn up the frontier railway tracks and posted red mobilization notices, did a light break upon the diplomats in the Wilhelmstrasse and bring about their own collapse and that of their powers of resistance. They had not *wished* to *believe* in the possibility of war.

This plainly shows, as I have already narrated, how little we had expected, much less prepared for, war in July, 1914. When, in the spring of 1914, Tsar Nicholas II was questioned by his court marshal as to his spring and summer plans, he replied : " Je resterai chez moi cette année, parce que nous aurons la guerre." [" I shall stay at home this year, because we shall have war."] (This fact, it is said, was reported to Imperial Chancellor von Bethmann ; I heard nothing of it then, and learned about it for the first time in November, 1918.) This was the same Tsar who gave me, on two separate occasions—at Björkö and Baltic Port—entirely without being pressed by me and in a manner that surprised me, his word of honour as a sovereign—to which he added emphasis by a clasp of the hand and an embrace—that he would never draw his sword against the German Emperor, least of all as an ally of England, in the event of an outbreak of war in Europe, owing to his gratitude to the German Emperor for his attitude in the Russo-Japanese War, in which Russia was involved solely by England. He added that he hated England, because of the great wrong she had done him and Russia by inciting Japan against them.

At the very time that the Tsar was announcing his summer war programme I was busy at Corfu excavating antiquities ; then I went to Wiesbaden, and, finally, to Norway. A monarch who desires war and prepares for it in such a manner that he can suddenly fall upon his neighbours—a task requiring lengthy and secret preparations for mobilization and concentration of troops—does not spend months outside his own country and does not allow his Chief of the General Staff to go to Carlsbad on leave of absence. My enemies, in the meantime, planned their preparations for attack.

Our entire diplomatic machine failed. The menace of war was not realized because the Foreign Office was so hypnotized with its idea of "*surtout pas d'histoires*" ["Above all, no yarns"] and by its belief in peace at any cost, that it had completely eliminated from its calculations war as a possible instrument of Entente statesmanship and, therefore, did not rightly estimate the importance of the portents of war.

Herein, also, is proof of Germany's peaceful inclinations. The above-mentioned standpoint of the Foreign Office brought it to a certain extent into conflict with the General Staff and the Admiralty Staff, both of whom, in accordance with their duty, uttered warnings, and desired to make preparations for defence. The effect of this conflict in views was evident for a long time ; the army could not forget that it had been taken by surprise, through the fault of the Foreign Office, and the diplomats were piqued because, in spite of their stratagems, war after all ensued.

The evidence that as early as the spring and summer of 1914—when nobody in Germany believed as yet in the Entente's attack—war was prepared for in Russia, France, Belgium and England is incontestable. I included the most important proofs of this, in so far as they are known to me, in the "Comparative

Historical Tables " compiled by me.   On account of
their great number I shall cite only a few here.   If, in
doing so, I do not mention all names, the reasons
can be easily understood.   Let me remark, furthermore, that this mass of material only became known
to me little by little, partly during the war, mostly
after it.

(1) As far back as April, 1914, the accumulation
of gold reserves was commenced by the English banks.
Germany, on the other hand, as late as July, was still
exporting gold and grain—to the Entente countries,
among others.

(2) In April, 1914, the German Naval Attaché in
Tokio, Captain von Knorr, reported that he was
greatly struck by the certainty with which everyone
there foresaw a war between the Triple Alliance and
Germany in the near future . . . that there was
something in the air as if, so to speak, people were
expressing their condolences over a death sentence not
yet pronounced.

(3) At the end of March, 1914, General Sherbet-
sheff, director of the St. Petersburg War Academy,
in the course of an address to his officers, said, among
other things : that war with the Powers forming the
Triple Alliance had become unavoidable on account
of Austria's anti-Russian Balkan policy . . . that
the strongest probability existed that it would break
out as early as that same summer ; that, for Russia, it
was a point of honour immediately to assume the
offensive.

(4) In the report of the Belgian Ambassador at

Berlin regarding a Japanese Military Mission which had arrived from St. Petersburg in April, 1914, it was stated, among other things : that in the regimental messes the Japanese officers had heard quite open talk of an imminent war against Austria-Hungary and Germany ; that it was stated, moreover, that the army was ready to take the field, and the moment was as auspicious for the Russians as for their allies, the French.

(5) According to the memoirs of the then French Ambassador at St. Petersburg, M. Paléologue, published in 1921 in the *Revue des Deux Mondes*, the Grand Duchesses Anastasia and Militza told him, on July 22, 1914, at Tsarskoe Selo, that their father, the King of Montenegro, had informed them in a cipher telegram, " we shall have war before the end of the month [that is, before the 13th of August, Russian style] . . . nothing will be left of Austria . . . . You will take back Alsace-Lorraine. . . . Our armies will meet at Berlin. . . . Germany will be annihilated."

(6) The former Serbian Chargé d'Affaires at Berlin, Bogitshevich, relates in his book " Causes of the War," published in 1919, the following statement which the then French Ambassador at Berlin, Cambon, made to him on the 26*th or* 27*th of July*, 1914, " If Germany wishes matters to come to a war, she will have England also against her. The English fleet will take Hamburg. We shall beat the Germans." Bogitshevich states that this talk made him sure that the war had been decided upon at the time of the meeting of Poincaré

with the Russian Tsar at St. Petersburg, if not sooner.

(7) Another Russian of high rank, a member of the Duma and a good friend of Sazonoff, told me later of the secret Crown Council held, with the Tsar presiding, in February, 1914 ; moreover, I obtained corroboration from other Russian sources mentioned in my " Historical Tables " of the following : at this Crown Council Sazonoff gave an address wherein he suggested to the Tsar that Constantinople should be seized, a step that the Triple Alliance would not acquiesce in, and would cause a war against Germany and Austria. He added that in the natural course of events Italy would break away from these two ; that France was to be trusted absolutely, and England probably.

The Tsar, it was said, had agreed, and had given orders for the necessary preliminary steps to be taken. The Russian Minister of Finance, Count Kokovzeff, wrote to the Tsar advising against this course—I was informed of this by Count Mirbach after the Peace of Brest-Litovsk—recommending a firm union with Germany, and warning him against war, which, he said, would be unfavourable to Russia and lead to revolution and the fall of the dynasty. The Tsar did not follow this advice, but pushed on towards war.

(8) The same gentleman told me this : *Two* days after the outbreak of war he had been invited by Sazonoff to breakfast. The latter came up to him, beaming with joy and rubbing his hands together,

and asked : " Come now, my dear baron, you must admit that I have chosen the moment for war excellently, haven't I ? " When the baron, rather worried, asked him what stand England would take, the minister smote his pocket, and, with a sly wink, whispered : " I have something in my pocket which, within the next few days, will bring joy to all Russia and astound the entire world ; I have received the *English promise* that England will go with Russia against Germany ! "

(9) Russian prisoners belonging to the Siberian Corps, who were taken in East Prussia, said that they had been transported by rail in the summer of 1913, to the vicinity of Moscow, as manœuvres were to be held there by the Tsar. The manœuvres did not take place but the troops were not taken back ; they were stationed for the winter in the neighbourhood of Moscow. In the summer of 1914 they were brought forward to the neighbourhood of Vilna, as big manœuvres were to be held there by the Tsar ; at and near Vilna they were deployed and then, suddenly, the "sharp cartridges" (war ammunition) were distributed, and they were informed that there was a war against Germany ; they were unable to say why and wherefore.

(10) In a report by an American concerning his trip through the Caucasus in the spring of 1914, made public in the Press during the winter of 1914–15, the following was stated : when he arrived in the Caucasus at the beginning of *May*, 1914, he met, while on his way to Tiflis, long columns of troops of all arms, in war

equipment. He had feared that a revolt had broken out in the Caucasus. When he made inquiries of the authorities at Tiflis, while having his passport inspected, he received the quieting news that the Caucasus was quite peaceful, that he might travel wheresoever he wished, that what he had seen had to do only with practice marching and manœuvres.

At the close of his trip at the end of *May*, 1914, he desired to embark at a Caucasian port, but all the vessels there were so filled with troops that only after much trouble could he manage to get a cabin for himself and his wife. The Russian officers told him that they were to land at Odessa and march from there to take part in some great manœuvres.

(11) Prince Tundutoff, Hetman of the Kalmuk Cossacks—living between Tsaritsin and Astrakhan—who was, before and during the war, personal *aide* of the Grand Duke Nicholas Nicholaievitch, came to General Headquarters at Bosmont in 1918 seeking to establish connexion with Germany, because the Cossacks were not Slavs at all and were thoroughly hostile to the Bolsheviki.

He stated that before the outbreak of war, he had been sent by Nicholas Nicholaievitch to the General Staff in order to keep the Grand Duke posted on happenings there, and that he had been present at the notorious telephone talks between the Tsar and the Chief of the General Staff, General Januskevitch ; that the Tsar, deeply impressed by the earnest telegram of the German Emperor, had resolved to forbid mobilization and had ordered Januskevitch by telephone not to carry out mobilization, i.e. to break it off; that the latter had not obeyed the unmistakable order, but had inquired by telephone of Sazonoff, Minister for Foreign Affairs—with whom, for weeks, he had kept in touch, intrigued and incited to war—what he was to do now; that Sazonoff had answered that the Tsar's order was nonsensical, that all the general need do was to carry out mobilization, that he (Sazonoff) would bring the Tsar around again next day and talk him out of heeding the German Emperor's stupid telegram; that, thereupon, Januskevitch had informed the Tsar that mobilization was already under way and could no longer be broken off.

Prince Tundutoff added: " This was a lie, for I myself saw the mobilization order lying beside Januskevitch on his writing-table, which shows that it had not then been acted upon."

The psychologically interesting point about the above is that Tsar Nicholas, who helped to prepare the world war and had already ordered mobilization, wished to recede at the last moment. My earnest, warning telegram, it seems, made him realize clearly for the first time the colossal responsibility which he was bringing upon himself by his warlike preparations. He therefore wished to stop the war machine, the murderer of entire peoples, which he had just set in motion. This would have been possible and peace might have been preserved if Sazonoff had not frustrated his desires.

When I asked whether the Grand Duke, who was known as a German-hater, had incited much to war, the Cossack chief replied that the Grand Duke had certainly worked zealously for war, but that incitement on his part would have been superfluous as there was already a strong feeling against Germany all through the Russian officer corps; that this spirit was transmitted, principally, from the French army to the Russian officers; that there had been a desire, in fact, to go to war in 1908-9 [Bosnian question], but France was not then ready; that, in 1914, Russia likewise was not quite ready; that Januskevitch and Sukhomlinoff had really planned the war for 1917, but Sazonoff and Isvolsky, as well as the French, could not be restrained any longer; that the two former were afraid of revolution in Russia and of the influence of the German Emperor on the Tsar, which might dissuade the Tsar from the idea of waging war; and that the French, who for the time being were certain of England's help, were afraid that England might come to an understanding later on with Germany, at the expense of France.

When I asked whether the Tsar had been aware of the warlike spirit in Russia and had tolerated it, the Cossack prince answered that it was worthy of note that, as a matter of precaution, the Tsar had forbidden once for all invitations to German diplomats or military attachés to luncheons or evening meals given by Russian officers at which he himself was to be present.

(12) When our troops advanced in 1914 they found in Northern France and along the Belgian frontier great stores of English soldiers' great-coats. Accord-

ing to statements by the inhabitants, these were placed there during the *last years of peace*. Most of the English infantrymen who were made prisoners by us in the summer of 1914 had no great-coats; when asked why, they answered quite naïvely: " We are to find our great-coats in the stores at Maubeuge, Le Quesnoy, etc., in the North of France and in Belgium."

It was the same with regard to maps. In Maubeuge great quantities of English military maps of Northern France and Belgium were found by our men; copies of these have been shown to me. The names of places were printed in French and English and all sorts of words were translated in the margin for the convenience of soldiers; for instance: *Moulin*— mill; *pont*—bridge; *maison*—house; *ville*—town; *bois*—wood, etc. These maps date from 1911 and were engraved at Southampton.

The stores were established by England with the permission of the French and Belgian Governments *before* the war, in the midst of peace. What a tempest of horror would have broken out in Belgium, the " neutral country," and what a rumpus England and France would have kicked up, if we had wished to establish stores of German soldiers' great-coats and maps in Spa, Liège and Namur!

§ 2

Among the statesmen who, besides Poincaré, particularly helped to unleash the world war, the Sazonoff-Isvolsky group should probably be given first rank. Isvolsky, when in Paris, it is said, proudly placed his hand upon his breast, and declared : " I made the war. Je suis le père de cette guerre." [" I am the father of this war."]

Delcassé, also, has a large share in the guilt for the world war, and Grey an even larger share, because he was the spiritual leader of the " encirclement " policy, which he faithfully pushed forward and brought to completion as the " legacy " of his dead sovereign.

I have been informed that an important role was played in the preparation of the world war directed against the monarchical Central Powers, by the policy of the international " Grand Orient Lodge," a policy extending over many years and always envisaging the goal at which it aimed. The German Grand Lodges, I was furthermore told—with two exceptions in which non-German financial interests are paramount and which maintain secret connexion with the " Grand Orient " in Paris—had no relationship to the " Grand Orient." According to the assurance given me by the distinguished German Freemason who explained to me this whole inter-relationship—which, until then, had been unknown to me—they were entirely loyal and faithful. He said that, in 1917, an international meeting of the lodges of the " Grand Orient " was held, after which there was a subsequent conference in Switzerland. There the following programme was adopted : dismemberment of Austria-Hungary, de-mocratization of Germany, elimination of the House of Habsburg, abdication of the German Emperor, restitution of Alsace-Lorraine to France, union of Galicia with Poland, elimination of the Pope and the Catholic Church, elimination of every State Church in Europe.

I am not now in a position to investigate the very damaging information concerning the organization and activities of the Grand Orient Lodges, which has been transmitted to me in the very best of faith. Secret and public political organizations have played important parts in the life of peoples and states, ever since history has existed. Some of them have been beneficial; most of them have been destructive if they had to have secret passwords which shunned the light of day. The most dangerous of these organizations hide under the cloak of some ideal object or other—such as Christian love of their neighbours, readiness to help the weak and poor, etc.—in order that, with such pretexts as a blind, they may work for their real secret ends. It is certainly advisable to study the activities of the Grand Orient Lodges, for one cannot adopt a definite attitude towards this world-wide organization until it has been thoroughly investigated.

§ 3

I shall not refer to the war operations in this work. I shall leave this task all the more readily to my officers and to the historians, for, writing as I am without a single document, I should only be able to describe events in very broad outline.

When I look back upon the four arduous years of war, with their hopes and fears, their brilliant victories and losses in precious blood, what is uppermost in my mind is the feeling of ardent gratitude to, and undying admiration for, the unequalled achievements of the German nation in arms.

Just as no sacrifice in endurance and privation was too great for those who were at home, so also the army, in defending itself during the war so criminally forced upon us, did not merely overcome the crushing superiority of twenty-eight hostile nations, but on land and water, and in the air, won victories. Their glory may have somewhat paled in the mists of the present day but, for that very reason, will shine forth all the more brightly in the light of history. Nor is that all. Wherever our allies were hard pressed, German intervention — often with weak forces — always restored the situation and often won noteworthy successes. Germans fought on all the battlefields of the far-flung world war.

Surely the heroic bravery of the German nation deserved a better fate than to fall a victim to the dagger that treacherously stabbed it from behind ! It seems to be the German destiny that Germany shall always be defeated by Germans. I recently read the, unfortunately not entirely unjustified, words : " In Germany every Siegfried has Hödur behind him."

Finally, let me say a word concerning the German " atrocities " and give two instances thereof !

After our advance into Northern France I immediately ordered that art treasures should be protected. Art-historians and professors were assigned to each army, and these travelled about inspecting, photographing and describing churches, châteaux and castles.   Among them, Professor Clemen, Curator of the Rhine Province, especially distinguished himself and reported to me, when I was at the front, on the protection of art treasures.

All the collections in towns, museums and castles were catalogued and numbered; whenever they seemed to be imperilled by the fighting they were taken away and stored in two splendid museums at Valenciennes and Maubeuge.   There they were carefully preserved and the name of the owner marked on each article.

The old windows of the cathedral of St. Quentin were removed by German soldiers, at the risk of their lives, under English shell-fire.   The story of the destruction of the church by the English was told by a German Catholic priest, who published it with photographs, and, by my orders, it was sent to the Pope.

At the château of Pinon, which belongs to the Princess of Poix—who had been a guest of mine and of the Empress—was located the headquarters of the general commanding the Third Army Corps. I visited the château and lived there for a time. Previously the English had been quartered there and had ravaged the place terribly.   The commanding general, von Lochow, and his staff, had a great deal of trouble to get it into some sort of shape again after the devastation wrought by the English.

Accompanied by the general I visited the private apartments of the princess, which, up to then, our soldiers had been forbidden to enter. I found that her entire wardrobe had been thrown out of the clothes-presses by the English soldiers and, together with her hats, was lying about on the floor. I had every garment carefully cleaned, hung in the presses, and locked up. The writing-desk had also been forced open and the princess's correspondence scattered about. At my command, all the letters were gathered together, sealed in a package, placed in the writing-desk, and locked up.

Afterwards, all the silver was found buried in the garden. According to the villagers, this had been ordered as early as the *beginning of July,* so that the princess had known that war was imminent long before its outbreak! I at once ordered that an inventory of the silver should be made, and the articles deposited in the bank at Aix-la-Chapelle and returned to the princess after the war. Through neutral channels I caused information to be transmitted by my court marshal, Freiherr von Reischach, to the princess in Switzerland, concerning Pinon, her silverware, and my care for her property. No answer was received. Instead, the princess published a letter in the French Press to the effect that General von Kluck had stolen all her silver!

On account of my care and the self-sacrificing work of German art experts and soldiers—often at the risk of their lives—art treasures worth billions were preserved for their French owners and for French towns. This was done by the Huns; the *boches !*

R

XI

THE POPE AND PEACE

IN the summer of 1917 I received a visit at Kreuznach from the Papal Nuncio, Pacelli, who was accompanied by a chaplain. Pacelli is a distinguished, likeable man, of high intelligence and excellent manners, the perfect pattern of an eminent prelate of the Catholic Church. He knows German well enough to understand it easily when he hears it, but not sufficiently to speak it with fluency.

Our conversation was conducted in French, but the Nuncio now and then employed German expressions of speech. The chaplain spoke German fluently and—even when not asked—took part in the conversation whenever he feared that the Nuncio was becoming too much influenced by what I said.

Very soon the conversation turned on the possibility of mediation and the bringing about of peace, in which connexion all kinds of projects and possibilities were touched upon, discussed and dismissed.

I suggested, finally, seeing that my peace offer of December 12th, 1916, had been rejected in such an unprecedented manner, that the Pope should make an effort. The Nuncio remarked that he thought such a step would be attended with great difficulties ; that the Pope had already been rebuffed when he had made certain advances in this direction ; that apart from this, the Pope was absolutely in despair on account of the slaughter, and wondered ceaselessly how he might help towards freeing the world of European culture from the scourge of war. Any suggestion in this direction, he added, would be most valuable to the Vatican.

I stated that the Pope, as the highest in rank of all the priests of the Roman Catholic Christians and Churches, should, first of all, issue instructions to his priests in all countries to banish hate, once for all, from their minds, for hate was the greatest obstacle in the path of peace ; that it was, unfortunately, true that the clergy in the Entente countries were, to a positively frightful extent, the standard-bearers and instigators of hatred and fighting.

I called attention to the numerous reports from soldiers at the beginning of the war concerning abbés and parish priests captured with arms in their hands ; to the machinations of Cardinal Mercier and the Belgian clergy, members of which often worked as spies ; to the sermon of the Protestant Bishop of London who, from the pulpit, glorified the *Baralong* murderers ; and to other similar cases. I added that it would therefore be a great achievement if the Pope should succeed in having the Roman Catholic clergy in all the countries at war condemn hatred and recommend peace, as was already being done by the German clergy, either from the pulpit or by means of pastoral letters.

Pacelli considered this suggestion excellent and worthy of attention, but he remarked that it would be difficult to enlist the efforts of the various prelates in its support. I replied that in view of the severe discipline of the hierarchy of the Roman Catholic Church, I could not imagine that if the Pope should solemnly call upon the prelates of the Church to preach reconciliation and consideration for the foe, none of any country whatsoever would refuse obedience ; that the prelates, on account of their eminent rank, were above all party influence, and that since reconciliation and Christian love were fundamental principles of the Christian religion, they were absolutely in duty bound to work towards inducing people to observe these principles.

Pacelli agreed with this and promised to give the idea his earnest attention and report upon it to the Vatican. In the further course of the conversation the Nuncio asked what form—beyond the purely ecclesiastical step suggested by me—the intervention of the Pope might take to bring about the possibilities of peace. I pointed out that Italy and Austria were both Roman Catholic states upon which the Pope could bring influence to bear easily and effectively ; that one of these was his native country and place of residence, in which he was greatly revered by the people and exerted direct influence upon his fellow-countrymen ; that Austria was ruled by a sovereign who actually bore the title " apostolic," who, together with all his family, had direct relations with the Vatican and was among the most faithful adherents of the Catholic Church; that I was, therefore, of the opinion that it would not be difficult for the Pope, at least, to try to make a beginning with these two countries and induce them to discuss peace.

I added that the diplomatic skill and wide vision of the Vatican were known the world over; that, if once a beginning were made in this way—and that it had a good chance of success—the other Powers could scarcely refuse later on an invitation from the Vatican to an exchange of views, which should, at first, not be binding upon them.

The Nuncio remarked that it would be difficult for the Vatican to make the Italian Government agree to such a course, seeing that it had no direct relations with that Government, and no influence with its members; that the Italian Government would never look with favour upon such an invitation, even to mere conferences.

Here the chaplain interposed that such a step by the Pope was absolutely out of the question, since it might entail consequences which might be actually dangerous to the Vatican; the Government would at once mobilize the " *piazza* " [man in the street] against the Vatican, and the Vatican certainly could not expose itself to that. When I refused to attach importance to this objection the chaplain grew more and more excited. He said that I did not know the Romans; that, when they were incited they were simply terrible; that, just as soon as the *piazza* took action, things would get

disagreeable ; that, if it did, there was even a possibility of an attack on the Vatican, which might
actually imperil the very life of the Pope.

I replied that I, too, was well acquainted with the
Vatican ; that no rabble or *piazza* could storm it ;
that, in addition, the Pope had a strong party of
adherents in society circles and among the people,
which would at once be ready to defend him. The
Nuncio agreed with me, but the chaplain continued
unabashed to expatiate upon the terrors of the
piazza and paint in the blackest of colours—the risks
that would be run by the Pope.

I then remarked that anyone wishing to capture
the Vatican must first get a battery of heavy mortars
and howitzers, together with pioneers and storm
troops and institute a regular siege ; that all this
was scarcely possible for the *piazza ;* that, therefore,
it was highly improbable that the latter would undertake anything of the sort. Moreover, I mentioned
having heard that measures had already been taken
in the Vatican to guard against such an emergency.
At this the priest was silent.

The Nuncio then remarked that it was difficult
for the Pope to do anything really practical towards
peace without giving offence and arousing opposition in lay Italy, which would place him in danger ;
that it must be borne in mind that he was, unfortunately, not free ; that, had the Pope a country,
or, at least, a province of his own where he could
govern autonomously and do as he pleased, the
situation would be quite different ; that, as matters

stood, he was too dependent upon lay Rome and quite unable to act according to his own free will.

I remarked that the aim of bringing peace to the world was so holy and great that it was impossible for the Pope to be frightened by purely worldly considerations from accomplishing such a task, which seemed created especially for him; that, should he succeed in it, a grateful world would assuredly bring influence to bear upon the Italian Government in support of his wishes and of his independence.

This made an impression on the Nuncio; he remarked that I was right, after all; that the Pope must do something in the matter.

Then I called the attention of the Nuncio to the following point: he must have noticed, I said, how the Socialists of all countries were zealously working in favour of peace efforts. I told him that we had always allowed the German Socialists to travel to foreign countries in order to discuss the question of peace at conferences, because I believed them to be acquainted with the desires and views of the lower classes; that we placed no obstacles in the path of anybody desiring to work honestly and without veiled purpose in the interests of peace; that the same desire for peace also existed among the Entente nations and among their Socialists, but that the latter were prevented by refusal of passports from attending congresses in neutral countries; that the desire for peace was gaining strength in the world, nations were acquiring it more and more, and

if nobody in any Government should be found willing
to work for peace—I, unfortunately, had failed in
my attempt—the peoples would finally take the
matter into their own hands. I added that this would
not occur without serious shocks and revolutions—
as history proved—through which the Roman Church
and the Pope would not come unscathed.

What must a Catholic soldier think, I asked,
when he reads always of efforts by Socialists only,
never of an effort by the Pope, to free him from the
horrors of war ? If the Pope did nothing, I continued, there was danger of peace being forced upon
the world by the Socialists, which would mean the
end of the power of the Pope and the Roman Church,
even among Catholics !

This argument struck home to the Nuncio. He
stated that he would at once report it to the Vatican
and give it his support ; that the Pope would have
to act.

Greatly worried, the chaplain again interposed,
remarking that the Pope would endanger himself
by such a course ; that the *piazza* would attack him.

To this I replied that I was a Protestant and
hence, a heretic in the chaplain's eyes, notwithstanding which I was obliged to point out that the Pope
was designated by the Catholic Church and the
world—the " viceroy of Christ upon earth " ; that I
had, in studying the Holy Scriptures, occupied
myself earnestly and carefully with the person of
the Saviour, and sought to immerse myself pro-
foundly therein ; that the Lord never feared the

piazza, although no fortress-like building, with guards and weapons, was at His disposal ; that the Lord had always walked in the midst of the *piazza*, spoken to it, and finally gone to His death on the cross for the sake of this hostile *piazza*.

Was I now to believe, I asked, that His " viceroy upon earth " was afraid of the possibility of becoming a martyr, like his Lord, in order to bring peace to the bleeding world, all on account of the ragged Roman *piazza ?* I, the Protestant, thought far too highly of a Roman priest, particularly of the Pope, to believe such a thing. Nothing could be more glorious for him, I went on, than to devote himself unreservedly body and soul, to the great cause of peace, even despite the remote danger of thus becoming a martyr !

With shining eyes, the Nuncio grasped my hand and, deeply moved, said : " Vous avez parfaitement raison ! C'est le devoir du Pape, il faut qu'il agisse, c'est par lui que le monde doit être régagné à la paix. Je transmettrai vos paroles a Sa Sainteté." [" You are absolutely right ! It is the duty of the Pope, he must act, it is through him that the world must be won back to peace. I shall transmit your words to His Holiness."]

The chaplain turned away, shaking his head, and murmured to himself : " Ah, la piazza, la piazza."

XII

THE END OF THE WAR AND MY ABDICATION

§ 1

A FEW days after August 8, 1918, I summoned a Crown Council, in order to get a clear conception of the situation and to draw therefrom the necessary conclusions upon which to base the policy to be followed by Count Hertling. The Chief Military Command approved the idea that the Imperial Chancellor should keep in sight the possibility of getting into closer touch with the enemy, but laid stress on the necessity of first occupying the Siegfried Line and there decisively beating off the foe, and on the point that negotiations must not begin before this occurred. Thereupon I directed that the chancellor should get into communication with a neutral Power—Holland—in order to ascertain whether it was willing to undertake steps towards mediation.

What rendered the contemplated action through Dutch channels very difficult was that Austria could not be brought to a definite agreement, but continually postponed the declaration which had been requested of her. Even a verbal agreement given to me by Emperor Charles was under Burian's influence afterwards broken by him.

The Dutch Government had already been in-

formed by me and had signified its readiness to act.
Meanwhile, unbeknown to us, Austria made her
first separate peace offer, which set the ball rolling.
Emperor Charles, indeed, had got into touch secretly
with the Entente and had long since resolved to
abandon us. He acted according to the plan which
he had explained thus to his entourage : " When I
go to the Germans, I agree to everything they say,
and when I return home, I do whatever I please."

Thus it happened that my Government and I
were constantly deceived by Vienna's action, without being able to do anything against it, for we constantly received the hint from there : " If you make
things difficult for us, we shall leave you in the lurch ;
in other words, our army will no longer fight by
your side." In view of the situation, such action
on Austria's part had to be avoided in any way
possible, both on military and political grounds.

The defection of Austria-Hungary brought about
a crisis for us. Had Emperor Charles kept control
of his nerves for three weeks longer many things
would have turned out differently. But Andrassy—
as he himself admitted—had been negotiating behind
our backs with the Entente for a long time in Switzerland. Thus Emperor Charles believed that he
would assure himself of good treatment at the hands
of the Entente.

After our failure of August 8, General Ludendorff
declared that he could no longer guarantee a military
victory, and the opening of peace negotiations
became necessary. As diplomacy did not succeed

in initiating any promising negotiations and as in the meantime, on account of revolutionary agitation, the military situation became even worse, Ludendorff, on the 29th of September, demanded that negotiations should be opened for an armistice instead of for peace.

At this critical time a strong movement began at home in favour of setting up a new Government for the now necessary termination of the war. I could not ignore this movement, for the old Government, during the seven weeks from August 8 to the end of September, had not managed to initiate peace negotiations that offered any hope of success.

Meanwhile, General von Gallwitz and General von Mudra, summoned from the front, appeared before me. They gave a picture of the internal condition of the army, laying due emphasis upon the great number of shirkers behind the front, the frequency of insubordination, the displaying of the red flag upon trains filled with soldiers returning from furlough at home, and other similar phenomena. The two generals considered that the principal cause of these bad conditions was to be sought in the unfavourable influence exercised upon the soldiers by the spirit that predominated behind the front and in the general desire to end the fighting and get peace, which was spreading from the homeland along the lines of communication, and was even then becoming noticeable among some of the troops at the front itself. The generals advanced the opinion that owing to these reasons, the army must immediately be withdrawn behind the Antwerp—Meuse line.

On that same day I commanded Field Marshal von Hindenburg by telephone to effect the retreat as soon as possible to the Antwerp—Meuse line. The falling back of the tired—but nowhere decisively beaten—army to this position merely signified the occupation of an essentially shorter line, which possessed far greater natural advantages. True, it was not yet completed, but the fact is to be borne in mind that we had engaged in battle on the Somme while occupying positions composed largely of shell-craters. What we had to do was to regain operative freedom, which, to my way of thinking, was by no means impossible ; in the course of the war had we not often retreated in order to put ourselves in a situation that was more advantageous from the military point of view ?

The army, certainly, was no longer the old army. The new 1918 troops, particularly, were badly tainted with revolutionary propaganda and often took advantage of the darkness of night to sneak away from the firing-line and vanish to the rear : but the majority of my divisions fought flawlessly and preserved their discipline and military spirit to the very end. To the very end they were always a match for the foe in *moral ;* despite superiority in numbers, guns, munitions, tanks and aeroplanes, the foe invariably succumbed when he encountered serious resistance. The associations of our ex-service men are therefore right in bearing upon their banners the motto : " Unbeaten on land and sea ! "

The achievements of the German fighters and of the German nation in arms, during four and a half years of war, are beyond all praise. One does not know what to admire most : the enthusiasm with which the magnificent youth of 1914, without waiting for our artillery fire to take effect, joyfully charged the enemy, or the self-sacrificing fidelity to duty and tenacity with which our men in field-grey, sparingly fed and seldom relieved, year in year out, digging by night, living in dug-outs and holes by day, or crouching in shell-holes, defied the hail of steel from the enemy artillery, flyers and tanks. And this army, which one might have expected to be rated as utterly fought to a finish, was able, after nearly four years of war, to carry out successful offensive operations such as our foes could nowhere boast of, despite their colossal superiority.

In spite of all this, it was not right to believe the German army capable of accomplishing the super-human ; it was necessary for us to fall back, in order to get breath.

The Field Marshal objected to the order to retreat ; the army, he thought, should, for political reasons (peace negotiations, etc.), stay where it was ; he also pointed out, among other things, that it was first necessary to arrange for the withdrawal of war material, etc., to the rear.

I now resolved to acquiesce in the desire ex-pressed to me by the army and go to the front, that I might be with my hard-fighting troops and convince myself personally of their spirit and condition.

I could carry out this resolve all the easier in view of the fact that, ever since the new Government had been set up, claims were no longer made upon my time either by it or by the Imperial Chancellor, which made my staying at home seem useless.

The Notes to Wilson were discussed and written by Solf, the War Cabinet and the Reichstag, after sessions which lasted for hours, without my being informed thereof; until, finally, on the occasion of the last Note to Wilson, I caused Solf to be given to understand very plainly, through my chief of cabinet, that I demanded information concerning the note *before* it was sent.

Solf appeared and showed me the Note; he was proud of his antithesis between *laying down* of arms (*Waffenstreckung*), which was demanded by Wilson, and *armistice* (*Waffenstillstand*), which was proposed. When I spoke about the rumours of abdication and demanded that the Foreign Office should protest through the Press, against the unfairness of the newspaper polemics, Solf replied that already everybody on every street corner was talking about abdication and that, even in the best circles, people were discussing it quite unreservedly.

When I expressed my indignation at this, Solf sought to console me by observing that should His Majesty go, *he* would go also, as he could no longer serve under such conditions. I went, or—to put it much more correctly—I was overthrown by my own Government, and—Herr Solf remained.

When the Imperial Chancellor, Prince Max, heard of my resolve to go to the front he did all he could to prevent me. He asked why I wished to go, and received the answer that I considered it my duty, as Supreme Commander, to return to the front seeing that I had been separated for almost a month from the hard-fighting army. When the chancellor raised the objection that I was indispensable at home, I retorted that we were at war and that the Emperor belonged to his soldiers. Finally, I declared, once for all, that I would go; that if Wilson's armistice Note arrived, it would in any event have to be discussed at the General Headquarters of the army, and the chancellor and other members of the Government would be obliged to go to Spa for the conferences.

I went to the army in Flanders, after having once more given the General Staff at Spa definite orders to fall back as quickly as possible to the Antwerp—Meuse line, in order that the troops might finally be taken out of the fighting-line and given a rest. Despite objections that this would take time, that the position was not yet ready, that the war material must first be taken back, etc., I insisted and the retreat was begun.

In Flanders I saw delegations from the different divisions, spoke with the soldiers, distributed decorations, and was everywhere joyfully received by officers and men. Particularly ardent enthusiasm reigned among the soldiers of a royal Saxon recruit depot, who, when I was returning to my train, greeted me with wild cheers at the railway station. While I was giving out decorations to members of the Reserve Guard Division, an enemy bombing-squadron—followed by heavy fire from anti-aircraft guns and machine guns—flew directly over us, and dropped bombs near the special train.

The commanders of the army were unanimous in declaring that the spirit of the troops at the front was good and reliable ; that, further to the rear, among the supply columns, it was not so good ; that the worst of all were the soldiers back from leave, who, it was plain to be seen, had been worked upon and infected at home, whence they had brought back a poor spirit. The young recruits at the depots, it was stated furthermore, were good.

At Spa, whither I now went, news came constantly from home of the ever increasing violent agitations and hostile attitude against the Emperor, and of the growing slackness and helplessness of the Government, which, without initiative or strength, was letting itself be pushed around at will. It was alluded to contemptuously in the newspapers as the " debating society," and Prince Max was called by leading newspapers the " Revolution Chancellor." As I learned afterwards, he lay in bed for ten days, suffering from influenza and was incapable of really directing affairs. His Excellency von Payer and Solf, together with the so-called War Cabinet, which was in permanent session, governed the German Empire.

8

It seemed to me that at such a critical time, the imperilled ship of State should not be steered by representatives of the Imperial Chancellor, inasmuch as they certainly could not have the authority possessed by the responsible head of the Government. What was particularly needed at this juncture was authority; yet, so far as I know, no wide powers to act had been conferred upon the vice-chancellor.

The right solution—i.e. the one that those concerned were in duty bound to adopt—would have been to set Prince Max aside as chancellor and summon in his place some man of strong personality. Seeing that we had the parliamentary form of Government it devolved upon the political parties to bring about the change in the chancellorship and present me with a successor to Prince Max. This did not occur.

§ 2

Now began the efforts of the Government and the Imperial Chancellor to induce me to abdicate. Drews, the Minister of the Interior, came to me at the behest of the chancellor, in order to supply me with information concerning the feeling in the country. He described the now well-known happenings in the Press, high finance and with the public, and laid emphasis on the fact that the Imperial Chancellor himself had adopted no definite attitude upon the question of my abdication, but, nevertheless, had sent him to me. Drews, in short, well-nigh suggested to me that I myself should decide to abdicate, in order that it might not appear that the Government had exerted pressure upon me.

I spoke to the minister about the fateful consequences of my abdication and asked how he, as a Prussian official, could reconcile such a suggestion with his oath as an official of his King. The minister grew embarrassed and excused himself by reference to the command of the Imperial Chancellor, who had been unable to find any other man for the task. I was informed later that Drews was one of the first officials to speak of the abdication of his master and King.

I refused to abdicate and declared that I would gather troops together and return with them in order to help the Government to maintain order in the land.

After that, Drews was received, in my presence, by Field Marshal von Hindenburg and General Gröner, whom he informed of the mission entrusted to him by the Imperial Chancellor, and by both of whom he was very sharply rebuked in the name of the army. Gröner's characterization of Prince Max, in particular, was expressed in such plain terms that I had to appease and comfort the minister.

The Field Marshal also called Drews's attention to the fact that, in the event of my abdication, the army would cease to fight and would disperse; that the majority of the officers, in particular, would probably resign and thus leave the army without leaders.

Soon after that I learned from one of my sons
that the Imperial Chancellor had tried to ascertain
whether he was prepared to undertake the mission
which subsequently was undertaken by Drews. My
son indignantly declined to suggest abdication to
his father.

In the meantime I had sent the chief of cabinet,
von Delbrück, to Berlin, in order to lay before the
chancellor a general address, also intended for publication, which should take the place of my address
to the ministry (not published by the chancellor),
deal more broadly with the matters taken up therein,
and make clear my attitude towards the Government and towards the new trend of public opinion.
At first the chancellor failed to publish this. Not
until several days later did he find himself forced
to permit publication, owing to a letter written
to him, as I afterwards learned, by the Empress.
Thereupon Herr von Delbrück informed me that
the address had made a good impression in Berlin,
and the Press had relieved the situation and tended
to quieten the people, so that the idea of abdication had begun to disappear and that even the
Socialists of the Right had decided to postpone
action concerning it.

During the next few days there were constant
reports that the Socialists in Berlin were planning
trouble and that the chancellor was steadily growing
more nervous. The report given by Drews to the
Government after his return from Spa, had not
failed to cause an impression ; the gentlemen cer-

tainly wished to get rid of me, but, for the time being, they were scared of the consequences.

Their point of view was as obscure as their conduct. They acted as if they did not want a republic, yet failed completely to realize that their course was bound to lead straight to a republic. Many, in fact, explained the action of the Government by maintaining that the creation of a republic was the very end that its members had in view; from the puzzling conduct of the chancellor towards me plenty of people drew the conclusion that he was working to eliminate me in order to become himself President of the German Republic, after being, in the interim, the administrator of the Empire.

To believe this is undoubtedly to do the prince an injustice; such a train of thought is impossible in a man belonging to an old German princely family.

General Gröner—who had gone to Berlin to study the situation—reported on his return that he had formed very bad impressions regarding the Government and the sentiment prevailing in the country; that matters were drifting to revolution; that the Government was merely tearing down without setting up anything positive; that the people at any cost wanted peace, no matter what kind of peace; that the authority of the Government was down to zero, the agitation against the Emperor in full swing, and that my abdication could scarcely be avoided longer.

He added that the troops at home were unreliable and disagreeable surprises might come in case of a revolt; that the courier chests of the Russian Bolshevik Ambassador, seized by the criminal police, had disclosed some very damaging evidence that the Russian Embassy, in conjunction with the Spartacus group, had long since thoroughly prepared, without being disturbed, a Bolshevik revolution on the Russian model. (This had gone on with the knowledge of the Foreign Office—which had received constant warnings, but had either laughed at them all or dismissed them with the remark that the Bolsheviki must not be angered; likewise under the very eyes of the police, who were continually at loggerheads with the Foreign Office.) The men back from leave, he went on, infected by propaganda, had carried the poison to the army, which was already partially affected and would, as soon as it had been made free by an armistice, refuse to fight against the rebels upon its return home.

Therefore, he declared, it was necessary to accept immediately and unconditionally, any sort of armistice, no matter how hard its conditions might be; that the army was no longer to be trusted and revolution was imminent behind the front.

On the morning of the 9th of November* the Imperial Chancellor, Prince Max of Baden, caused me again to be informed—as he had already done on the 7th—that the Social Democrats, and also

---

* Concerning the course of events up to the fateful 9th of November and this day itself there are authentic statements by an eye-witness in the book (well worth reading) of Lieutenant-Colonel Niemann, who was sent by the Chief Army Command to me, entitled "War and Revolution" ("Krieg und Revolution"); Berlin, 1922.

the Social Democratic secretaries of State, demanded my abdication; that the rest of the members of the Government, who had stood out so far against it, were now in favour of it, and that the same was true of the majority parties in the Reichstag. For these reasons, he continued, he requested me to abdicate immediately, or, otherwise, extensive street fighting attended by bloodshed would take place in Berlin; it had already commenced on a small scale.

I immediately summoned Field Marshal von Hindenburg and the Quartermaster-General, General Gröner. General Gröner again announced that the army could fight no longer and desired rest above all else, and that, therefore, any sort of armistice must be unconditionally accepted; that the armistice must be concluded as soon as possible, inasmuch as the army had supplies for only six to eight days more and was cut off from all further supplies by the rebels, who had occupied all the supply storehouses and Rhine bridges; that, for some unexplained reason, the armistice commission sent to France—consisting of Erzberger, Ambassador Count Oberndorff and General von Winterfeldt—which had crossed the French lines two evenings before had sent no report as to the nature of the conditions.

The Crown Prince also appeared, with his Chief of Staff, Count Schulenburg, and took part in the conference. During our conversation several telephone inquiries came from the Imperial Chancellor which, pointing out that the Social Democrats had left the Government and that delay was dangerous, became most insistent. The Minister of War reported uncertainty among part of the troops in Berlin—4th Jägers, Second Company Alexander Regiment, Second Battery, Jüterbog, gone over to the rebels — no street fighting.

I wished to spare my people civil war. If my abdication was indeed the only way to prevent bloodshed, I was willing to *renounce the Imperial throne, but not to abdicate as King of Prussia*; I would remain, as such, with my troops, for the military leaders had declared that if I abdicated completely the officers would leave in crowds, and the army would then pour back, without leaders, into the Fatherland, damage it, and place it in peril.

A reply had been sent to the Imperial Chancellor to the effect that my decision must first be carefully weighed and formulated, after which it would be transmitted to him. When, a little later, this was done, there came the surprising answer that my decision had arrived too late! The Imperial Chancellor, on his own initiative, had summarily announced my abdication—which had not yet occurred!—as well as the renunciation of the throne by the Crown Prince—who had not even been questioned! He had turned over the Government to the Social Democrats and summoned Herr Ebert as Imperial Chancellor. All this had been spread by wireless, so that the entire army could read of it.

Thus the decision as to my going or staying, as to my renunciation of the Imperial Crown and retention of the Royal Crown of Prussia, was summarily snatched from me. The army was shaken to the core by the erroneous belief that its King had abandoned it at the most critical moment of all.

If the conduct of the Imperial Chancellor, Prince Max of Baden is considered as a whole, it appears as follows : first, solemn declaration that he will place himself, together with the new Government, before the Emperor's throne, to protect it ; then, suppression of the address—which might have impressed public opinion favourably—elimination of the Emperor from all co-operation in the Government, sacrifice of the respect due to the Emperor by suppression of the censorship ; failure to come to the support of the monarchy in the matter of abdication ; then, attempts to persuade the Emperor to abdicate voluntarily ; and, finally, announcement of my abdication by wireless, in which the chancellor went over my head.

This sequence of events shows the course—a perilous one to the nation—adopted by Scheidemann, who held the chancellor in the hollow of his hand. Scheidemann left his colleagues in the dark as to his real purpose, drove the prince from one step to another and finally summoned Ebert, declaring that the leaders no longer had the masses under control. Thus he caused the prince to sacrifice the Emperor, the princes and the empire, and made him the destroyer of the empire. After that, Scheidemann overthrew the weak princely " statesman."

The situation following the arrival of the wireless message was difficult. It is true that troops were being transported to Spa for the purpose of carrying on undisturbed the work at Great Central Headquarters, but the Field Marshal now thought it no longer possible to reckon absolutely on their reliability in case rebellious forces should advance from Aix-la-Chapelle and Cologne, and confront our troops with the dilemma of whether or not to fight against their own comrades. In view of this he advised me to leave the army and go to some neutral country, for the purpose of avoiding " civil war."

I went through a fearful mental struggle. On the one hand, I, as a soldier, was outraged at the idea of abandoning my still faithful, brave troops. On the other hand, there was the declaration of our foes that they were unwilling to conclude with me any peace endurable to Germany, as well as the statement of my own Government that only by my departure for foreign parts was civil war to be prevented.

In this struggle I set aside all personal considerations. I consciously sacrificed myself and my throne in the belief that by so doing I was best serving the interests of my beloved Fatherland. The sacrifice was in vain. My departure brought us neither better armistice conditions nor better peace terms, nor did it prevent civil war ; on the contrary, it hastened and intensified, in the most pernicious manner, the disintegration of the army and the nation.

For thirty years the army was my pride. For it I lived, upon it I laboured, and now, after four and a half brilliant years of war with unprecedented

victories, it was forced to collapse by the stab in
the back from the dagger of the revolutionists, at
the very moment when peace was within reach!

The fact that it was in my navy, my proud
creation, that there was first open rebellion, cut me
most deeply to the heart.

§ 3

There has been much talk about my having
abandoned the army and gone to neutral foreign
parts.

Some say that the Emperor should have gone
to some regiment at the front, hurled himself with it
upon the enemy, and sought death in one last attack.
That would not only have rendered impossible the
armistice, ardently desired by the nation, concerning which the commission sent from Berlin to General
Foch was already negotiating, but would also have
meant the useless sacrifice of the lives of many
soldiers—of some of the very best and most faithful,
in fact.

Others say that the Emperor should have returned
home at the head of the army. But a peaceful
return was no longer possible ; the rebels had already
seized the Rhine bridges and other important points
in the rear of the army. Certainly, I could have
forced my way back at the head of loyal troops
taken from the fighting front, but, by so doing, I
should have put the finishing touch to Germany's

collapse, because, in addition to the struggle with the enemy who would certainly have pressed forward in pursuit, civil war would also have ensued.

Still others say that the Emperor should have killed himself. That was made impossible by my firm Christian beliefs; and would not people have exclaimed : " How cowardly ! Now he shirks all responsibility by committing suicide ! " This alternative was also eliminated, because I had to consider how to help and be useful to my people and my country in the evil time that was to be foreseen.

I knew also that I was particularly called upon to champion the cause of my people in the clearing up of the question of war-guiltiness—which was disclosing itself more and more as the pivotal point in our future destiny—for, better than anyone else, I could bear witness to Germany's desire for peace and to our clear conscience.

After unspeakably arduous soul-struggles, and following the most urgent advice of my counsellors of the highest rank who were present at the moment, I decided to leave the country, for, in view of the reports made to me, I must needs believe that, by so doing, I should most faithfully serve Germany, make possible better armistice and peace terms for her, and spare her further loss of human life, distress and misery.

XIII

THE ENEMY TRIBUNAL AND THE NEUTRAL TRIBUNAL

WHEN the Entente's demand became known that I and the German army leaders should be surrendered for trial before Entente tribunals, I immediately asked myself whether I could be of use to my Fatherland by giving myself up before the German people and the German Government had expressed themselves regarding this demand. It was clear to me that, in the opinion of the Entente, such a surrender would so seriously shake for all time the prestige of Germany as a State and a people, that we could never again take our place with equal rights, equal dignity and equal title to alliances, in the first rank of nations, where we belonged. I recognized it as my duty not to sacrifice the honour and dignity of Germany. The question resolved itself into deciding whether there was any way to give myself up which might benefit the German nation and not subject it to the above-mentioned disadvantages. Had there been such a way, I should have been ready without hesitation to add yet another sacrifice to those I had already made.

The question of my giving myself up has been—as I know—debated well-meaningly and earnestly

in German circles.   Wherever this was due to psycho-
logical depression or failure to realize the impression
which self-chastisement, self-debasement and fruitless martyrdom in the face of the Entente must arouse,
all that was needed was to recall the distinctly political origin of the Entente's demand, to which I
have incidentally referred, in order to arrive at a
clean-cut decision—in other words, at an emphatic
refusal.

It was otherwise with the considerations based
upon the assumption that I might, by taking upon
myself before the eyes of the whole world, the responsibility for all important decisions and acts of my
Government connected with the war, assist towards
making easier the fate of the German nation.   Here
was not an act of non-political sentimentality but, on
the contrary, a deed which in my view had much to
commend it.   The consideration that according to the
Constitution of the Empire then in force, not I, but
the chancellor alone—as was well known—bore the
responsibility, would naturally not have bothered
me.

Had there been even the slightest prospect of
bettering Germany's situation by taking such a step,
there would have been no possible doubt for me
personally as to what I should do.   Already I had
shown my willingness to sacrifice myself when I
left the country and gave up the throne of my
fathers, because I had been erroneously and deceiv-
ingly assured that I could, by so doing, make possible better peace terms for my people, and prevent

civil war. I should likewise have made this further attempt to help my people, despite the fact that in the meantime one of the considerations that had been urged upon me in its favour—viz. : the prevention of civil war—had already proved to be false.

There was, however, no possibility of helping the German people by such an act. Surrender of my person would have had no result beyond our obedience to the demand from the Entente that I should be given up, for no tribunal in the world can pronounce a just sentence before the State archives of *all* the nations participating in the war are thrown open, as has been done, and is still being done by Germany.

Who, after the unprecedented judgment of Versailles, could still summon up optimism enough to believe that the Entente nations would place their secret documents at the disposal of such a tribunal ! After careful reflection on my part, therefore, I gave the decisive importance that was their due to the above-mentioned weighty considerations of personal and national dignity and honour, and rejected the idea of giving myself up. It was not for me to play the role of Vercingetorix, who, as is well known, relying upon the magnanimity of his foes, surrendered himself to them in order to obtain a better fate for his people. In view of the conduct of our enemies during the war and in the peace negotiations, it was surely not to be assumed that the Entente would show any greater magnanimity than did Cæsar when he threw the noble Gaul into chains, subsequently had him executed, and, in spite of what Vercingetorix had done, enslaved his people just the same.

I wish to remark in a general way that it has always proved wrong to follow the suggestions of the enemy or even to heed them to any extent. The well-meant suggestions regarding my giving myself up that emanated from Germans, germinated in the soil of the enemy demands, though perhaps this was but partly known to those who made them. For that very reason it was necessary to refuse to heed them.

Thus the only solution remaining is an international, non-partisan court, which, instead of trying individuals shall examine and pronounce judgment upon all the events that led up to the world war, in all the countries taking part therein, after all the national archives—not merely those of Germany— have been opened up. Germany can well agree to this mode of procedure. Whosoever opposes it pronounces judgment upon himself!

My standpoint on the subject here discussed is expressed in the letter, which I addressed, under date of April 5, 1921, to Field Marshal von Hindenburg, and which the latter in the meantime has made public. To make matters clearer, the letter which preceded it, from the marshal, is also given.*

---

* This letter and the letter from the Field Marshal which preceded it are here reprinted *in extenso*. The parts that are most important in relation to the matter in question are italicized in the text.

Hanover, March 30th, 1921.

Your Imperial and Royal Majesty :

I beg to thank Your Majesty most respectfully for his gracious interest in the illness of my wife. She is not yet out of danger.

I have little that is pleasant to report from our country. The troubles in Central Germany are more serious than they are represented to be by the Prussian Government. I hope that they will soon be suppressed.

The effects of the Versailles peace decree lie ever more crushingly upon the German people, and the object of this peace—our enemies' policy of annihilation—comes more plainly to the fore every day. For the purpose of justifying this policy of force the fairy tale of German war-guiltiness must be adhered to.

The spokesman of the enemy alliance, Mr. Lloyd George, is little disturbed by the fact that, on December 20 of last year, he declared that no statesman desired war in the summer of 1914, that all the nations had slipped or stumbled into it. In his speech at the London Conference on March 3 he calmly remarked that Germany's responsibility for the war was fundamental, that it was the basis on which the Peace of Versailles was erected, and that, if the admission of this guilt should be refused or withheld, the treaty would become untenable.

Now, as before, the question of war-guiltiness is the cardinal point in the future of the German nation.

T

The admission of our alleged " guilt " regarding the war, forced from the German representatives at Versailles against their judgment, is wreaking frightful vengeance; equally so the untrue acknowledgment of Germany's " complicity " which Minister Simons gave at the London Conference.

I agree with Your Majesty to the uttermost depths of my soul—in my long term of military service I have had the good fortune and honour to enter into close personal relations with Your Majesty. I know that the bent of all the efforts of Your Majesty throughout your reign were towards the maintenance of peace. I can realize how immeasurably hard it is for Your Majesty to be eliminated from active co-operation for the Fatherland.

The " Comparative Historical Tables " compiled by Your Majesty, a printed copy of which Your Majesty sent me recently, is a good contribution to the history of the origin of the war and is calculated to remove many an incorrect conception. I have regretted that Your Majesty did not make the tables public, but limited them instead to a small circle. Now that the tables, owing to indiscretions, have been published in the foreign Press, partly in the form of incomplete excerpts, it seems to me advisable to have them published in full in the German Press

To my great joy I have heard that there has been an improvement recently in the health of Her Majesty. May God help further !

With the deepest respect, unlimited fidelity and

gratitude, I am Your Imperial and Royal Majesty's most humble servant,

(signed) VON HINDENBURG, Field Marshal.

House Doorn, April 5th, 1921.

My Dear Field Marshal :

Accept my warmest thanks for your letter of March 30th ult. You are right. The hardest thing of all for me is to be obliged to live in foreign parts, to follow, with burning anguish in my soul, the awful fate of our dear Fatherland, to which I have devoted the labours of my entire life, and to be barred from co-operation on its behalf.

You stood beside me during the dark, fatal days of November, 1918. As you know, I forced myself to the difficult, terrible decision to leave the country only upon the urgent declaration of yourself and the rest of my counsellors who had been summoned, that only by my so doing would it be possible to obtain more favourable armistice terms for our people and spare it a bloody civil war.

The sacrifice was in vain. Now, as well as before, the enemy wishes to make the German people expiate the alleged guilt of " Imperial Germany."

In my endeavour to subordinate all personal considerations to the welfare of Germany I keep myself completely in the background. I am silent in the face of all the lies and slanders which are spread abroad concerning me. I consider it beneath my dignity to defend myself against attacks and abuse.

In accordance with this policy of restraint, I have also kept the " Historical Tables " mentioned by you strictly objective and made them accessible only to a narrow circle of acquaintances ; I am utterly at a loss to understand how they have now become public through some sort of indiscretion or theft (?). The purpose inspiring me when I prepared these tables was this : to bring together strictly historical material by a systematic enumeration of sober facts, such as might enable the reader to form his own judgment of the historical events preceding the war. I found my most convincing sources, be it remarked, in the literature which has sprung up after the war, particularly in the works of natives of the enemy countries. Therefore, I am glad that you find my modest contribution to history useful.

As to your suggestion to make the tables, which have been completed in the meantime, accessible to the German Press, I thank you and will follow it.*

Truth will hew a way for itself—mightily, irresistibly, like an avalanche. Whoever does not close his ears to it against his better judgment must admit that, during my twenty-six years' reign previous to the war, Germany's foreign policy was directed solely to the maintenance of peace. Its one and only aim was to protect our sacred native soil, threatened from the west and the east, and the peaceful development of our commerce and political economy.

* This has meanwhile been done. The " Comparative Historical Tables from 1878 to the Outbreak of the War in 1914 " were published in December, 1921, by K. F. Koehler, Leipzig.

Had we ever had warlike intentions we should have struck the blow in 1900, when England's hands were tied by the Boer War, Russia's by the Japanese War, at which time almost certain victory beckoned us. In any event, we assuredly would not have singled out the year 1914, when we were confronted by a compact, overwhelmingly superior foe. Also, every impartial man must acknowledge to himself that Germany could expect nothing from the war, whereas our enemies hoped to obtain from it the complete realization of the aims which they had based, long since, upon our annihilation.

The fact that my zealous efforts and those of my Government were concentrated during the critical July and August days of 1914 upon maintaining world peace, is being proved more and more conclusively by the most recent literary and documentary publications, in Germany and, most especially, in the enemy countries. The most effective proof thereof is Sazonoff's statement: " The German Emperor's love of peace is a guarantee to us that we ourselves can decide upon the moment of war." What further proof of our innocence is needed ? The above means that the intention existed to make an attack upon one who was absolutely unsuspecting.

God is my witness that, in order to avoid war, I went to the uttermost limit compatible with responsibility for the security and inviolability of my dear Fatherland.

It is futile to accuse Germany of war-guiltiness. To-day there is no longer any doubt that not Germany, but the alliance of her foes, prepared the war according to a definite plan, and intentionally caused it.

For the purpose of concealing this, the allied enemies extorted the false " admission of guilt " from Germany in the shameful peace treaty and demanded that I should *be produced before a hostile tribunal.* You, my dear Field Marshal, know me too well not to be aware that no sacrifice for my beloved Fatherland is too great for me. Nevertheless, *a tribunal in which the enemy alliance would be at once plaintiff and judge would be not an organ of justice but an instrument of political arbitrariness, and would serve only, through the sentence which would inevitably be passed upon me, to justify subsequently the unprecedented peace conditions imposed upon us.* Therefore, the enemy's demand naturally had to be rejected by me.

But, in addition, the idea of *my being produced before a neutral tribunal,* no matter how constituted, cannot be entertained by me. *I do not recognize the validity of any sentence pronounced by any mortal judge whatsoever, be he never so exalted in rank, upon the measures taken by me most conscientiously as Emperor and King—in other words, as the constitutional, not responsible, representative of the German nation*—because, were I to do so, I should thereby be sacrificing the honour and dignity of the German nation of which I was the representative.

Legal proceedings having to do with guilt and punishment, instituted solely *against the head* of one of the nations which took part in the war, *deprive that one nation of every vestige of equality of rights with the other nations,* and, thereby, of its prestige in the community of nations. Moreover, this would cause, as a consequence, *the impression desired by the enemy* that *the entire " question of guilt " concerns only this one head of a nation and the one nation represented by him.* It must be taken into consideration, moreover, that *a non-partisan judgment of the " question of guilt "* is impossible, if the *legal proceedings are not made to include the heads and leading statesmen of the enemy Powers,* and if their conduct is not subjected to the same investigation, for it goes without saying that the conduct of the aforesaid one nation at the outbreak of the war can only be judged correctly if there is simultaneous consideration of the actions of its opponents.

A *real clearing up of the " question of guilt,"* in which surely Germany would have no less interest than her foes, could be accomplished only if *an international, non-partisan tribunal, instead of trying individuals as criminals, should establish all the events which led to the world war,* as well as all other offences against international law, in order, thereafter, to measure correctly the guilt of individuals implicated in every one of the nations participating in the war.

Such an honest suggestion was officially made by Germany after the end of the war, but, so far as I know, it was partly refused, partly found unworthy of any answer at all. Furthermore, Germany immediately after the war unreservedly threw open her archives, whereas the enemy alliance so far has taken good care not to follow such an example. The secret documents from the Russian archives, now being made public in America, are but the beginning.

This method of procedure on the part of the enemy alliance in itself, combined with overwhelming damaging evidence coming to hand, shows where the " war-guiltiness " is really to be sought! This makes it all the more a solemn duty for Germany to collect, sift, and make public, by every possible means, every bit of material bearing on the " question of guilt," in order, by so doing, to unmask the real originators of the war.

Unfortunately, the condition of Her Majesty has become worse. My heart is filled with the most grievous worry.

God with us!

Your grateful,
(signed) WILHELM.

XIV

THE QUESTION OF GUILT

§ 1

HISTORY can show nothing to compare with the world war of 1914–18. It can also show nothing like the perplexity which has arisen as to the causes leading up to that war. This is all the more astounding in that the great war befell a highly cultivated, enlightened, politically trained race of men and the causes leading up to it were plainly evident.

The apparent complicity in the crisis of July, 1914, should deceive nobody. The telegrams exchanged at that time between the cabinets of the Great Powers and their rulers, the activities of statesmen and leading private individuals in verbal negotiations with important personages of the Entente, were certainly of the greatest importance because of the decisive significance assumed by almost every word that came from responsible lips, by every line that was written or telegraphed. The essential basis of the causes of the war, however, is not altered by such things ; it is firmly established and people must never hesitate from freeing it—calmly and with an eye to facts—from the bewildering outcroppings arising from the events that accompanied the outbreak of war.

The general situation of the German Empire in the period before the war had become increasingly brilliant and, for that very reason, increasingly difficult from the point of view of foreign politics. Unprecedented progress in industry, commerce, and world traffic had made Germany prosperous. The curve of our development tended steadily upward.

The concomitant of this peaceful penetration of a considerable part of the world's markets, to which German diligence and achievement justly entitled us — was bound to be unwelcome to the older nations of the world, particularly to England. This is quite a natural phenomenon, with nothing remarkable about it. Nobody is pleased when a competitor suddenly appears and compels one to look on while old customers desert to the new-comer. For this reason I cannot reproach the British Empire because of English ill-humour at Germany's progress in the world's markets.

Had England, by introducing better commercial methods, been able to restrict or even overcome German competition, she would have been quite within her rights in so doing and no objections could have been raised. It would simply have been a case of the better man winning. In the life of nations nobody can find it objectionable if two of them contend peacefully against each other by the same methods — i.e. peaceful methods—yet with all their energy, daring and organizing ability, each striving to benefit itself.

On the other hand, it is quite another matter if one of these nations, realizing that its assets on the world's balance-sheet are threatened by the industry, achievements and superior business methods of the other, and not being in a position to apply ability equal to that of its young competitor, resorts to force —i.e. to methods that are not peaceful but war-like—in order to call a halt upon the other nation in its peaceful campaign of competition, or to attempt to annihilate it.

Our situation became more serious when we were obliged to build a navy for the protection of our interests, which, in the last analysis, were not based on the nineteen billions yearly to which German exports and imports amounted. The supposition that we built this navy for the purpose of attacking and destroying the far stronger English fleet is absurd, for owing to the discrepancy of strength between the two navies it would have been impossible for us to win a victory on the water. Moreover, we were striding forward in the world's markets in accordance with our desires and had no cause for complaint. Why, then, should we wish to jeopardize the results of our peaceful labours ?

In France, the idea of revenge had been sedulously cultivated ever since 1870–71 ; it was fostered with every possible variation in literary, political and military writings, in the officer corps, in schools, associations, and political circles.

I can well understand this spirit. Looked at from the healthy national standpoint, it is, after all, more honourable for a nation to desire revenge for a blow received than to endure it without complaint.

But Alsace-Lorraine has been German soil for many centuries ; it was stolen by France and taken back by us in 1871 as our property. Hence, a war of revenge which had as its aim the conquest of thoroughly German territory was unjust and immoral. For us to have yielded on this point would have been a slap in the face to our sentiments of nationality and justice. Since Germany could never voluntarily return Alsace-Lorraine to France, the French dream could only be realized by means of a victorious war, which would push forward the French frontier-posts to the left bank of the Rhine. Germany, on the contrary, had no reason for staking what she had won in 1870–71, so the course for her to pursue was to maintain peace with France, all the more so because the combination of the Powers against the German-Austro Dual Alliance was becoming ever more apparent.

As to Russia, the mighty empire of the Tsars was clamouring for an outlet to the sea in the south. This was a natural ambition and not to be judged harshly. In addition, there was the Russian-Austrian conflict of influence, especially in Serbia, which also concerned Germany, in so far as Germany and Austria-Hungary were allies.

The Russia of the Tsars, moreover, was in a state of continual internal ferment and every Tsaristic Government had ever to be prepared with a possible war, in order to be able to deflect attention from her internal troubles to foreign difficulties ; to have a safety-valve as an outlet for the passions that might lead to trouble at home.

Another point was that Russia's enormous demand for loans was met almost exclusively by France; more than twenty billions of French gold francs found their way to Russia, and France, to some extent, had a voice in determining how they should be expended. As a result the matter resolved itself entirely into one of expenditure on strategic measures and preparations for war. The golden chain of the French billions not only bound Russia to France financially but forced Russia to serve the French idea of revenge.

Thus England, France and Russia had—though for different reasons—one aim in common, viz.: to overthrow Germany. England wished to do so for commercial-political reasons, France on account of, her policy of revenge, Russia because she was a satellite of France, for reasons of internal politics and because she wished to reach the southern sea. These three great nations, therefore, were bound to act together. The union of these ambitions in a common course of action, duly planned, is what we call the "policy of encirclement."

In addition to all this there was also the "Gentlemen's Agreement," which has only recently come to light and has already been thoroughly discussed in the "Hohenlohe" chapter of this book. Of this agreement I knew absolutely nothing during my reign and the German Foreign Office was only superficially and unreliably informed.

When I learned of it I immediately sought information concerning it from Herr von Bethmann. He wrote me a rather puzzling letter to the effect that there certainly was something about it among the documents of the Foreign Office; that the German Ambassador at that time in Washington, von Holleben, had undoubtedly made a confidential report on it, but as he had not given his source of information the Foreign Office had not attached any importance to the matter and had not reported further on it to me. Hence the said agreement actually had no influence upon Germany's policy, but it constitutes supplementary proof that the Anglo-Saxon world, as far back as 1897, had combined against us and therein is explained a number of obstacles encountered by Germany in her foreign policy. It also explains America's attitude in the war.

On the other hand we were quite well acquainted with the Entente Cordiale, its foundations and its purposes, and it decisively influenced the course of our policy.

In view of the grouping of England, France and Russia—three very strong Powers—only one political course lay open to Germany; the threat of deciding Germany's future by force of arms must be avoided until we had secured for ourselves such an economic, military, naval and politically national position in the world as to make it seem advisable to our opponents to refrain from risking a decision by arms, and to yield us the share in the apportionment and management of the world to which our ability entitled us. We neither desired nor were we entitled to jeopardize our hard-won position.

The aims of the Entente could be attained only through a war, those of Germany only without a war. It is necessary to hold fast to this basic idea; it is of more decisive value than all accessory matters; hence I shall not here go into detail, nor deal with Belgian or other reports, nor the telegrams sent just before the outbreak of war. The thorough treatment of these details lies in the domain of research.

In Germany our situation was correctly understood and we acted accordingly.

§ 2

To refer once more to our relations with England. We did everything in our power to bring about a *rapprochement*; we consented to the demand for limitation of naval construction, as I have shown in my report of Haldane's visit to Berlin. I even went so far as to try to utilize my family connexions. But in vain. The actions of King Edward VII are explained by the simple fact that he was an Englishman and was trying to bring to realization the plans of his Government. Maybe the political ambition of the King, who did not begin to reign until well on in years, contributed to this.

We certainly did all that was possible to meet England half-way, but it was useless because the German export figures showed an increase; naturally we could not limit our world-commerce in order to satisfy England. That was asking too much.

As regards our policy towards England, we have been much blamed for refusing the offer of an alliance made to us by Chamberlain, the English Colonial Minister, towards the close of the 'nineties. On closer examination, however, this matter proved far different in character from what it was represented to be.

Firstly, Chamberlain brought with him a letter from Salisbury, the English Premier, to Bülow, which contained the declaration that Chamberlain was acting on his own account only, that the English Cabinet was not behind him. This certainly might have meant the adoption of a course that was diplomatically permissible, and gave a free hand to the English Cabinet which was responsible to Parliament; but it turned out later, be it remarked, that the Liberal Party in England was at that time hostile to a German-English alliance.

Nevertheless, in view of the possibility that the course adopted was a mere diplomatic formality—that Chamberlain might have been sent on ahead and complete freedom of action retained for the English Cabinet (which is a favourite method in London)—Prince Bülow, with my consent, went thoroughly into the matter with Chamberlain.

It then transpired that the English-German alliance was unquestionably aimed at Russia. Chamberlain spoke openly about a war to be waged later by England and Germany against Russia. Prince Bülow, in full agreement with me, declined politely but emphatically thus to disturb the peace of Europe. In so doing he was but following the lead of the great chancellor in the phrase coined by Prince Bismarck—I myself have heard it repeatedly in the Bismarck family circle—" Germany must never become England's dagger on the European continent."

So we did nothing further at that time than to go straight ahead with our policy; that is to say, we refused all agreements which might lead to a war that was not based directly on the defence of our native soil. The refusal of the Chamberlain offer is a proof of the German love of peace.

As to France, we sought to bring about an endurable state of affairs. This was difficult, for, in French eyes, we were the arch-enemy and it was impossible for us to acquiesce in the demands inspired by the policy of revenge. We settled the Morocco quarrel peacefully; no man of standing in Germany entertained the idea of war on account of Morocco. For the sake of peace we allowed France at that time to encroach upon the essentially legitimate interests of Germany in Morocco—strengthened as the French were by the agreement concluded secretly with England as to mutual compensation in Egypt and Morocco.

At the Algeciras Conference the shadow of the Great War was already visible. It is assuredly not pleasant to be forced to retreat politically as we did in the Morocco matter, but Germany's policy subordinated everything to the great cause of preserving the peace of the world.

We tried to attain this end by courtesy, which

U

was partially resented. I recall the journey of my mother, the Empress Frederick, to Paris. We expected for her a tolerably good reception, seeing that she was an English princess and went, as an artist, to be the guest of French art circles. Twice I visited the Empress Eugénie; once, from Aldershot, at her residence of Farnborough Hill, the other time aboard her yacht, in Norwegian waters, near Bergen. These were acts of politeness that seemed to me perfectly natural, seeing that I happened to be very near her. When the French General Bonnal was in Berlin with several officers, these gentlemen dined with the Second Infantry Regiment. I was present and toasted the French army—something that was quite out of the ordinary, but it was done with the best intentions. I brought French female and male artists to Germany. All these things, of course, were but trifles in the great game of politics, but they at least showed our good will.

With Russia I went to the utmost trouble. My letters, which in the meantime have been published, naturally were never sent without the knowledge of the Imperial Chancellors, but always in agreement with them and largely at their desire. Russia would doubtless never have gone to war with Germany under Alexander III, for he was reliable. Tsar Nicholas was weak and vacillating; whoever was last with him was right; and it was impossible, of course, for me always to be that individual.

With this Tsar, too, I made every effort to restore the traditional friendship between Germany and

Russia. I was moved to do so, not only by political reasons, but by the promise which I had made to my grandfather on his death-bed.

I repeatedly most urgently advised Tsar Nicholas to introduce liberal reforms in his country, to summon the so-called Great Duma, which existed and functioned even as far back as the reign of Ivan the Terrible. In doing so it was not my intention to interfere in Russian internal affairs; what I wanted was to eliminate, in the interests of Germany, the ferment going on in Russia, which had often enough been deflected to foreign conflicts, as I have already described. I wished to help towards the elimination of, at least, this one phase of the internal situation in Russia, which threatened to cause war, and I was all the more willing to make the effort since I might thereby serve both the Tsar and Russia.

The Tsar paid no heed to my advice, but instead, created a new Duma which was quite inadequate to cope with the situation. Had he summoned the old Duma he might have dealt and talked personally with all the representatives of his huge realm and won their confidence.

When the Tsar resolved upon war against Japan I told him that I would cause him no annoyance and assure him security in the rear, and Germany kept this promise.

When the course taken by the war did not fulfil the Tsar's expectations, and the Russian and Japanese armies finally lay before each other for weeks without serious fighting, the young brother of the Tsar, the

Grand Duke Michael, arrived at Berlin on a visit. We could not quite make out what he wanted. Prince Bülow, who was then chancellor, requested me at some time to ask the Grand Duke how matters really stood with Russia; the prince said that he had received bad news and thought it was high time for Russia to bring the war to an end.

I undertook this mission. The Grand Duke was visibly relieved when I spoke frankly to him; he declared that things looked bad for Russia. I told him that it seemed to me that the Tsar ought soon to make peace, for what the Grand Duke told me about the unreliability of troops and officers appeared to me quite as serious as the renewed internal agitation.

The Grand Duke Michael was grateful for my having given him an opportunity to talk. He said that the Tsar was vacillating as always, but he must make peace and would make it if I advised him to do so. He asked me to write a few lines to the Tsar to that effect for him to deliver.

I drafted a letter in English to Tsar Nicholas, went to Bülow, told him what the Grand Duke had said to me and showed him the draft of my letter. The prince thanked me and found the letter suitable. The Grand Duke informed the Russian Ambassador in Berlin, Count Osten-Sacken, and, after he had repeatedly expressed his thanks, went direct to the Tsar, who then had peace negotiations opened.

When next we met, Count Osten-Sacken told me that I had done Russia a great service. I was glad that this was recognized, and, on account of it, felt justified in hoping that my conduct would contribute towards the bringing about of friendly relations with Russia. In acting as I did, I also worked towards the prevention, during the Russo-Japanese war, of the possible spread of a Russian revolution across the frontiers of Germany. Germany earned no thanks thereby. Our conduct during the Russo-Japanese War, however, is another proof of our love of peace.

The same purpose underlay my suggestion which led to the Björkö Agreement (July, 1905). It contemplated an alliance between Germany and Russia, which other nations should be at liberty to join. Ratification of this agreement failed through the opposition of the Russian Government (Isvolsky).

§ 3

It remains to say a few words about America. Apart from the " Gentlemen's Agreement " already mentioned—which assured America's standing beside England and France in a world war—America did not belong to the Entente Cordiale created by King Edward VII, at the behest of his Government, and, most important of all, America, in so far as it is possible at present to judge events, did not contribute towards bringing on the world war. Perhaps the unfriendly answer given by President Wilson to the German Government at the beginning of the war may have had some connexion with the " Gentlemen's Agreement."

There can be no doubt, however, that America's entry into the war, and her supply of enormous quantities of ammunition and other war material, which preceded her entry, seriously affected the chance of the Central Powers to bring the war to a successful termination by force of arms.

It is necessary, however, to avoid all emotional criticism of America, because, in the great game of politics, real factors only can be considered. America was at liberty (despite the " Gentlemen's Agreement ") to remain neutral or to enter the war on the other side. One cannot reproach a nation for a decision as to war or peace made in accordance with its sovereign rights, so long as the decision is not a violation of definite agreements. Such is not the case here.

Nevertheless, it must be noted that John Kenneth Turner, in his previously mentioned book, " Shall it Be Again ? " gives extensive proofs that all Wilson's reasons for America's entry into the war were fictitious ; that it was far more a case of acting solely in the interest of Wall Street high finance.

The great profit derived by America from the world war is evident in the fact that the United States was able to attract to itself nearly 50 per cent. of the world's gold, so that the dollar, instead of the English pound, now determines the world's rate of exchange. Here again no reproach is justified, for any other nation in a position to do so would have rejoiced in attracting to itself this increase of gold, and its consequent paramount prestige in the world's money-market. It was certainly regrettable for us that America did not effect this stroke of business with the Central Powers.

In the same way that Germany objects, with perfect justification, to having had her peaceful labours contested by the Entente not by peaceful but by warlike means, so also she can and must enter constant protest—as she is already trying to do by means of the publication of material—against America's violation of right at the close of the world war.

Personally, I do not believe that the American people would have consented to this ; American women particularly would not have participated in the denial of President Wilson's Fourteen Points if at that time they could have been enlightened as to the facts. America, more than any other country, had been misled by English propaganda, and therefore allowed President Wilson, who had been provided with unprecedented powers, to act on his own initiative at Paris—in other words, to be beaten down on his Fourteen Points. Just as later on Mr. Wilson omitted mention of the English blockade, against which he had previously protested, so also he acted with regard to his Fourteen Points.

The German Government had accepted Wilson's Fourteen Points, although they were severe enough. The Allies likewise had accepted the Fourteen Points, with the exception of those dealing with reparations and the freedom of the seas. Wilson had guaranteed the Fourteen Points.

I fail to find the most important of them in the Versailles instrument, but only such as expressed the Entente's policy of violence, and even parts of these in a greatly falsified form. Relying on Wilson's guarantee, Germany evacuated the enemy territory occupied by her and surrendered her weapons—in other words, made herself defenceless. In this blind confidence and the abandonment of the Fourteen Points on the one side, and in the outbreak of the German Revolution on the other, lies the key to our present condition. According to Turner, as far back as the drawing up of the armistice terms the Fourteen Points were to Wilson no more than a means of making Germany lay down her arms ; as soon as this end was achieved, he dropped them.

A very large section of the American people has already arrayed itself against Mr. Wilson and is unwilling to be discredited along with him. I am not dreaming of spontaneous American help for Germany ; all I count upon is the sober acknowledgment by the American people that it has to make good the gigantic wrong done to Germany by its former president. For the atmosphere of a victory does not last for ever and, later on, not only in Germany but elsewhere, people will remember the unreliability of the American President and consider it rather as American national unreliability.

That is not a good thing for the American people. To have the policy of a nation branded with the stigma of unreliability is not advantageous. When hereafter judgment is passed on American policy, people will forget that Mr. Wilson, unversed in the ways of the world, was trapped by Lloyd George and Clemenceau.

I have met—particularly at the Kiel Regatta—many American men and women whose political judgment and caution would make it impossible for them to approve such a flagrant breach of faith as was committed by Mr. Wilson, because of its effect on America's political prestige. It is upon such considerations of national egotism, and not upon any of a sentimental nature, that I base my hope that Germany's burden will be lightened from across the ocean.

Besides the injustice in the abandonment of the Fourteen Points, it must also be remembered that Mr. Wilson was the first to demand the voluntary withdrawal of the German reigning dynasty; in doing so he hinted that if such action were taken, the German people would be granted a better peace. It is very probable at that time that Mr. Wilson was already under the dominant influence of France. Before the Government of Prince Max joined in the demand for my abdication of the throne, which it based on the same grounds as Mr. Wilson—that Germany would thereby get better terms (prevention of civil war was used as a second means of bringing pressure on me)—it was in duty bound to get some sort of a binding guarantee from Mr. Wilson. At all events, the statements made, which became increasingly urgent and pressing, contributed towards my determination to quit the country, for I was constrained to believe that by so doing I could render my country a great service.

I subordinated my own interests and those of my dynasty—which certainly were not unimportant—and after the severest mental struggles forced myself to acquiesce in the wish of the German authorities. It transpired later that the German Government had obtained no real guarantees, but in the tumultuous sequence of events during those days, it was necessary for me to consider the unequivocal and definite announcement of the Imperial Chancellor as authoritative. For this reason I did not investigate it.

Why the Entente, through Mr. Wilson, demanded my abdication is now obvious. It felt perfectly sure that, following my dispossession of the throne, military and political instability would necessarily ensue and thus enable it to force upon Germany not easier but harder terms. At that time the revolution had not yet appeared as an aid to the Entente.

For me to have remained on the throne would have seemed to the Entente more advantageous to Germany than my abdication. I myself agree with this view of the Entente, now that it has turned out that Max of Baden's Government had no substantial foundation for its declaration that my abdication would secure better terms for my Fatherland.

I go even further and declare that the Entente would never have dared to offer such terms to an intact German Empire. It would not have dared to offer them to an Imperial realm upon which the parliamentary system had not yet been forced with the help of German Utopians, at the very moment of its final fight for existence ; to a realm whose monarchical government had not been deprived of the power to command its army and navy.

In view of all this, heavy guilt also lies on the shoulders of the American ex-President as a result of his having demanded my abdication under the pretence that it would secure better terms for Germany. Here also we certainly have a point of support for the powerful lever which is destined to drag the Treaty of Versailles from where it lies behind lock and key. In Germany, however, Mr. Wilson should never be confused with the American people.

§ 4

In setting forth my political principles in what follows, I am actuated solely by a desire to help towards proving Germany's innocence of having brought on the world war.

From the outset of my reign German policy was based upon compromise of the differences which it found existing between nations. My policy, in its entirety, therefore, was eminently peaceful. This policy of peaceful compromise became apparent in internal politics, at the very beginning of my reign, in the legislation prompted by me for the protection of the workers. The development of social legislation

—which placed Germany at the head of civilized nations in the domain of governmental protection— was based on a similar foundation.

The fundamental idea of a policy of compromise went so far in Germany, that the strength of the army remained far lower than universal compulsory military service and the increase of the population made possible. Here, as well as in the matter of naval construction, the curtailments demanded by the Reichstag were put up with by the Crown and the Government. Already at that time the question of Germany's capabilities of defence was left to the decision of the people's representatives. A nation that desired and prepared for war would have adopted quite different tactics.

The more apparent the Entente's policy of encirclement and attack became, the more the defensive means of protecting our welfare should have been strengthened. This idea of natural and justified self-protection, by means of defensive measures against a possible hostile attack, was carried out in a wretchedly inadequate manner.

Germany's desire for peace, in fact, hindered the development of these protective measures by land and sea in a manner compatible with her financial and national strength, and increased the risk which our welfare was bound to run in the event of war. We are now suffering, therefore, not from the consequences of the tendency towards aggression falsely imputed to us, but actually from the consequences of a blind confidence and a well-nigh incredible love of peace.

The entirely different political principles of the Entente have already been described by me, also our continuous efforts to live on friendly terms with the individual Entente nations.

I do not wish to ignore completely the less important work done by Germany, under the same inspiration as that accomplished on a greater scale in the field of politics, to effect a compromise on existing points of conflict. The Kiel Regatta brought us guests from all the leading nations. We sought compromise on the neutral territory of sport with the same zeal as in the domain of science by means of exchanges of professors, and foreign officers were most willingly allowed to inspect our army system. On looking back the latter might be adjudged a mistake, but, in any case, all these points are certain proofs of our honest desire to live at peace with all men.

Germany, moreover, did not take advantage of a single one of the opportunities that arose for waging war with a sure prospect of success.

I have already referred to the benevolent neutrality of Germany towards Russia at the time of the Russo-Japanese War.

At the time when England was deeply involved in the Boer War, we might have fought against England or against France, which, at that time, would have been compelled to forgo help from England. But we did not do so. While the Russo-Japanese War was in progress we might have fought not only against Russia, but against France also. But we did not do so.

In addition to the Morocco crisis already touched
upon, in connexion with which we set aside the idea
of going to war, we also gave evidence of our desire
for peace by overcoming the Bosnian crisis by diplomatic means.

When one considers these political events as a
whole, and adduces the declarations of Entente
statesmen such as Poincaré, Clemenceau, Isvolsky,
Tardieu and others, one is bound to ask oneself, in
amazement, how a peace treaty, founded upon the
assumption of Germany's guilt in causing the world
war, could have been drafted and signed. This
miscarriage of justice will not stand before the bar
of world history.

A Frenchman, Louis Guetant, a delegate from
Lyons to the Society for the Rights of Man, recently
made this statement :—

" If we once look upon events without prejudice, with
complete independence and frankness, without bothering
about which camp chance placed us in at birth, the following
is forced upon our attention first of all : The war of 1914
is a consequence of the war of 1870 ; for, ever since that earlier
date, the idea of revenge, more or less veiled, has never
left us.

" The war of 1870, however, was prepared and declared
by the French Government. The French Empire, indeed,
needed it very badly in order to contend against interior
troubles and its steadily growing unpopularity with the
public. Even Gambetta, the wild Tribune of the opposition, exclaimed : ' If the Empire brings us the left bank of
the Rhine, I shall become reconciled with it ! ' Thus, it
was a war of conquest ; nobody bothered about what the

conquered populations might have to say about it. We
shall bend their will to ours! Thus it is written in the law
of the victor!

"And now, suddenly, the opportunity for doing this
was to escape France. In view of the political difficulties
and dangers of war caused by his candidature, Prince
Leopold declares himself ready to withdraw. That is
bad! Without a pretext there can be no war!

"It was the same with France as with the milkmaid
and the broken pitcher in the fable, only, instead of ' Farewell,
calf, cow, pig, hens,' it was ' Farewell, bloody profits, glory,
victory, left bank of the Rhine, even Belgium! '—for the
latter, too, lay on that left bank of the Rhine, which France
coveted. No, that would have been too hard, the disillusionment would have been too great, the opportunity
must be created anew. The entire chauvinistic Press, the
entire clan of boasters, sets to work, and soon finds a way.
Gramont, Minister for Foreign Affairs, sends Ambassador
Benedetti to visit Emperor William, who was taking the cure
at Ems, to demand from him a written promise that, in case
Prince Leopold should change his mind about his withdrawal, he, William, as head of the family, would take issue
against this.

"The withdrawal of Prince Leopold was announced to
France in a valid manner and officially accepted by the
Spanish Government. There could be no doubt as to its
genuineness. Nevertheless, the Paris newspapers, almost
without exception, clamoured for war. Whoever, like
Robert Michell in the *Constitutional,* expressed his pleasure
at the prospects of peace and declared himself satisfied, was
insulted in the street. Gambetta shouted at him: ' You
are satisfied! What a base expression! ' Copies of his
newspaper were stolen from the news-stands, thrown into
the river, hurled in his face! Emile de Girardin wrote to
him : ' The opportunity is unique, unhoped-for ; if the

Empire misses it, the Empire is lost!' Then it was that
preparation for the war of 1914 was begun."

Voices like this, which are not unique either in
France or England, must also ever be adduced as
proof that the guilt is not ours.

Our political and diplomatic operations in the
course of decades were not, it must be admitted,
faultlessly conceived or executed, but where we
made mistakes, they were caused invariably by the
too-great desire to maintain the peace of the world.
Such mistakes do not constitute guilt.

As I have mentioned elsewhere, I even consider
the Congress of Berlin a mistake, for it made our relations with Russia worse. The congress was a victory
for Disraeli, an Anglo-Austrian victory over Russia,
which turned Russian anger upon Germany. Yet—
think of all that has been done since then to make
up with Russia! I have partly enumerated these
acts. And Bismarck's sole intention in planning the
Congress of Berlin was, as I have pointed out, the
prevention of a great general war.

Chancellor von Bethmann Hollweg, who had strict
orders from me to maintain peace if it was at all
possible, also made mistakes in 1914. As a statesman
he was not at all adequate to the world crisis, but
the blame for the war cannot be put upon us simply
because our opponents profited by our mistakes.
Bethmann, like all of us, wished to avoid the war—
sufficient proof of this is to be found in the one fact
alone that he persisted until the 4th of August in

his political inertia, negotiating with England in the erroneous belief that he could keep England out of the Entente.

While on this subject I wish to call attention to the delusion under which Prince Lichnowsky, the German Ambassador in London, also laboured. Soon after he had become ambassador, King George went to dinner at the Embassy. The King's example was followed automatically by the best society people in London. The prince and princess were singled out for marked attention and exceedingly well treated socially. From this the German Ambassador drew the conclusion that our relations with England had improved, until, shortly before the war, Sir Edward Grey coolly informed him that he must draw no political conclusions from social favours and good treatment accorded to him personally.

Nothing could give a better insight into the difference between English and German mentality than this. The German assumed social friendliness to be the expression of political friendliness, for the German is accustomed to express aversion and approval by means of social forms as well as otherwise. He is very outspoken about what he has on his mind.

The Englishman, however, makes a distinction; in fact, he is rather pleased if the man to whom he is speaking confuses form with substance, or, in other words, if he takes the form to be the expression of actual sentiments and political views. Judged from the English standpoint, the remarks of Sir Edward

v

Grey just referred to were a perfectly frank statement.

The much discussed non-renewal of the re-insurance treaty with Russia, already touched upon by me, is not to be considered as so decisive as to have influenced the question of whether there was to be war or peace. The re-insurance treaty, in my opinion, would not have prevented the Russia of Nicholas II from taking the road to the Entente; under Alexander III it would have been superfluous.

Prince Bismarck's view that the Russian Ambassador, Prince Shuvaloff, would have renewed the re-insurance treaty with him, but not with his successor, is naturally the honest, subjective way of looking at the matter. Judged in the light of fact, however, it does not hold water, in view of what the two parties concerned had to consider at that time. For instance, the under secretary of State of the prince, Count Berchem, stated officially, in a report to the prince, that the treaty could not be renewed, which meant that it could not be renewed through Shuvaloff either. I thought that not the old treaty, but only an entirely new and different kind of treaty was possible, in the drawing up of which Austria must participate, as in the old Three-Emperor-relationship. But, as I said, treaties with Nicholas II would not have seemed absolutely durable to me, particularly after the sentiments of the very influential Russian general public had also turned against Germany.

Our acts were founded upon the clear perception

that Germany could reach the important position in the world, and obtain the influence in world-affairs necessary to her, solely by maintaining world peace. This attitude was strengthened, moreover, by personal considerations.

Never have I had warlike ambitions. In my youth my father had given me terrible descriptions of the battlefields of 1870 and 1871, and I felt no inclination to bring such misery, on a colossally larger scale, upon the German people and the whole of civilized mankind. Old Field Marshal Moltke, whom I respected greatly, left behind him the prophetic warning : " Woe to him who hurls the firebrand of war upon Europe ! " and I considered as a political legacy from the great chancellor the fact that Prince Bismarck had said that Germany must never wage a preventable war, that German resistance would be neutralized if she did.

Thus the trend of the German policy of maintaining peace was determined by political insight, personal inclination, the legacies of two great men, Bismarck and Moltke, and the desire of the German people to devote itself to peaceful labours and not to plunge into adventures.

Whatever has been said in malevolent circles about the existence of a German party favourable to war is a conscious or unconscious untruth. In every country there are elements which, in serious situations, either from honest conviction or less lofty motives, favour the appeal to the sword, but never have such elements influenced the course of German policy.

The accusations, which have been made especially against the General Staff to the effect that it worked for war, are utterly untenable. The Prussian General Staff served its King and Fatherland by hard, faithful work, and, as was its duty, by labours extending over many years of peace, maintained Germany's ability to defend herself, but it exerted absolutely no political influence whatsoever. Interest in politics, as is well known, was never particularly strong in the Prussian-German army. Looking backward, one might almost say, in fact, that it would have been better for us if those in leading military circles had concerned themselves more with foreign policy.

§ 5

How, therefore, the Peace of Versailles, in view of this perfectly clear state of affairs, could have been founded upon Germany's guilt in having caused the world war, would seem an insoluble riddle if it were not possible to trace the tremendous effect of a new war weapon—viz., the political propaganda of England against Germany, planned on a large scale and applied with audacity and unscrupulousness. I cannot bring myself to dismiss this propaganda by branding it with catchwords such as " a piece of rascality," etc., since it constitutes an achievement which, in spite of its repugnant nature, cannot be ignored; it did us more harm than the arms in the hands of our opponents.

To us Germans such an instrument of insincerity, distortion and hypocrisy is not pleasing; it is something that is incompatible with the German character; our inclination is to convince our opponents with the weapon of truth as well as with weapons of war. But war is a cruel thing, and what matters in it is to win; after all, to fire heavy guns at civilized beings is not a pleasant matter, nor to bombard beautiful old towns, yet this had to be done by both sides in the war.

Moreover, we could not have developed a propaganda on a large scale such as that of our enemies during the war, for the very reason that they had no foes in their rear, whereas we were surrounded. In addition, most Germans have not the gift to fit a scheme of propaganda to the different mentalities of the nations upon which it is supposed to work. But, just as the English were more than our match with that terrible weapon of theirs, the tank—against which we could bring nothing of equal efficiency—so also were they superior to us with their very effective weapon of propaganda.

This weapon still continues its work and over and over again we are compelled to defend ourselves against it. For there can be no doubt that the Unjust Peace of Versailles could not have been founded upon Germany's war-guiltiness unless propaganda had previously accomplished its task, and, partly with the support of German pacifists, instilled into the brains of one hundred million human beings the belief in Germany's guilt, so that to many the Unjust Peace of Versailles seemed justified.

Meanwhile, things have changed, the barriers between nations have fallen, and the peoples are gradually awakening to the realization of how their confidence was imposed upon.　The reaction will be crushing to the makers of the Versailles peace, but helpful to Germany.　It goes without saying that, among the statesmen, politicians and publicists of the Entente who really know, not a single one is sincerely convinced of Germany's guilt in having caused the world war. Every one of them knows the real inter-relation of events, and assuredly there never was an instance where so many augurs smiled at each other over a secret held in common, as that of the responsibility for the world war.　In fact, one may even speak of a chorus of such individuals, since twenty-eight nations took part in the war against Germany.

In the long run, however, not even the shrewdest augurs will suffice to make world history ; truth will make its way forward and thus Germany will come into her rights.

The various stipulations of the Versailles treaty are in themselves null and void, since they can be observed neither by the Entente nor by Germany. For months it has been possible to note what difficulties are arising in the path not only of Germany but of the victors, as a result of such an extravagant instrument.

In many ways the treaty has been punctured by the Entente itself, and the reason for this is easily found. In the present highly-developed state of the world, which rests upon free, systematic exchange of material

and intellectual property, regulated solely by production itself, it is quite out of the question for three
men—no matter how eminent they may be—to sit
down anywhere and dictate paragraphed laws to
the world. Yet that is what the Treaty of Versailles
does, not only for Germany, but also, indirectly,
for the Entente and America, since all economic
questions must be solved by mutual, not one-sided,
action.

The life of nations is ever regulated—and most
particularly in our day—not by paragraphs, but
simply and solely by the needs of nations. True, it
is possible to do violence temporarily to these national
needs by the imposition of arbitrary decisions, but,
in such cases, both parties concerned must suffer.

The world is at such a stage just now. Conditions like those at present prevailing cannot last;
not guns, nor tanks, nor squadrons of aeroplanes
can perpetuate them. Therefore, their removal has
already begun; for, if the Peace of Versailles were
really such a judicious, unimpeachable instrument,
bringing blessings upon the world, there would not
be constant need for new conferences, discussions,
and meetings having to do with this " marvellous "
document. The constant necessity for new inter-
pretations is due, indeed, to the fact that the needs
of highly-cultivated and civilized nations were not
taken into account when the peace was concluded.

One must not be pharisaical, however : up to a
certain point the extravagance of the terms imposed
by the victor after a life-and-death struggle is a

natural consequence of the relief felt at having
escaped alive from deadly danger.

Nevertheless, I know that Germany, if we had
emerged victorious from the war, would have imposed quite different terms—i.e. terms that would
have been just and endurable. The peace treaties
of Brest-Litovsk and Bukarest—which indeed are
not at all comparable with the Treaty of Versailles—
cannot be adduced against us. They were concluded in the very midst of the war and had to
include conditions which would guarantee our safety
until the end of the war. Had it come to a general
peace, the treaty made by us in the East would have
had a far different aspect ; had we won the war, we
should ourselves have revised it. At the time when
it was made it was necessary to give preference to
military requirements.

But enlightenment regarding the Unjust Treaty
of Versailles is on the way, and the necessities of life
among present-day nations will speak in imperious
tones to victors and vanquished.

After years of the heaviest trial will come the
liberation from a yoke imposed unjustly upon a
great, strong, honest nation. Then every one of
us again will be glad and proud that he is a German.

XV

THE REVOLUTION AND GERMANY'S FUTURE

I DO not care what my foes say about me. I cannot recognize them as my judges. When I see how the same people who exaggeratedly spread incense before me in other days are now vilifying me, the most that I can feel is pity. The bitter things that I hear about myself from home disappoint me. God is my witness that I have always wished what was best for my country and my people, and I believed that every German had recognized and appreciated this. I have always tried to keep my political actions, everything that I did as a ruler and a man, in harmony with God's commandments. Much turned out differently from what I desired, but my conscience is clean. *The welfare of my people and my empire was the goal of my actions.*

I bear my personal fate with resignation, for the Lord knows what He does and what He wishes. He knows why He subjects me to this test. I shall bear everything with patience and await whatsoever God still holds in store for me.

The only thing that grieves me is the fate of my country and my people. I am pained at the hard period of trial which my children of the German land are undergoing, which I—compelled to live in foreign parts—cannot suffer with them. *That is the sword-thrust which pierces through my soul;* that is what is bitter to me. Here in solitude I still feel and think solely for the German people, still wonder how I can better matters and help with enlightenment and counsel.

Nor can bitter criticism ever lessen my love for my land and people. I remain faithful to the Germans, no matter how individual Germans may now stand with regard to me. To those who remain by me in misfortune as they did in prosperity, I am grateful—they comfort me and relieve my gnawing homesickness for my beloved Germany. And I can respect those who, impelled by honest convictions, array themselves against me : as for the rest, let them look for justification to God, their consciences and history.

They will not succeed in separating me from the Germans. I can ever look upon country and people solely as a whole. They remain to me what they were when I said in the Imperial Palace on the occasion of the opening of the Reichstag, on the 1st of August, 1914 : " I know parties no more; I know only Germans."

The revolution broke the Empress's heart. She aged visibly from November, 1918, onward, and could not resist her bodily ills with her previous strength. Thus, her decline soon began. The hardest of all for her to bear was her homesickness for Germany, for the German people. Notwithstanding this, she still tried to afford consolation to me.

The revolution destroyed things of enormous

value. It was brought about at the very moment when the German nation's fight for existence was to have been ended, and every effort should have been concentrated upon reconstruction. It was a crime against the nation.

I am well aware that many who rally around the Social Democratic banner did not wish for revolution ; some individual Social Democratic leaders likewise did not desire it at that time, and more than one among them was ready to co-operate with me. Yet these Social Democrats were incapable of preventing the revolution and therein lies their share of guilt for what is now going on, all the more so because the Socialist leaders stood closer to the revolutionary masses than the representatives of the monarchical government and could, therefore, exert more influence upon them.

Even in the days before the war the leaders had suggested the idea of revolution to the masses and fostered it, and the Social Democrats had been from time immemorial openly hostile to the earlier, monarchical form of government and had worked systematically towards its elimination. They sowed the wind and reaped the whirlwind.

The time and nature of the revolution were not to the liking of many of the leaders, but it was exactly these men who, at the decisive moment, abandoned the leadership to the most unbridled elements and failed to exert their influence towards the maintenance of the Government.

It was the duty of Prince Max and his colleagues

to protect the old form of government. They failed to fulfil their holy duty because they had become dependent on the Socialist leaders, the very men who had surrendered their influence on the masses to the Radical elements.

The greatest share of the guilt therefore falls upon the leaders, and, for that reason, history will not brand the German working-classes, but their leaders, with the curse of the revolution, in so far as these leaders participated in the institution of the revolution, or failed to prevent it—and it will also brand the Government of Prince Max of Baden with that curse.

The German workers fought brilliantly in battle under my leadership and laboured ceaselessly at home to provide munitions and war material. That is something which must not be forgotten. It was only later that some of them began to break away, but the responsibility for this lies at the door of the agitators and revolutionaries, not at that of the decent, patriotic section of the working-classes.

The conscienceless agitators are the men really responsible for Germany's total collapse. That will be recognized some day by the working-classes themselves.

The present is a difficult time for Germany. Of the future of this strong, healthy nation I do not despair. A nation which could achieve such unprecedented progress as that of Germany between 1871 and 1914, a nation which could maintain itself successfully for over four years in a defensive war against twenty-eight nations, cannot be driven from the earth. Economically, the world cannot do without us.

In order, however, that we may regain the position in the world which is Germany's due, we must not count upon or wait for outside help. Whatever happens such help will not be forthcoming; were it to come, it would but mean at best our being mere helots. The help from abroad for which the German Social Democratic Party hoped has not materialized. The international part of the Socialistic programme has proved a frightful mistake. The workers of the Entente countries took the field against the German people in order to destroy it; nowhere was there a trace of international solidarity among the masses.

This mistake, too, is a further reason why the war turned out so badly for Germany. The English and French working-classes were rightly directed— i.e. nationally—by their leaders; the German working-classes were wrongly directed—i.e. internationally.

The German people must rely upon no other people, but solely upon itself. When self-conscious, national sentiment returns to all classes of our people, our upward march will begin. The whole population must be united in national sentiment, no matter how far apart their ways may lie in different departments of the nation's life. Therein lies the strength of England, of France—even of the Poles.

If this comes to pass, the feeling of solidarity with all fellow-members of the nation, the consciousness of the dignity of our noble country, the pride in being German and in that genuinely German conception of ethics—which was one of the secret sources of strength that made Germany so great—will return to us.

In the community of cultured nations Germany will again play, as she did before the war, the role of the nation with the greatest capacity for labour, and will once more march victoriously in the van in peaceful competition, offering not only to herself but to all the nations of the earth whatever is best in the domain of technical achievement, of science, and of art.

I believe in the revocation of the Unjust Peace of Versailles by the judgment of the sensible elements of foreign countries and by Germany herself. I believe in the German people and in the continuation of its peaceful mission in the world, which has been interrupted by a terrible war for which Germany, since she did not will it, does not bear the guilt.

INDEX

Lightning Source UK Ltd.
Milton Keynes UK
UKOW051128050312

188367UK00001B/296/A